Legal Aspects of

Police
Supervision

Second Edition

Isaac T. Avery, III

Copperhouse
@ATOMICdogPUBLISHING

COPPERHOUSE PUBLISHING COMPANY
P.O. Box 5463, Incline Village, Nevada 89450

All Copperhouse titles are now distributed by

Atomic Dog Publishing

Atomic Dog is a higher education publishing company that specializes in developing and publishing HyBred Media™ textbooks that combine online content delivery, interactive media, and print.

You can contact Atomic Dog as follows:

1148 Main Street, Third Floor
Cincinnati, OH 45202-7236
Phone: 800-310-5661   Fax: 513-333-0498
Email: copperhouse@atomicdog.com
Website: www.atomicdog.com

Your Partner in Education
with
QUALITY BOOKS AT FAIR PRICES

Library of Congress Catalog Number 97-65245
ISBN 1-928916-18-X Paper Text Edition

4 5 6 7 8 9 10

Printed in the United States of America

Table of Contents

Chapter 10
The Ten (or So) Worst Mistakes an IA Investigator Can Make —or—How to Be Sued and Lose without Really Trying   89

Chapter 11
Freedom of Speech: Congress Shall Make No Law . . . Abridging the Freedom of Speech . . .   94

Chapter 12
Religious Freedom in the Workplace   108

Chapter 13
Drug Testing in the Workforce: Legal Ramifications 117

Chapter 14
Litigation under 42 U.S.C. § 1983 123

Chapter 15
Failure to Protect 137

CHAPTER 1

CONSTITUTIONAL LAW FOR PUBLIC MANAGERS

INTRODUCTION

A constitution is a system of fundamental principles or laws that have been adopted by a people for the government of a nation, state, or other group. No laws, rules, or policies adopted by a government or decisions by its employees which conflict with the constitution are enforceable. A constitution sets the parameters for all government actions and carves out areas of individual liberties that cannot be infringed upon. A constitution implies a permanent instrument that is intended to meet present and future conditions.

The United States Constitution is the charter creating a government and guaranteeing citizens their liberties. The United States Constitution has three primary functions: (1) organize government, (2) assign duties and responsibilities to the branches of the federal government and between the federal and state governments, and (3) act as a limitation on the authority of all governments.

HISTORY OF THE CONSTITUTION

The United States was first organized by the thirteen original colonies into a loose confederation. This organization was documented by the Articles of Confederation, ratified in 1781. Because the colonists' fear of a too-powerful central government similar to England's was at its peak, the federal government was given very little authority. It had no executive branch to enforce the laws and no judiciary branch to interpret the laws or settle disputes. Taxes could not be raised without the consent of the colonies, and the federal government's laws were not binding upon the colonies unless they agreed.

The colonies determined that the Articles needed to be amended to allow the central government more authority. A constitutional convention was called for the "sole and only" purpose of amending the Articles. Instead, a new document known as the "Constitution" was drafted. When the Articles were found to be inadequate to the exigencies of the country, the Constitution was ordained "to form a more perfect union." *Texas v. White*, 74 U.S. 700 (1869).

The constitution was ratified on June 21, 1788, when the ninth state agreed to its ratification. Virginia (June 25, 1788), New York (July 26, 1788), North Carolina (November 11, 1789), and Rhode Island (May 29, 1790) all ratified the document later so that approval was unanimous. The vast majority of the document has remained unchanged since then.

ORGANIZATION OF GOVERNMENT

ARTICLE I—LEGISLATIVE BRANCH

§ 1. All legislative powers herein granted shall be vested in a congress of the United States, which shall consist of a senate and house of representatives.

§ 2. The house of representatives shall be comprised of members chosen every second year by the people of the several states . . . .

No person shall be a representative who shall not have attained to the age of twenty-five years, and been seven years a citizen of the United States, and who shall not, when elected, be an inhabitant of the state in which he shall be chosen.

Representatives . . . shall be apportioned among the several states which may be included within this union . . . . The actual enumeration shall be made within three years after the first meeting of the congress of the United States, and within every subsequent term of ten years, in such manner as they shall by law direct. The number of representatives shall not exceed one for every thirty thousand, but each state shall have at least one representative . . . .

. . . .

The house of representatives . . . shall have the sole power of impeachment.

§ 3. The senate of the United States shall be composed of two senators from each state, <u>chosen by the legislature thereof</u> [underlined portion repealed by Amendment XVII], for six years; and each senator shall have one vote.

. . . .

No person shall be a senator who shall not have attained to the age of thirty years, and been nine years a citizen of the United States, and who shall not, when elected, be an inhabitant of that state for which he shall be chosen.

The vice president of the United States shall be president of the senate, but shall have no vote, unless they be equally divided.

. . . .

The senate shall have the sole power to try all impeachments. . . . And no person shall be convicted without the concurrence of two-thirds of the members present.
. . . .

§ 7. All bills for raising revenue shall originate in the house of representatives; but the senate may propose or concur with amendments as on other bills.

Every bill which shall have passed the house of representatives and the senate shall, before it become a law, be presented to the president of the United States. If he approves, he shall sign it; but if not, he shall return it with his objections, to that house in which it shall have originated . . . . If after . . . reconsideration two-thirds of that house shall agree to pass the bill, it shall be sent . . . to the other house, . . . and if approved by two-thirds of that house, it shall become a law. . . . If any bill shall not be returned by the president within ten days (Sundays excepted) after it shall have been presented to him, the same shall be a law, in like manner as if he had signed it, unless the congress by their adjournment prevent its return, in which case it shall not be a law.

. . . .

§ 8. The congress shall have power

To lay and collect taxes, duties, . . . and provide for the common defense and general welfare of the United States . . . ;

To borrow money on the credit of the United States;

To regulate commerce with foreign nations, and among the several states, and with the Indian tribes;

To establish an uniform rule of naturalization . . . ;

To coin money . . . and fix the standard of weights and measures;

To provide for the punishment of counterfeiting . . . ;

To establish post offices and post roads;

. . . .

To constitute tribunals inferior to the supreme court;

To define and punish piracies and felonies committed on the high seas . . . ;

To declare war . . . ;

To raise and support armies . . . ;

To provide and maintain a navy;

To make rules for the government and regulation of the land and naval forces;

. . . .

To make all laws which shall be necessary and proper for carrying into execution the foregoing powers, and all other powers vested by this constitution in the government of the United States . . . .

§ 9. . . . The privilege of the writ of habeas corpus shall not be suspended, unless when in cases of rebellion or invasion the public safety may require it.

No bill of attainder or ex post facto law shall be passed.

. . . .

§ 10. No state shall enter into any treaty, alliance, or confederation; . . . coin money; . . . pass any bill of attainder, ex post facto law, or law impairing the obligations of contracts, or grant any title of nobility.

The Legislative Branch is comprised of the two houses of congress: the Senate and the House of Representatives. The decision to have two houses of Congress was a compromise between the larger states and the smaller ones. The House of Representatives is composed of 435 members. Each state is assigned representatives based upon its population established by the census. Each member is elected for a two-year term. The terms are not staggered, so the entire House of Representatives is up for reelection every two years. Because the number of representatives is based upon population, the larger states have more members in the House of Representatives than the smaller ones. Thus, they also have more power.

The Senate, on the other hand, is comprised of two senators from each state. The senators serve six-year terms. The terms are staggered so that approximately one-third of the Senate is up for reelection every two years. The smaller states have the same voice within the Senate as the larger ones.

Congress is charged with the responsibility of passing laws, imposing taxes, establishing the general policies of government, and funding government agencies. In order for a law to become effective, it must be passed by a majority of both houses. Except for revenue bills, which must originate within the House of Representatives, a bill may be introduced in either house. It is then assigned to a committee, where it is studied. The committee will vote a favorable or unfavorable report on the bill and send it to the entire house for a vote. If the bill passes one house, it goes to the other for the same procedure. When the second house changes the bill, it must be returned to the first house for concurrence in the change. When the first house does not concur, a conference committee is appointed to try and resolve the differences. Both houses must vote on any compromise. If both houses pass the bill, it goes to the President for signature. If he signs it, the bill becomes a law or the money is appropriated. If the President refuses to sign the bill or vetoes it, the bill goes back to the Congress. If two-thirds of both houses vote to override the veto, the bill becomes a law without the President's signature.

ARTICLE II—EXECUTIVE BRANCH

§ 1. The executive power shall be vested in a president of the United States of America. He shall hold his office during the term of four years, . . . together with the vice president, chosen for the same term . . . .

. . . .

§ 2. The president shall be commander in chief of the army and navy of the United States, and of the militia of the several states, when called into the actual service of the United States; . . . he shall have power to grant reprieves and pardons for offences against the United States, except in cases of impeachment.

He shall have power, by and with the advice and consent of the senate to make treaties, provided two-thirds of the senators present concur; and he shall nominate, and by and with the advice and consent of the senate, shall appoint ambassadors, other public ministers and consuls, judges of the supreme court, and all other officers of the United States whose appointments are not herein otherwise provided for . . . .

. . . .

§ 3. He shall from time to time give to the congress information of the state of the union, and recommend to their consideration such measures as he shall judge necessary and expedient; . . . he shall take care that the laws be faithfully executed . . . .

§ 4. The president, vice president and all civil officers of the United States shall be removed from office on impeachment for, and conviction of, treason, bribery, or other high crimes and misdemeanors.

The Executive Branch, headed by the President, is required to enforce the laws and carry out the policies of the Congress. The executive agencies assist the President. These agencies include the Department of Justice, which is headed by the Attorney General and which contains most of the federal law enforcement agencies, including the Federal Bureau of Investigation and the Drug Enforcement Agency. The President is also the commander in chief of all military forces.

The President and the Vice President run for election as a team. They serve a term of four years and may only serve two terms. *See* Amendment XXII.

ARTICLE III—JUDICIAL BRANCH

§ 1. The judicial power of the United States shall be vested in one supreme court, and in such inferior courts as the congress may from time to time ordain and establish. The judges, both of the supreme and inferior courts, shall hold their offices during good behavior, and shall, at stated times, receive for their services a compensation which shall not be diminished during their continuance in office.

§ 2. The judicial power shall extend to all cases, in law and equity, arising under this constitution, the laws of the United States, and treaties made . . . ;—. . . to all cases of admiralty . . . ;—to controversies to which the United States shall be a party;—to controversies between two or more states;—between a state and citizens of another state;—between citizens of different states . . . .

The trial of all crimes, except in cases of impeachment, shall be by jury; and such trial shall be held in the state where the said crimes shall have been committed . . . .

The United States Supreme Court heads the Judicial Branch. The Court is comprised of a chief justice and eight associate justices who are nominated by the President and confirmed by a majority vote of the Senate. Like all judges of the federal judiciary, the appointment is for life.

The Constitution establishes the Supreme Court, and the Congress is authorized by the Constitution to establish the inferior courts. The federal court system is divided into districts. Each state has at least one district court with one or more district judges. North Carolina is divided into three districts: Eastern, Middle, and Western. Each district court is placed within one of the thirteen circuit courts of appeals. The courts of appeals review the decisions of the district judges, and their decisions may be reviewed by the Supreme Court. North Carolina, South Carolina, Virginia, West Virginia, and Maryland are all in the Fourth Circuit Court of Appeals.

The Judicial Branch must interpret the Constitution and laws and apply these laws and rules to everyday circumstances and settle disputes between parties to a lawsuit.

ARTICLE IV—OBLIGATIONS OF THE STATES

§ 1. Full faith and credit shall be given in each state to the public acts, records, and judicial proceedings of every other state. . . .

§ 2. The citizens of each state shall be entitled to all privileges and immunities of citizens in the several states.

A person charged in any state with treason, felony, or other crime, who shall flee from justice, and be found in another state, shall, on demand of the executive authority of the state from which he fled, be delivered up, to be removed to the state having jurisdiction of the crime.

FULL FAITH AND CREDIT

The Full Faith and Credit Clause, Article IV, Section 1, requires each state to enforce the judgments and public acts of the other states. This agreement to recognize the decisions and policies of the other states creates a nation rather than a confederation of independent countries. For example, the State of North Carolina must recognize a divorce granted by the State of Nevada.

PRIVILEGES AND IMMUNITIES CLAUSE

Article IV, Section 2 was primarily intended to help fuse into one nation a group of independent colonies. It confers upon citizens of every state a general citizenship. It prevents discrimination by states against citizens of another state in respect to fundamental privileges of citizenship. 16A Am. Jur. 2d *Purpose of Provisions* § 714, at 732-34. The Fourteenth Amendment also has a Privileges and Immunities Clause.

EXTRADITION

The provisions of Article IV, Section 2 also forged the colonies into a nation by providing for a criminal to be returned from one state to another for trial or to serve a prison term upon capture after escape. This provision requires a law enforcement officer to obtain criminal process for the escapee. The governor from the state that wants the defendant sends a request to the state where the defendant is found and requests extradition. The governor of the state receiving the request may review the paperwork and may even hold a hearing to be sure the defendant is wanted. If the defendant is the person wanted, the governor of the state receiving the request must return the defendant for trial or to complete his prison sentence.

ARTICLE V—AMENDING THE CONSTITUTION

The congress, whenever two-thirds of both houses shall deem it necessary, shall propose amendments to this constitution, or, on the application of the legislatures of two-thirds of the several states, shall call a convention for proposing

amendments, which, either case, shall be valid . . . when ratified by the legislatures of three-fourths of the several states, or by conventions in three-fourths thereof . . . .

The Constitution, once ratified, was almost immediately amended. Many of the states approved the Constitution, but objected to the basic document on the grounds that it failed to specifically protect certain rights. As a result, the first ten amendments known as the "Bill of Rights" were proposed by Congress on September 25, 1789, and were ratified by the states and became effective on December 15, 1791.

Since that time, the Constitution has been amended sixteen more times. Each amendment was intended to make the Constitution specifically address concerns at the time when the amendment was proposed. There have also been several attempts to amend the Constitution that received the necessary two-thirds of both houses of Congress but failed to receive approval of three-fourths of the state legislatures as is required by Article V. The "Equal Rights Amendment" is the most recent example.

CHECKS AND BALANCES

The three branches of government each have been assigned authority that limits the power of the other branches. A law enacted by Congress can be vetoed by the President or declared unconstitutional by the Supreme Court. Congress can override a veto and can propose amendments to the Constitution. The President can limit the authority of the Supreme Court by the justices that he nominates. Congress, likewise, must consent to each nominee and can reject persons submitted by the President. Congress also controls the budget and sets spending priorities. There are numerous other ways that each branch prevents the other from becoming too powerful.

ARTICLE VI—SUPREMACY CLAUSE

This constitution, and the laws of the United States which shall be made in pursuance thereof, and all treaties made, or which shall be made, under the authority of the United States, shall be the supreme law of the land; and the judges in every state shall be bound thereby, anything in the constitution or laws of any state to the contrary notwithstanding.

The senators and representatives before mentioned, and the members of the several state legislatures, and all executive and judicial officers, both of the United States and of the several states, shall be bound by oath or affirmation, to support this constitution; but no religious test shall ever be required as a qualification to any office or public trust under the United States.

When the colonies voted for a strong central government by ratifying the Constitution of 1787, Article VI assured a strong federal system. A state constitutional provision, law, rule, or local ordinance that conflicts with the Constitution as interpreted by the federal judiciary is invalid and not enforceable. The colonies gave the ultimate authority to the federal government.

Likewise, federal laws, rules, and regulations made pursuant to federal law take precedent over state constitutions, laws, rules, and local ordinances. If there is a conflict, federal regulations prevail. Also, if the federal government has exercised its power, a state may not have regulations in the same field if Congress has indicated its intent to be the sole regulator. *DeCanas v. Bica*, 424 U.S. 351 (1976).

SELECTIVE INCORPORATION

The most significant of the amendments from the state and local law enforcement standpoint is the Fourteenth Amendment. This amendment was passed after the Civil War and directly limited the authority of state governments. This amendment has spawned the doctrine of "selective incorporation" from the United States Supreme Court. Selective incorporation is a procedure whereby the Supreme Court has applied certain provisions of the Bill of Rights through the Fourteenth Amendment to the states by interpreting the Due Process Clause to encompass certain of the basic rights protected by the first ten amendments. The amendments originally acted only as a limitation upon the power of the federal government; now, they also limit the power of state governments. For example, the First Amendment provides, in part, that "Congress shall make no law respecting an establishment of religion." Through selective incorporation, the Supreme Court now holds that no state may make a law respecting establishment of religion. Not all provisions of the Bill of Rights apply to the states. The Second Amendment, providing the right of people to bear arms, has never been applied to the states. The United States Supreme Court determines which amendments are incorporated.

AMENDMENT I

Congress shall make no law respecting an establishment of religion, or prohibiting the free exercise thereof; or abridging the freedom of speech or of the press; or the right of the people peaceably to assemble, and to petition the government for a redress of grievances.

FREEDOM OF RELIGION CLAUSE

The Freedom of Religion Clause has two parts: (1) the Establishment Clause, and (2) the Free Exercise Clause. This amendment was proposed to prevent the national government from establishing a particular religion as the only one, like England had. Also, the Free Exercise Clause was intended to prevent persecution for worshiping or believing in a particular way. Many of the colonists came to the New World to escape such persecution.

Although the language of this amendment limits the authority of Congress to make any law respecting religion, the Supreme Court has incorporated this amendment through the Fourteenth Amendment to act as a limitation on state and local government also. *Everson v. Board of Education,*

330 U.S. 1 (1947) (Establishment Clause); *Hamilton v. Regents of the University of California*, 293 U.S. 245 (1934) (Free Exercise Clause).

ESTABLISHMENT CLAUSE

The Establishment Clause prohibits more than the establishment of a national church. It prohibits acts by any government preferring one religion to another or preferring religion generally as against nonbelief. *Cantwell v. Connecticut*, 310 U.S. 296 (1940). If the government action has a secular purpose, and the principal effect neither advances nor inhibits religion and does not foster excessive government entanglement with religion, such action is constitutional. *Comm. for Public Education and Religious Liberty v. Regan*, 444 U.S. 646 (1980). Government action may accommodate religious practices without violating the Establishment Clause. *Church of Latter-Day Sts. v. Amos*, 483 U.S. 327 (1987).

For example, a Christmas creche located outside a county building along with secular seasonal symbols does not violate the Establishment Clause. The creche located inside, alone, does. *County of Allegheny v. American Civil Liberty Union*, 492 U.S. 573 (1989). A state requirement that creationism be taught if evolution is taught in a school violates the Establishment Clause. *Edwards v. Aguillard*, 482 U.S. 578 (1987).

FREE EXERCISE CLAUSE

Government may not prevent the free exercise of religion or deny a benefit because of the exercise of a religious belief. However, government may assist in the free exercise of religion. *Church of Latter-Day Sts. v. Amos*, 483 U.S. 327 (1987). Also, government action that has an inadvertent, detrimental effect upon the free exercise of religion is still constitutional. *Braunfeld v. Brown*, 366 U.S. 599 (1961).

An individual's sincerely held religious beliefs are entitled to protection by the Free Exercise Clause, regardless of whether the individual is a member of any particular religious organization and regardless of whether the individual's belief is based upon a tenet or any organized religious denomination. *Frazee v. Illinois Dep't of Employment Security*, 489 U.S. 327 (1989).

A state cannot deny unemployment benefits to a person fired from a job for refusing to work on her Sabbath because of a religious conviction adopted after beginning employment. *Hobbie v. Unemployment App. Comm.*, 480 U.S. 136 (1987). Also, a state may not require an applicant for a drivers license to have a color picture put on his license in violation of his sincerely held belief that such a picture violates the Second Commandment, which forbids graven images. *Quaring v. Peterson*, 728 F.2d 1121 (8th Cir.), *aff'd*, 472 U.S. 478 (1985).

Any government regulation must be based upon proof that the regulation advances a compelling governmental interest. *Cantwell v. Connecticut*, 310 U.S. 296 (1940). Prohibitions against use of drugs, handling dangerous reptiles, or human sacrifices advance compelling governmental interests. For example, a state can deny unemployment benefits to a person fired for unlawfully using peyote during a religious ceremony. *Employment Div. v. Smith*, 485 U.S. 660 (1988

FREEDOM OF SPEECH AND THE PRESS

The major purpose of the First Amendment, as it relates to freedom of speech, is to protect free discussion of government affairs. The First Amendment, at least, embraces the liberty to discuss publicly and truthfully all matters of public concern without prior restraint or fear of subsequent prosecution. *First Nat'l. Bank v. Bellotti*, 435 U.S. 765 (1978). The protection also extends not only to spoken and written words, but to expressions through actions or drawings. *Texas v. Johnson*, 491 U.S. 397 (1989) (burning of American flag as part of a protest of government policy); *Hustler Magazine v. Falwell*, 485 U.S. 46 (1990) (superimposed photograph of preacher within sexually explicit surroundings).

These provisions apply to the states through the Fourteenth Amendment and act as a limitation upon the authority of state and local governments to limit speech or the press. *Hague v. CIO*, 307 U.S. 496 (1939). This amendment does not apply to purely private restrictions on speech; it applies only to actions by a government. There must be some government action. *Sinn v. The Daily Nebraskan*, 829 F.2d 662 (8th Cir. 1987) (government action not present when a student paper refused to publish "roommate wanted" ad with plaintiff's preference for a homosexual roommate).

Commercial speech, such as advertising, receives limited protection. *Shapero v. Kentucky Bar Ass'n.*, 486 U.S. 466 (1988) (lawyers are entitled to advertise services). However, deceptive advertising is not entitled to protection by the First Amendment. *Friedman v. Rogers*, 440 U.S. 1 (1979).

Freedom of speech and the press are not absolute and are subject to restriction, but only to prevent grave and immediate danger to legitimate state interests. *West Virginia St. Bd. of Education v. Barnette*, 319 U.S. 624 (1943). The main purpose of the First Amendment is to prevent all previous restraints upon publication or speech as practiced by government. *Patterson v. Colorado,* 205 U.S. 454 (1907). Laws that punish for improper speech or press are more likely to survive a constitutional challenge than those laws preventing the speech. *Joseph Burstyn, Inc. v. Wilson*, 343 U.S. 495 (1952).

In order to restrain or punish speech or press, there must be a "clear and present danger" of bringing about substantial evil that the state or federal government has the power to prevent. *Schenck v. United States*, 249 U.S. 47 (1919). "Fighting words" may be punished, but a statute enacted for this purpose must not be overly broad to prevent legitimate criticism. *Houston v. Hill*, 482 U.S. 451 (1987) (city ordinance that made it unlawful to "assault, strike, oppose, molest, or interrupt" a police officer is overbroad and violative of the First Amendment since part of the ordinance also prohibits criticism, which is protected speech). On the other hand, dissemination of obscenity may be punished. *Kaplan v. California*, 413 U.S. 115 (1973).

Freedom of the press does not guarantee the media access to information, nor does it grant reporters the right to protect their sources of information about crimes from disclosure. The media, however, may not be held libel for publication of false information about a "public figure" absent a showing that the reporter knew information was false or that the reporter did not know that his or her story showed a reckless disregard for the truth or falsity of what was printed. *New York Times Co. v. Sullivan*, 376 U.S. 254 (1964). In order to be a public figure, a person voluntarily places himself into or is drawn into the possibility of a particular public controversy. *Gertz v. Robert Welch, Inc.*, 418 U.S. 323 (1974).

Freedom of speech and the press extends to many forms of artistic expression, and the government's interest in regulating any actions protected by the First Amendment must be substantial. *New York State Liquor Auth. v. Bellanca*, 452 U.S. 714 (1981) (ordinance prohibiting nude dancing in an establishment with a liquor license does not violate the First Amendment because the twenty-first Amendment authorizes state control of liquor and controls over the First Amendment); *Schad v. Mt. Ephraim*, 452 U.S. 61 (1981) (local ordinance prohibiting all live entertainment in town violates First Amendment); *Young v. American Mini Theaters*, 427 U.S. 50 (1976) (zoning ordinance that prevents adult movie theaters within 1,000 feet of each other is constitutional).

The First Amendment does not prevent disciplinary action against a government employee who criticizes his superiors for the employee's own personal reasons. *Connick v. Myers*, 461 U.S. 138 (1983). On the other hand, an employee cannot be adversely affected for commenting on matters of public concern. *Rankin v. McPherson*, 483 U.S. 378 (1987) (after President Reagan was shot, deputy constable said, "if they go for him again I hope they get him"; this is protected speech). The speech on matters of public concern must be viewed as any other speech, and government cannot use its position as an employer to accomplish what it could not do otherwise. *Perry v. Sinderman*, 408 U.S. 393 (1972).

A police officer may be fired for circulating a letter within the department which criticizes the manner in which the chief ran the department, since the letter deals with internal matters and not with matters of public concern. *Brown v. Trenton*, 867 F.2d 318 (6th Cir. 1989). A police officer who, in an off-duty conversation, referred to the chief as a "son-of-a-bitch" and a "bastard" cannot be subject to disciplinary action unless the department can show that the statements will harm efficiency, discipline, or harmony within the department. *Waters v. Chaffin*, 684 F.2d 833 (11th Cir. 1982). A police chief cannot be subjected to disciplinary action under any circumstances for making truthful statements that town council members asked him to "fix" or withdraw citations. Even though this totally disrupts the working relationship with the council, the First Amendment completely protects this statement. *O'Donnell v. Yanchulis*, 875 F.2d 1059 (3rd Cir. 1989).

Political beliefs are also protected. A deputy sheriff cannot be dismissed merely because he is of a different political party. The sheriff must show impact on the agency. *Elrod v. Burns*, 427 U.S. 347 (1976). Campaigning for an opposing candidate for sheriff which disrupts the functioning of the agency is not protected. *Joyner v. Lancaster*, 815 F.2d 20 (4th Cir. 1987). A sheriff may have a right to demand "political loyalty" from all deputies. *Jenkins v. Medford*, 119 F.3d 1156 (4th Cir.) *cert. den.* 522 U.S. 1090 (1998).

FREEDOM TO ASSEMBLE

The right to peaceably assemble is not protected by the First Amendment unless the purpose of the assembly is to petition the government for redress of grievances. The right to assemble for social purposes unrelated to governmental expression is not protected under this amendment. *Presser v. Illinois*, 116 U.S. 252 (1886). This right is protected by the Fourteenth Amendment and restricts the authority of the states. *DeJonge v. Oregon*, 299 U.S. 353 (1937).

Freedom of assembly is susceptible to restriction only to prevent grave and immediate danger. Speculative apprehension that there will be trouble is insufficient to prohibit assembly. It is the duty of the police to prevent such occurrences and to protect expression of viewpoints. *United Servicemen's Fund v. Shands*, 440 F.2d 44 (4th Cir. 1971).

Reasonable restrictions on assembly are allowed. For example, prohibitions of picketing within a specified distance of a courthouse are allowed. *Cox v. Louisiana*, 379 U.S. 559 (1965).

FREEDOM OF ASSOCIATION

Although the First Amendment does not specifically mention a right of association, it is implicit within the amendment. Freedom of association includes the right to associate with others for political, economic, and other legal interests. *NAACP v. Burton*, 371 U.S. 415 (1963). This freedom is included in the bundle of First Amendment rights that are applicable to the states through the Due Process Clause. *Gideon v. Wainwright*, 372 U.S. 335 (1963).

The right to associate is not absolute but is subject to many restrictions. *Rotary International v. Rotary Club of Duarte*, 481 U.S. 537 (1987) (California state law that requires all-male club to admit women does not violate freedom of association); *U.S. Civil Serv. Comm'n v. National Ass'n. of Letter Carriers*, 413 U.S. 548 (1973) (limitation on political activity is constitutional). Personal but illegal sexual activity is not protected by the First Amendment. *Fleisher v. Signal Hill*, 829 F.2d 1491 (9th Cir. 1987). A question on an application for special assignment regarding a police officer applicant and his family's off-duty social and political activities constitutes invasion of the officer's rights absent legitimate need to know by employer. *Fraternal Order of Police, Lodge No. 5 v. Philadelphia*, 812 F.2d 105 (3rd Cir. 1987).

RIGHT TO PRIVACY

There is no right to privacy mentioned in the First Amendment. Like the right of association, the right to privacy is implicit within the First Amendment. *Roe v. Wade*, 410 U.S. 113 (1973). This right actually arises from a combination of many of the rights found within the First, Third, Fourth, Fifth, and Ninth Amendments. The states may not interfere with this right of privacy. *Griswold v. Connecticut*, 381 U.S. 479 (1965).

This right protects a person from governmental interference with such things as the right of contraception, *id.*, or the right to possess obscene materials in the privacy of one's home, *Stanley v. Georgia*, 394 U.S. 557 (1969). It does not protect cohabitation by two police officers, *Shawgo v. Spradlin*, 701 F.2d 470 (5th Cir.), *cert. denied*, 464 U.S. 965 (1983), or knowing receipt of child pornography, *United States v. Marchant*, 803 F.2d 174 (5th Cir. 1986).

AMENDMENT II

A well regulated militia, being necessary to the security of a free state, the right of the people to keep and bear arms shall not be infringed.

The Second Amendment does not guarantee the right to keep and bear arms, except to preserve a well-regulated militia. *United States v. Miller*, 307 U.S. 174 (1939). The Second Amendment is a limitation upon the power of Congress and the national government and not upon the states. *Presser v. Illinois*, 116 U.S. 252 (1886). Even the federal government may regulate possession and use of firearms as long as it does not prevent the states from maintaining a militia. *United States v. Warin*, 530 F.2d 103 (6th Cir.), *cert. denied*, 426 U.S. 948 (1976). Because the Second Amendment does not apply to the states or to possession of a firearm by an individual, state and local governments can regulate sales and possession of firearms with violating the guarantees of the Second Amendment. See *People Rights Organization, Inc. v. City of Columbus, Ohio*, 152 F.3d 522 (6th Cir. 1998).

AMENDMENT III

No soldier shall, in time of peace, be quartered in any house without the consent of the owner, nor in time of war but in a manner to be prescribed by law.

The Third Amendment's prohibition against unconsented peacetime quartering of soldiers protects one aspect of privacy from governmental intrusion. *Katz v. United States*, 389 U.S. 347 (1967). The Third Amendment is incorporated into the Fourteenth Amendment and prohibits forced housing of soldiers of the federal government or National Guardsmen of the states. *Engblom v. Carey*, 677 F.2d 957 (2nd Cir. 1982).

AMENDMENT IV

The right of the people to be secure in their persons, houses, papers, and effects, against unreasonable searches and seizures, shall not be violated, and no warrants shall issue but upon probable cause, supported by oath or affirmation and particularly describing the place to be searched and the persons or things to be seized.

The Constitution does not forbid all searches and seizures, only unreasonable ones. *Elkins v. United States*, 364 U.S. 206 (1960). The primary purpose of this amendment is to protect the individual and personal rights. *United States v. White*, 322 U.S. 694 (1944). The touchstone of the Fourth Amendment analysis of the legality of a search or seizure is always reasonableness in the circumstances of a particular government's invasion of a citizen's personal security or privacy. Reasonableness depends upon a balance between the public interest in the intrusion and the right of the citizen to be free from arbitrary interference by law enforcement officers. *Pennsylvania v. Mimms*, 434 U.S. 106 (1977). Success of the search or seizure in revealing evidence of a violation of the law is immaterial in determining whether the actions of the government official were reasonable. *Byars v. United States*, 273 U.S. 28 (1927). The Fourth Amendment is incorporated through the Fourteenth Amendment and prohibits unreasonable searches and seizures by state and local officials. *Mapp v. Ohio*, 367 U.S. 643 (1961).

The Fourth Amendment is also applied in the civil setting. The Supreme Court views the method of seizure or arrest of a person to be controlled by the Fourth Amendment. The use of deadly force, *Tennessee v. Garner*, 471 U.S. 1 (1985), and nondeadly force, *Graham v. Connor*, 490 U.S. 386 (1989), during an arrest by a police officer is limited by the Fourth Amendment. An officer may be sued in federal or state court, pursuant to 42 U.S.C. § 1983, for violations of the Fourth Amendment during a stop or arrest.

Searches of an employee's property because of noncriminal misconduct are also controlled by this amendment, and the employer must have reasonable grounds to suspect that evidence of wrongdoing exists in order to search property in which the employee has a reasonable expectation of privacy. *O'Connor v. Ortega*, 480 U.S. 709 (1987).

Drug testing of employees is a search that must meet the reasonableness standard. The Supreme Court has held that a public safety employee may be subjected to suspicionless random drug tests. *Treasury Employees v. Von Rabb*, 489 U.S. 656 (1989). After an incident, suspicionless drug testing is also allowed. *Skinner v. Railway Labor Executive Ass'n*, 489 U.S. 602 (1989) (engineers always tested after train wreck).

AMENDMENT V

No person . . . shall be compelled in any criminal case to be a witness against himself . . . .

The Fifth Amendment grants certain rights to persons suspected of or charged with a crime. The purpose is to limit the power of the legislature and the prosecuting officers. *Ex parte Wilson* 114 U.S. 417 (1885).

The Fifth Amendment protection from compulsory testimony against oneself is aimed at preventing the recurrence of the inquisition and the star-chamber used in Europe. Prevention of these greater evils was deemed of more importance than the occurrence of the lesser evil that this privilege may on occasion save a guilty man from his just deserts. *Ullmann v. United States*, 350 U.S. 422 (1956). Although this privilege is to be liberally construed, *Hoffman v. United States*, 341 U.S. 479 (1951), it does not prevent a defendant's incriminating testimony from being used against him; it prevents only compelled testimony from being used against a defendant. This provision applies to state as well as federal prosecutions. *Malloy v. Hogan*, 378 U.S. 1 (1964).

The prohibition applies only to "compelled testimony." Routine statements or information are not prohibited. A state statute requiring a motorist involved in a motor vehicle accident to stop at the scene and give his name and address does not violate the Fifth Amendment. *California v. Byers*, 402 U.S. 424 (1971). Likewise, blood tests for alcohol, *Schmerber v. California*, 384 U.S. 757 (1966), or videotapes that demonstrate impairment of a defendant's ability to walk and talk, *Pennsylvania v. Muniz*, 496 U.S. 582 (1990) (content of statements may be privileged), are not privileged.

A public employee may not be compelled to surrender his Fifth Amendment rights in order to avoid loss of his job. *Gardner v. Broderick*, 392 U.S. 273 (1968). However, the Fifth Amendment does not protect a public employee from being dismissed from his job for refusing to answer questions narrowly and directly related to his job; the answers may not, however, be used against him in a criminal trial. *Garrity v. New Jersey*, 385 U.S. 493 (1967).

AMENDMENT VI

In all criminal prosecutions the accused shall enjoy the right to a speedy and public trial, by an impartial jury of the state and district wherein the crime shall have been committed, which district shall have been previously ascertained by law, and to be informed of the nature and caused of the accusation; to be confronted with the witnesses against him; to have compulsory process for obtaining witnesses in his favor, and to have the assistance of counsel for his defense.

The Sixth Amendment is a limitation upon the government's trial procedures in criminal trials. It does not apply to civil proceedings. *Middendorf v. Henry*, 425 U.S. 25 (1976).

SPEEDY TRIAL

The right to a speedy trial is such a basic part of due process of law that it applies to the states as well as the federal government. *Klopfer v. North Carolina*, 386 U.S. 213 (1967). The purposes of this provision are (1) to prevent undue and oppressive incarceration prior to trial, (2) to minimize anxiety and concern accompanying public accusations, and (3) to limit the possibilities that a long delay will impair the ability of the accused to prepare a defense. *United States v. Ewell*, 383 U.S. 116 (1966).

There is no set time period. The court will consider: (1) the length of the delay, (2) the reason for the delay, (3) the defendant's assertion of his rights under this clause, and (4) prejudice to the defendant. The time runs from arrest, not from the time of the crime. A delay of five years is not too long. *United States v. MacDonald*, 456 U.S. 1 (1982).

PUBLIC TRIAL

The guarantee of a "public trial" is based upon the deeply rooted concept that the trial must not only be fair, it must appear to be just. *Levine v. United States*, 362 U.S. 610 (1960). It is, however, a personal right of the accused and does not guarantee access to a criminal trial on the part of the public or the press. *Gannett Co. v. DePasquale* 443 U.S. 368 (1979). The purpose of the public trial requirement is to assure that the accused is dealt with fairly. History has shown that secret tribunals are effective instruments of oppression. *Estes v. Texas*, 381 U.S. 532 (1965). Another purpose is to create the possibility that persons unknown to the parties or their counsel, but having knowledge of the facts, may be drawn to the trial. *Tanksley v. United States*, 145 F.2d 58 (9th Cir. 1944). Since the purposes of a public trial are fundamental to due process, this requirement applies to state prosecutions pursuant to the Fourteenth Amendment. *In re Oliver*, 333 U.S. 257 (1948).

Even though there is a right to a public trial, it is not unlimited. The trial judge has a right to control access. The court must consider all other alternatives before closure and point to specific important reasons for the closure. *Waller v. Georgia*, 467 U.S. 39 (1984). Public trial does not grant the press the right to broadcast a trial. *Nixon v. Warner Communications, Inc.*, 435 U.S. 589 (1978).

TRIAL BY IMPARTIAL JURY

The right to trial by an impartial petit jury is a basic and fundamental feature of our system of jurisprudence. *Bailey v. Central V.R., Inc.*, 319 U.S. 350 (1943). It applies only to serious or nonpetty offenses. A crime that carries a potential prison sentence of more than six months is a nonpetty crime, and a jury trial must be guaranteed. *Burch v. Louisiana*, 441 U.S. 130 (1979). The fact that such a conviction has collateral consequences, such as loss of drivers license for driving while impaired, does not entitle the defendant to a jury trial when the first offense carries a maximum prison term of six months, or forty-eight hours of community service plus a maximum fine of $100.00 and attendance at an alcohol abuse course. *Blanton v. North Las Vegas*, 489 U.S. 538 (1989).

A petit jury need not be composed of twelve persons, nor is a unanimous verdict required, except in federal criminal trials. *Andres v. United States*, 333 U.S. 740 (1948). A jury in a state trial must be composed of at least six persons. *Burch v. Louisiana*, 441 U.S. 130 (1979). An Oregon provision allowing a conviction based upon a verdict of ten to two is constitutional. *Apodaca v. Oregon*, 406 U.S. 404 (1972). A jury of only six persons is constitutional only if the verdict is unanimous. *Burch v. Louisiana*, 441 U.S. 130 (1979).

A defendant is entitled to an impartial jury and not a jury of his own selection. *Ross v. Oklahoma*, 487 U.S. 81 (1988). A juror may be exclude for bias or refusal to follow the judge's instructions on the law. *Wainwright v. Witt*, 469 U.S. 412 (1985). A prosecutor may not remove a prospective juror because the prosecutor believes the juror will base his or her vote upon the race of the defendant. *Batson v. Kentucky*, 476 U.S. 79 (1986).

TRIAL IN DISTRICT WHERE COMMITTED

The right to trial in the district where the crime is committed applies to federal prosecutions. *Beavers v. Henkel*, 194 U.S. 73 (1904). State trials will occur within the state of the crime because state criminal statutes do not extend beyond the borders of the state.

NATURE AND CAUSE OF ACCUSATION

This provision is designed to assure that a defendant in a criminal action knows the charge against him. There are two primary reasons for this provision: (1) to enable the defendant to prepare a meaningful defense, *Partson v. United States*, 20 F.2d 127 (8th Cir. 1927); and (2) to permit the defendant to plead former jeopardy in any subsequent prosecution, *Russell v. United States*, 369 U.S. 749 (1962). Charging the crime in the language of the statute is sufficient if it alleges necessary elements of the offense and includes the time and place of the crime. The right of a defendant to request more information through a bill of particulars may also allow for a more general charging instrument.

There is no specific case making this provision applicable to a state prosecution. General notions of due process will require notice of the charges. Most states have a similar statutory or constitutional provision.

CONFRONTATION OF WITNESSES

The primary purpose of the right to confrontation is basically a trial right. It generally includes both an opportunity to cross-examine witnesses and an occasion for the jury to consider the witnesses' demeanor in determining whom to believe. *Barber v. Page*, 390 U.S. 719 (1968). This right to confrontation may be satisfied even without physical confrontation in court or the right to cross-examination. *Douglas v. Alabama*, 380 U.S. 415 (1965). The rules of evidence may allow hearsay testimony to be used in court, and the defendant is not denied his right to confrontation. Many of the exceptions to this right to confrontation have been upheld: (1) testimony from a prior proceeding or preliminary hearing, where a witness is currently unavailable but had been subject to cross-examination, *Barber v. Page*, 390 U.S. 719; (2) co-conspirator's out-of-court statement, *United States v. Inadi*, 475 U.S. 387 (1986); and (3) business records, *California v. Green*, 399 U.S. 149 (1970). There are numerous other exceptions to this right to confrontation which have developed over the years.

The right to confrontation is so basic that it is part of the Due Process Clause of the Fourteenth Amendment and applies to state criminal proceedings. *Pointer v. Texas*, 380 U.S. 400 (1965). Like all other provisions of the Sixth Amendment, the right to confrontation applies only to proceedings that are criminal in nature. *Morrissey v. Brewer*, 408 U.S. 471 (1972).

COMPULSORY PROCESS

The right to compulsory process guarantees a criminal defendant the right to present relevant testimony at any proceeding governed by the Sixth Amendment. The criminal defendant has a right to the government's assistance in compelling attendance of witnesses in his favor which may influence the outcome of the case against him. *Pennsylvania v. Richie*, 480 U.S. 39 (1987). This right is not unlimited and may bow to other legitimate interests in the criminal process. *Rock v. Arkansas*, 483 U.S. 44 (1987). The defendant has no right to testimony of witnesses that is incompetent, privileged, or otherwise inadmissible under the standard rules of evidence. *Taylor v. Illinois*, 484 U.S. 400 (1988). This right is applicable to state criminal proceedings. *Id.*

EFFECTIVE ASSISTANCE OF COUNSEL

The point at which the right to counsel attaches distinguishes the right to counsel under the Sixth Amendment and the Fifth Amendment right to counsel under *Miranda*. *Miranda v. Arizona*, 384 U.S. 436 (1966). *Miranda* applies during a custodial interrogation occurring at any time, even when criminal charges have not been filed. The Sixth Amendment right to counsel applies to all proceedings after a defendant has been formally charged with a crime and is thus facing the criminal justice apparatus, which is geared to prosecute him. *Arizona v. Roberson*, 486 U.S. 675 (1988). This right is so fundamental that it is incorporated into the Due Process Clause of the Fourteenth Amendment and applies to state proceedings. *McCoy v. Court of Appeals*, 486 U.S. 429 (1988).

This right is not only to an attorney but to reasonably effective assistance of counsel at trial, *Strickland v. Washington*, 466 U.S. 668 (1984), and upon any appeal of right, *Anders v. California*, 386 U.S. 738 (1967). Even if the lawyer makes errors, as long as his representation was the same as a reasonably competent lawyer in the area, the defendant's Sixth Amendment right is not violated. *United States v. Cronic*, 466 U.S. 648 (1984).

The Sixth Amendment right to counsel also prevents the government from engaging in conduct after the attorney has been appointed which undermines his representation or prevents proper representation. For example, planting an informant in a defendant's cell and requesting that he try to get the defendant to confess is a violation. *Maine v. Moulton*, 474 U.S. 159 (1985).

AMENDMENT VII

In suits at common law, where the value in controversy shall exceed twenty dollars, the right of trial by jury shall be preserved, and no fact tried by jury shall be otherwise reexamined in any court of the United States than according to the rules of the common law.

The provision of the Seventh Amendment is a limitation on the federal courts in a civil proceeding and not in a criminal trial. *Ross v. Bernhard*, 396 U.S. 531 (1970). This provision does not affect state civil trials. *Alexander v. Virginia*, 413 U.S. 836 (1973).

AMENDMENT VIII

Excessive bail shall not be required, nor excessive fines imposed, nor cruel and unusual punishment inflicted.

EXCESSIVE BAIL

The Eighth Amendment does not guarantee a defendant a right to pretrial release on bail, but bail statutes must be followed in order to assure that the government's interests of preventing flight from prosecution and protecting society are the bases for the bail amount, if any. Pretrial punishment cannot be a basis for denying bail or setting a high amount. *United States v. Salerno*, 481 U.S. 739 (1987).

EXCESSIVE FINES

Fines that fall within the statutory limits are usually found to be constitutional. An appellate court will not reverse a lower court's decision unless the amount is outrageously excessive for the crime committed. Civil fines and property forfeiture may be considered as punishment and will be limited by the excessive fines clause. *Austin v. United States*, 509 U.S. 602 (1993); *United States v. Halper*, 490 U.S. 435 (1989).

CRUEL AND UNUSUAL PUNISHMENT

A jail sentence usually will not be determined unconstitutional under the Eighth Amendment if it falls within the limits set by the legislature. There are, however, limitations to the authority of the Congress and the states in setting prison terms. The Supreme Court will take into account objective evidence of contemporary values in determining whether punishment comports with this clause. *Ford v. Wainwright*, 477 U.S. 399 (1986). This clause does limit state courts in the imposition of punishment. *Robinson v. California*, 370 U.S. 660 (1962).

The punishment is unconstitutional if it makes no measurable contribution to purpose of punishment or is grossly out of proportion to the severity of the crime. *Coker v. Georgia*, 433 U.S. 584 (1977). Punishments of torture or unnecessary cruelty are unconstitutional. *Wilkerson v. Utah*, 99 U.S. 130 (1879). The death penalty for murder, if certain procedures are followed, is not unconstitutional. *Furman v. Georgia*, 408 U.S. 238 (1972). Death for the rape of an adult woman without inflicting serious physical injury is cruel and unusual punishment. *Coker v. Georgia*, 433 U.S. 584. Criminal sanction for public intoxication is constitutional, *Texas v. Powell*, 392 U.S. 514 (1968), although punishment for being an alcoholic is unconstitutional, *Robinson v. California*, 370 U.S. 660 (1962).

Not only does this amendment speak to the length of the sentence imposed, it also addresses the manner of confinement within prison. It is the basis for a prisoner's lawsuit attacking jail conditions or use of force by prison guards. *Farmer v. Brennan,*. 511 U.S. 825 (1994). This amendment applies only to prisoners or persons confined after conviction and not prior to conviction. *Whitley v. Albers*, 475 U.S. 312 (1986).

AMENDMENT IX

The enumeration in the constitution of certain rights shall not be construed to deny or disparage others retained by the people.

The Ninth Amendment is intended to assure that those rights inherent to citizenship in a democracy which are not specifically stated in the Constitution are still guaranteed. *United States v. Cook*, 311 F. Supp. 618 (W.D. Pa. 1970). The primary right found inherent within the Constitution is the right of personal privacy found by reading the First, Third, Fourth, and Ninth Amendments together. This right to privacy includes: The right to make a decision about abortion under certain circumstances is not subject to government regulation, *Roe v. Wade*, 410 U.S. 113 (1973); neither is the right to choose a means of contraception, *Griswold v. Connecticut*, 381 U.S. 479 (1965). Inherent rights do not include the right to private use of marijuana, *Wolkind v. Selph*, 495 F. Supp. 507, *aff'd*, 649 F.2d 865 (4th Cir. 1980) (unpublished); for persons of the same sex to marry, *Baker v. Nelson*, 291 Minn. 310, *appeal dismissed*, 409 U.S. 810 (1971); or to ride a motorcycle without a helmet, *State v. Albertson*, 93 Idaho 640 (1970). This right to privacy does limit the authority of the states. *Griswold v. Connecticut*, 381 U.S. 479 (1965).

AMENDMENT X

The powers not delegated to the United States by the constitution, nor prohibited by it to the states, are reserved to the states, respectively, or to the people.

The Tenth Amendment is intended to prevent the national government from exercising powers it does not have and prohibiting the states from exercising powers it does have. *United States v. Darby*, 312 U.S. 100 (1941). This reserved power will not prevent the federal government from choosing a particular method of enforcing its authority. States may not rely upon the Tenth Amendment to prevent the federal government from enforcing the authority it has under any of the provisions of the Constitution. The federal government can preempt a state in regulation of private activities which affect interstate commerce. *Hodel v. Virginia Surface Mining & Reclamation Ass'n,* 452 U.S. 264 (1981). The federal government may also impose minimum wage and hour requirements on state and local government employees. *Garcia v. San Antonio Transit Auth.*, 469 U.S. 528 (1985). The reserved power merely protects the states from being abolished. The federal government can accomplish any objective, either through tax incentives or exercise of power under specific provisions of the Constitution.

AMENDMENT XI

The judicial power of the United States shall not be construed to extend to any suit in law or equity, commenced or prosecuted against one of the United States by citizens of another state, or by citizens or subjects of any foreign state.

The Eleventh Amendment prevents a civil suit by a citizen against a state, a state agency, or a state employee in his "official capacity" for money damages. *Will v. Michigan Dep't of State Police,* 491 U.S. 58 (1990). A state may be sued for prospective injunctive relief. *Edelman v. Jordan,* 415 U.S. 651 (1974). On the other hand, cities and counties may be sued for money damages. This amendment protects only states and their agencies. *Monell v. Department of Social Servs.*, 436 U.S. 658 (1978).

AMENDMENT XII

The electors shall meet in their respective state, and vote by ballot for president and vice president, one of whom, at least, shall not be an inhabitant of the same state with themselves; they shall name in their ballots the person voted for as president, and in distinct ballots the person voted for as vice president, and they shall make distinct lists of all persons voted for as president, and of all persons voted for as vice president, and of the number of votes for each, which lists they shall sign and certify, and transmit sealed to the seat of government of the United States, directed to the president of the

senate;—the president of the senate shall, in the presence of the senate and house of representatives, open all the certificates and the votes shall then be counted;—the person having the greatest number of votes for president shall be the president, if such number be a majority of the whole number of electors appointed; and if no person have such majority, then from the persons having the highest numbers not exceeding three on the list of those voted for as president, the house of representatives shall choose immediately, by ballot, the president. But in choosing the president, the votes shall be taken by states, the representation from each state having one vote; a quorum for this purpose shall consist of a member or members from two-thirds of the states, and a majority of all the states shall be necessary to a choice. And if the house of representatives shall not choose a president whenever the right of choice shall devolve upon them before the fourth day of March next following, then the vice president shall act as president, as in the case of death or other constitutional disability of the president. The person having the greatest number of votes as vice president shall be vice president, if such number be a majority of the whole number of electors appointed, and if no person have a majority, then from the two highest numbers on the list the senate shall choose the vice president; a quorum for the purpose shall consist of two-thirds of the whole number of senators, and a majority of the whole number shall be necessary to a choice. But no person constitutionally ineligible to the office of president shall be eligible to that of vice president of the United States.

The Twelfth Amendment established the electoral college for election of the President and Vice President. The voters do not elect a President directly but vote for electors who actually cast votes for President and Vice President. The number of electors is based upon the number of senators and representatives each state has. This system creates the possibility that one candidate could win the popular vote but another be elected President by winning the large states by a narrow margin and losing the small states by a large margin. This happened in the 2000 presidential election between George W. Bush and Al Gore.

AMENDMENT XIII

§ 1. Neither slavery nor involuntary servitude, except as a punishment for crime whereof the party shall have been duly convicted, shall exist within the United States, or any place subject to their jurisdiction.

§ 2. Congress shall have power to enforce this article by appropriate legislation.

The Thirteenth Amendment ended state-authorized slavery in the United States and was ratified just after the Civil War ended. There are still cases of involuntary servitude that are discovered in such places as migrant labor camps. *United States v. Mussry*, 726 F.2d 1448 (9th Cir. 1984).

AMENDMENT XIV

§ 1. . . . No state shall make or enforce any law which shall abridge the privileges or immunities of citizens of the United States; nor shall any state deprive any person of life, liberty, or property, without due process of law; nor deny to any person within its jurisdiction the equal protection of the laws.

The Fourteenth Amendment was enacted just after the Civil War. It amounted to the greatest restriction upon the authority of the states since the Constitution replaced the Articles of Confederation. This amendment is designed to safeguard citizens' fundamental rights from arbitrary or oppressive state actions. *Thomas Cusack Co. v. Chicago*, 242 U.S. 526 (1917).

PRIVILEGES AND IMMUNITIES

The Privileges and Immunities Clause is designed to place citizens of each state upon the same footing as citizens of other states. *Supreme Court of Virginia v. Friedman*, 487 U.S. 59 (1988). This clause had the effect of creating a national citizenship and forced the independent states to recognize that they are part of a nation. This clause is also the basis of the Selective Incorporation Doctrine.

The limitation of the Privileges and Immunities Clause applies only to the action of state or local government and not to private individuals. *District of Columbia v. Carter*, 409 U.S. 418 (1973). The privileges that have been recognized as protected by this clause include the right to travel within the United States, *Griffin v. Breckenridge*, 403 U.S. 88 (1971), and the right to acquire, possess, or dispose of property, *Marchie Tiger v. Western Invest. Co.*, 221 U.S. 286 (1911). They do not include such businesses as the sale of intoxicating liquor. *Cox v. Texas*, 202 U.S. 446 (1906).

DUE PROCESS

The Due Process Clause is identical to language found in the Magna Carta, which established democracy in England. 16A Am. Jur. 2d *Synonymity of Due Process and Law of the Land* ∋ 811, at 965. Due process incorporates fundamental fairness and universally accepted concepts of justice for dealings between a state or local government and the persons it governs. The concept of due process by its very nature contemplates flexible procedures and concepts of fairness. *Ingraham v. Wright*, 430 U.S. 651 (1977).

Due process has dual aspects: procedural and substantive. Both aspects protect only life, liberty, or property from action by a state or local government. For example, if a public employee does not have a property interest in his job, then the Due Process Clause does not apply.

Procedural due process refers to the process or proceedings which the government must follow when taking life, liberty, or property from a person. The essence of procedural due process is notice and an opportunity to be heard in reasonable time. Notice is a written or verbal statement that life, liberty, or property will be or has been taken; the reason for the action; and how to challenge the action. "Opportunity to be heard" means a meaningful right to state why the life, liberty, or property should not be taken. Due process embodies different rules for different protected interests. A criminal defendant is entitled to more formality than a person who has his car towed. The primary concerns are fair play and substantial justice. 16A Am. Jur. 2d *Procedural Due Process; Definition and Requisites* § 813, at 967-70.

Substantive due process, on the other hand, prevents deprivation of life, liberty, or property by government action that is arbitrary or capricious. That is, laws must be rationally related to some legitimate government interest. *Pennell v. San Jose*, 485 U.S. 1 (1988).

All types of government action are covered under this standard of rationality. It also includes a requirement that all laws, rules, and policies be definite. This means that a law, rule, or policy must convey a sufficiently definite warning of the conduct that is proscribed—or that people of common intelligence need not guess at its meaning. *Keyishan v. Board of Regents*, 385 U.S. 589 (1972). Otherwise, the law, rule, or policy is void for vagueness and violates substantive due process.

EQUAL PROTECTION

The guiding principle of the Equal Protection Clause is that all persons shall be treated alike under like circumstances and conditions, both in privileges conferred and liabilities imposed. 16A Am. Jur. 2d *Nature of Guaranty* § 738, at 774-75. Although this clause protects persons from the actions of state and local government, it does not limit actions of private individuals who do not use the law to treat persons unequally. *Lombard v. Louisiana*, 373 U.S. 267 (1963). This clause is not absolute and does not prevent state and local governments from making reasonable classifications. *Levy v. Louisiana*, 319 U.S. 68 (1968). Likewise, the Equal Protection Clause does not require that reasonable classifications be made with a mathematical nicety, *William v. Vermont*, 472 U.S. 14 (1985), or that equal results occur, *Personnel Admin. of Mass. v. Fenney*, 442 U.S. 256 (1979).

Classifications created by law, rule, or policy that do not affect a "suspect classification" will be found to be reasonable and not arbitrary if the distinction rests upon some ground of difference having a fair and substantial relationship to the object of the legislation. *Eisenstadt v. Baird*, 405 U.S. 438 (1972). In other words, is some legitimate governmental policy furthered by this different treatment? *Police Dep't of Chicago v. Mosley*, 408 U.S. 92 (1972) (Prohibiting picketing by labor unions within 150 feet of a school from 30 minutes before school to 30 minutes after school ends violates equal protection because it only applies to labor unions). For example, the government may treat military veterans differently than nonveterans by granting them preference in hiring. A governmental policy of rewarding persons for military service is legitimate, and the classification is valid under the Equal Protection Clause. *Hooper v. Bernalillo County Assessor*, 472 U.S. 612 (1985). Also, treating minors differently than adults is a valid classification. *Dallas v. Stranglin*, 490 U.S. 519 (1989).

There are several "suspect classifications" that require substantially more justification than just a legitimate reason. Those "suspect classifications" include distinctions based upon race, color, national origin, religion, *Personnel Admin. of Mass. v. Fenney*, 442 U.S. 256 (1979), and sex, *Frontiero v. Richardson*, 411 U.S. 677 (1973). In order to base a distinction upon a "suspect classification," the government must show that there is a compelling state interest and that this distinction furthers that interest with no other reasonable alternative available. *Fenney*, 442 U.S. 256 (1979). Few classifications based upon suspect criteria have been upheld.

AMENDMENT XV

§ 1. The right of the citizens of the United States to vote shall not be denied or abridged by the United States or by any state on account of race, color, or previous condition of servitude.

§ 2. The congress shall have power to enforce this article by appropriate legislation.

The legal effect of this amendment is to prohibit racial discrimination in all aspects of state and federal elections. *Gray v. Sanders*, 372 U.S. 368 (1972).

AMENDMENT XVI

The congress shall have power to lay and collect taxes on incomes, from whatever source derived, without apportionment among the several states, and without regard to any census or enumeration.

The Sixteenth Amendment removed a limitation on taxation that was present in the main body of the Constitution which required all taxes to be apportioned among the states. This change allowed direct taxes upon a person's income. *William E. Peck & Co. v. Lowe*, 247 U.S. 165 (1918).

AMENDMENT XVII

The senate of the United States shall be composed of two senators from each state, elected by the people thereof, for six years; and each senator shall have one vote. The electors in each state shall have the qualifications requisite for electors of the most numerous branch of the state legislatures.

When vacancies happen in the representation of any state in the senate, the executive authority of such state shall issue writs of election to fill such vacancies: Provided, that the legislature of any state may empower the executive thereof to make temporary appointments until the people fill the vacancies by election as the legislature may direct.

This amendment shall not be so construed as to affect the election or term of any senator chosen before it becomes valid as part of the constitution.

The Seventeenth Amendment, ratified on May 31, 1913, changed the method of electing senators from election by a vote of the state legislature to election by popular vote of the people. It also established a system for filling vacancies that occur in the Senate.

AMENDMENT XVIII

§ 1. After one year from the ratification of this article, the manufacture, sale, or transportation of intoxicating liquors within, the importation thereof into, or the exportation thereof from the United States and all territory subject to the jurisdiction thereof, for beverage purposes, is hereby prohibited.

§ 2. The congress and the several states shall have concurrent power to enforce this article by appropriate legislation.

§ 3. This article shall be inoperative unless it shall have been ratified as an amendment to the constitution by the legislatures of the several states, as provided in the constitution, within seven years from the date of the submission hereof to the states by the congress.

Ratified on January 29, 1919, the Eighteenth Amendment imposed a ban on the possession and sale of alcoholic beverages, known as "prohibition." This amendment was repealed by the Twenty-First Amendment.

AMENDMENT XIX

§ 1. The right of citizens of the United States to vote shall not be denied or abridged by the United States or by any state on account of sex.

§ 2. Congress shall have power to enforce this article by appropriate legislation.

The Nineteenth Amendment was enacted as a result of the women's suffrage movement. Effective August 26, 1920, it prohibits states and the federal government from denying men and women the right to vote if the denial is based upon sex.

AMENDMENT XX

§ 1. The terms of the president and vice president shall end at noon on the 20th day of January, and the terms of senators and representatives at noon on the 3rd day of January, of the years in which such terms would have ended if this article had not been ratified; and the terms of their successors shall then begin.

§ 2. The Congress shall assemble at least once in every year, and such meeting shall begin at noon on the 3rd day of January, unless they shall by law appoint a different day.

§ 3. If, at the time fixed for the beginning of the term of the president, the president elect shall have died, the vice president elect shall become president. If a president shall not have been chosen before the time fixed for the beginning of his term, or if the president elect shall have failed to qualify, then the vice president elect shall act as president until a president shall have qualified; and the congress may by law provide for the case wherein neither a president elect nor a vice president elect shall have qualified, declaring who shall then act as president, or the manner in which one who is to act shall be selected, and such person shall act accordingly until a president or vice president shall have qualified.

§ 4. The congress may by law provide for the case of the death of any of the persons from whom the house of representatives may choose a president whenever the right of choice shall have devolved upon them, and for the case of death of any of the persons from whom the senate may choose a vice president whenever the right of choice shall have devolved upon them.

§ 5. Sections 1 and 2 shall take effect on the 15th day of October following the ratification of this article.

§ 6. This article shall be inoperative unless it shall have been ratified as an amendment to the constitution by the legislatures of three-fourths of the several States within seven years from the date of its submission.

The Twentieth Amendment establishes a date for the term of office for the President, Vice President, and members of Congress to begin and end. It also establishes a line of succession for the President and Vice President elect.

AMENDMENT XXI

§ 1. The eighteenth article of amendment to the constitution of the United States is hereby repealed.

§ 2. The transportation or importation into any state, territory, or the possession of the United States for delivery or use therein of intoxicating liquors, in violation of the laws thereof, is hereby prohibited.

§ 3. **This article shall be inoperative unless it shall have been ratified as an amendment to the constitution by conventions in the several states, as provided in the constitution, within seven years from the date of the submission hereof to the states by the congress.**

Amendment Twenty-One was ratified on December 3, 1933, and ended prohibition by repealing the Eighteenth Amendment. This constitutional provision specifically allowed regulation of transportation, importation, and possession of alcoholic beverages by government. It did not create a constitutional right to possess, transport, or consume alcoholic beverages.

AMENDMENT XXII

§ 1. **No person shall be elected to the office of the president more than twice, and no person who has held the office of president, or acted as president, for more than two years of a term to which some other person was elected president shall be elected to the office of the president more than once. But this article shall not apply to any person holding the office of president when this article was proposed by the Congress, and shall not prevent any person who may be holding the office of president, or acting as president, during the term within which this article becomes operative from holding the office of president or acting as president during the remainder of such term.**

§ 2. **This article shall be inoperative unless it shall have been ratified as an amendment to the constitution by the legislatures of three-fourths of the several States within seven years from the date of its submission to the States by the congress.**

A President is barred from serving more than two terms, consecutive or not, by the Twenty-Second Amendment. If the President assumes an unexpired term, he cannot serve more than a total of ten years.

AMENDMENT XXIII

§ 1. **The District constituting the seat of Government of the United States shall appoint in such manner as the Congress may direct:**

A number of electors of President and Vice President equal to the whole number of Senators and Representatives in Congress to which the District would be entitled if it were a State, but in no event more than the least populous State; they shall be in addition to those appointed by the States, but they shall be considered, for the purpose of the election of President and Vice President, to be electors appointed by a State; and they shall meet in the District and perform such duties as provided by the twelfth article of amendment.

§ 2. The Congress shall have power to enforce this article by appropriate legislation.

The Twenty-Third Amendment gave the residents of Washington, DC, the right to vote for President and Vice President by creating an electoral college for the District of Columbia.

AMENDMENT XXIV

§ 1. The right of citizens of the United States to vote in any primary or other election for President or Vice President, for electors for President or Vice President, or for Senator or Representative in Congress, shall not be denied or abridged by the United States or any State by reason of failure to pay any poll tax or other tax.

§ 2. The Congress shall have power to enforce this article by appropriate legislation.

The Twenty-Fourth Amendment outlawed the practice of requiring persons to pay a tax in order to vote or requiring them to be up to date on all property or income taxes before being eligible to vote. The view was that such requirements discriminated against the poor and discouraged voting in general.

AMENDMENT XXV

§ 1. In case of the removal of the President from office or of his death or resignation, the Vice President shall become President.

§ 2. Whenever there is a vacancy in the office of the Vice President, the President shall nominate a Vice President who shall take office upon confirmation by a majority vote of both Houses of Congress.

§ 3. Whenever the President transmits to the President pro tempore of the Senate and the Speaker of the House of Representatives his written declaration that he is unable to discharge the powers and duties of his office, and until he transmits to them a written declaration to the contrary, such powers and duties shall be discharged by the Vice President as Acting President.

§ 4. Whenever the Vice President and a majority of either the principal officers of the executive departments or of such other body as Congress may by law

provide, transmit to the President pro tempore of the Senate and the Speaker of the House of Representatives their written declaration that the President is unable to discharge the powers and duties of his office, the Vice President shall immediately assume the powers and duties of the office as Acting President.

Thereafter, when the President transmits to the President pro tempore of the Senate and the Speaker of the House of Representatives his written declaration that no inability exists, he shall resume the powers and duties of his office unless the Vice President and a majority of either the principal officers of the executive department or of such other body as Congress may by law provide, transmit within four days to the President pro tempore of the Senate and the Speaker of the House of Representatives their written declaration that the President is unable to discharge the powers and duties of his office. Thereupon Congress shall decide the issue, assembling within forty-eight hours for that purpose if not in session. If the Congress, within twenty-one days after receipt of the latter written declaration, or, if Congress is not in session, within twenty-one days after Congress is required to assemble, determines by two-thirds vote of both Houses that the President is unable to discharge the powers and duties of his office, the Vice President shall continue to discharge the same as Acting President; otherwise, the President shall resume the powers and duties of his office.

The Twenty-Fifth Amendment provides a procedure for succession when the President dies, resigns, or is removed from office. A procedure is also provided to replace the Vice President. Disability of the President results in assumption of the duties by the Vice President.

AMENDMENT XXVI

§ 1. The right of citizens of the United States, who are eighteen years of age or older, to vote shall not be denied or abridged by the United States or any State on account of age.

§ 2. The Congress shall have power to enforce this article by appropriate legislation.

The Twenty-Sixth Amendment was ratified on July 5, 1971. It is the last amendment and lowered the voting age for all state and federal elections from age twenty-one to eighteen.

CHAPTER 2

CONSTITUTIONAL LIMITATIONS ON CODES OF CONDUCT

All law enforcement agencies adopt policies concerning on- and off-duty conduct of their employees. Such policies must meet constitutional restrictions. A public employee cannot be required to surrender a constitutionally protected right in order to be hired or remain employed. Also, the constitutional limitation on the authority of government applies to employment regulations just as it does to criminal laws or other laws of general application. Employment regulations must not be (1) unconstitutionally vague, (2) so broad that an employee's rights as a citizen are infringed, or (3) arbitrary. The policy must (1) be related to job performance of the employee, or (2) affect the ability of the public agency to deliver public services.

VAGUENESS

The United States Constitution prohibits enforcement of policies which are **vague**. One of the basic principles of due process is notice of conduct which is prohibited. A vague policy is one which fails to "give the person of ordinary intelligence a reasonable opportunity to know what is prohibited, so that he may act accordingly. Vague laws may trap the innocent by not providing fair warning." *Grayned v. City of Rockford,* 408 U.S. 104, 108 (1972). A vague policy offends two other notions of fair play. First, a vague policy does not contain standards for the manager to apply the policy. Consequently, the policy can be applied arbitrarily or discriminatorily. In other words, the policy can be applied at the whim of the manager. Second, a vague policy may cause employees to forego legitimate constitutional conduct just to be sure that the vague policy is not violated. Id. at 108-09. The threat of sanctions may deter almost as potently as the application of sanctions themselves. *NAACP v. Dutton,* 371 U.S. 415, 433 (1963).

The vagueness limitation does not prohibit all policies with general or broad application. A policy that imposes discipline on any officer who "fails to do the right thing" is clearly vague. A person of ordinary intelligence will not always know what the "right thing" is, and managers have unlimited discretion in deciding what is the "right thing." On the other hand, "conduct unbecoming an officer and a gentleman" is not unconstitutionally vague. *Parker v. Levy,* 417 U.S. 733, 757 (1974). The Supreme Court held that even though it may be difficult to determine whether certain marginal conduct is "unbecoming," as long as the conduct for which an employee is being punished is clearly "unbecoming," the employee is put on notice. Policies that prohibit "misconduct," "immorality," or conduct that does not promote efficiency are not too vague. *Arnett v. Kennedy,* 410 U.S. 134 (1974). On the other hand, an ordinance that prohibited treating the American flag "contemptuously" is too vague. *Smith v. Gaguen,* 415 U.S. 566 (1974).

In order to avoid vagueness challenges, the policy must provide sufficient standards to allow the employee and the supervisor to know what conduct is prohibited. The policy may be found too vague if the conduct to which it is applied is marginal or if the court finds it unrelated to job performance or delivery of police services.

OVERBREADTH

The Constitution also prohibits policies which are overly broad. A policy is overbroad "if in its reach it prohibits constitutionally protected conduct." *Grayned v. City of Rockford*, 408 U.S. 104, 114 (1972). The question is whether the policy can reasonably be construed to prohibit both privileged and not privileged conduct. If so, it is too broad and will not be enforced. For example, a law prohibiting all picketing is too broad and restricts legitimate free speech under the First Amendment. Prohibiting picketing in or near a courthouse so as to interfere with free ingress and egress is not too broad. *Cameron v. Johnson*, 390 U.S. 611 (1968). A police department policy which provides that no member shall engage in any activity, conversation, deliberation, or discussion which is derogatory to the department or any member or policy of the department is too broad and restricts legitimate freedom of speech. *Muller v. Conlisk*, 429 F.2d 901 (7th Cir. 1990).

Also, the Supreme Court has been reluctant to strike down a statute or policy where there are a substantial number of situations in which it might validly be applied. *U.S. Civil Serv. Comm'n v. National Ass'n of Letter Carriers*, 413 U.S. 548, 580-81 (1973). The court does require the employee attacking the policy to demonstrate that the conduct being punished could not be regulated by a narrowly drawn policy. *Dombrowski v. Pfister*, 380 U.S. 479, 486 (1965).

Just as the policy of "conduct unbecoming an officer and a gentleman" is not unconstitutionally vague, it is likewise not unconstitutionally overbroad. *Parker v. Levy*, 417 U.S. 733, 760 (1974).

SUBSTANTIVE DUE PROCESS

The Due Process Clause of the Fourteenth Amendment prohibits state and local governments from depriving a person of liberty or property without due process of law. There are two aspects of due process: (1) procedural, and (2) substantive. Procedural due process refers to the requirement of notice and an opportunity to be heard before or after the taking of liberty or property. Substantive due process imposes a limit on what a state or local government can do, regardless of the procedural protections provided. In other words, government action which is arbitrary and not being given notice and a hearing will adequately protect the employee's liberty or property interest.

In the employment context, the "substantive due process" inquiry is limited to whether department policy or investigations involve matters unrelated to the government's position as employer. Policies and investigations subject to such an attack usually involve off-duty conduct and relate to private activities of an employee. When such off-duty activities affect the employee's right to privacy, *see Griswold v. Connecticut*, 381 U.S. 479, 484-86 (1965), or right to free associations, *NAACP v. Alabama*, 357 U.S. 449, 460-63 (1958), the government even as an employer cannot regulate or inquire into them, when there is no impact on the job.

For example, two off-duty police officers slept together one night. The female officer's estranged husband learned of the encounter and made an "officer needs assistance" call to his wife's location. Ten police cars with twenty officers arrived to assist. The officers were discovered and disciplined. The officers appealed the discipline, contending that the investigation violated the Due Process Clause. The court agreed and reversed the discipline because the investigation inquired into protected areas and was not limited to the effect the officers' relationship would have on the department. "Moreover, the questions that ensued were not confined narrowly, directly, and specifically to matters within the scope of the specific duties of the officers. Questions directed to whether the parties used contraceptives, whether pregnancy was likely to ensue, or how the sexual acts were performed are not questions that can be asked by a public employer." *Oddsen v. Board of Fire & Police Comm.*, 321 N.W.2d 161, 168-69 (Wis. 1982).

Had the investigation been limited to the effect the relationship would have on the job and the future ability to work together, then the court would not find it arbitrary. Such relationships which affect the job are subject to disciplinary action*, see Allen v. City of Greensboro*, 452 F.2d 489 (4th Cir. 1971), whereas consensual off-duty heterosexual activity by non-married co-workers is not, *Shawgo v. Spradlin*, 701 F.2d 470 (5th Cir.), *cert. denied*, 464 U.S. 965 (1983).

CONCLUSION

Policies must have standards narrowly drawn and related to the job. When conduct that does not relate to job performance or delivery of police services is punished, the courts may find the policy unconstitutional.

CHAPTER 3

EMPLOYMENT AT WILL

INTRODUCTION

The legal status of an employee will govern the protection afforded an employee and the legal requirements of a supervisor in dealing with an employee. The phrase "employment at will" refers to the concept that there is no set time or conditions for continued employment. That is, the employer-employee relationship can be terminated at any time by the employer for any reason or for no reason or even for a reason that is morally wrong. "Employment at will" is not unlimited. The employee cannot be terminated for an illegal reason, in violation of statutory protection or in violation of public policy. In England, there was a presumption that employment was for one year unless otherwise stated. The United States courts generally followed this rule after the American Revolution. The Industrial Revolution and the concept of individual freedom to contract caused the courts to reexamine this presumption, and at the end of the nineteenth century, the courts had adopted the rule that an employee without a definite term of employment was an employee at will and may be discharged without reason. *Coman v. Thomas Mfg. Co.*, 325 N.C. 172 (1989).

Since the initial adoption of the employment-at-will doctrine, it has been constantly eroded. Today, there are no true employment-at-will situations. All employees are provided some protection from termination for "improper" reasons. The extent of the protection depends upon state laws and court decisions within a particular state. An improper demotion or dismissal may result in an employee being promoted, reinstated, or given back pay or front pay. Litigation involving employment decisions is very expensive in terms of time, legal resources, and morale. This chapter will discuss some of the common exceptions to the employment-at-will doctrine.

EXCEPTIONS

Illegal Reasons

The Congress and the state legislatures have passed laws that limit the right of an employer to terminate an at-will employee. Federal statutes include antidiscrimination statutes such as Title VII of the Civil Rights Act of 1964, which prohibits discrimination on the basis of race, sex, color, national origin, and religion; the Americans with Disabilities Act, which prohibits discrimination on the basis of disability; and the Age Discrimination in Employment Act, which prohibits discrimination based upon age. Anti-retaliation statutes also make it illegal to fire an employee for filing complaints about violation of rights or testifying on behalf of others who claim a violation of rights. Legislatures may also grant protection for specific conduct, in order to ensure the effectiveness of a program. Some such protections usually prohibit retaliation for exercising certain rights, such as filing of workers compensation claims, *see* N.C. Gen. Stat. § 97-6.1; engaging in labor disputes, N.C. Gen. Stat. § 95-83; and filing OSHA claims, N.C. Gen. Stat. § 95-130(8). Many states also have "whistleblower" statutes. These laws prohibit discipline or dismissal for reporting illegal activities. *See* N.C. Gen. Stat. § 126-84 (state employees). Other such protections are available to the employee.

Statutory Protection

State legislatures or cities and counties have enacted civil service or other such protection which provide that an employer cannot dismiss an employee who is satisfactorily performing the job. These statutes or ordinances provide that after a period of training or probationary period, the employee can only be dismissed upon the employer demonstrating a violation of a policy or repeated failure to satisfactorily perform the job. The term usually used is that an employee can only be dismissed for "just cause." The personnel systems usually include a right to appeal a decision to dismiss to an independent body which can overrule management's decision. For example, the North Carolina General Assembly has established the State Personnel System to provide protection for state employees, including state police officers in the Highway Patrol, State Bureau of Investigation (SBI), and Alcohol Law Enforcement (ALE). *See* N.C. Gen. Stat. ch. 126 (1995). This system provides that a "career" state employee cannot be dismissed except for "just cause." A career state employee is a person employed in a full-time permanent position for the immediate twenty-four preceding months. N.C. Gen. Stat. § 126-1.1. The employee cannot be fired for failing to meet job performance requirements without the department showing prior written warnings documenting poor job performance. A career state employee can be fired for "personal conduct" or "grossly negligent" job performance without a prior written warning but only if the conduct amounts to "just cause." The system also provides for predemotion and predismissal conferences as well as postdemotion and postdismissal hearings before an administrative law judge employed by the Office of Administrative Hearings. The final decision on a dismissal of a career state employee is made by the State Personnel Commission, not the head of the agency. These rights protect the employee but restrict the ability of the law enforcement manager to remove inefficient employees.

Public Policy Exceptions

The courts have granted employees job protection by allowing wrongful discharge claims when such dismissal violates a "public policy." Public policy has been defined as the principle of law which holds that no citizen can lawfully do that which has a tendency to be injurious to the public or against the public good. *Petermann v. International Brotherhood of Teamsters*, 344 P.2d 25 (Cal. 1959). Other courts reach a similar result but characterize the analysis as one of an implied term of any contract, even an at-will contract, of good faith and fair dealing. Consequently, a bad-faith discharge would violate the terms of the contract and allow a lawsuit for breach of contract.

Some courts have adopted a four-part test to determine whether there is a public policy which is violated by disciplinary action. The test is as follows:

1. **clarity**: the employee must prove the existence of a clear public policy, such as protecting life, obeying the law, telling the truth as a witness, etc.;

2.   **jeopardy**: the employee must prove that discouraging the conduct that is the basis of the disciplinary action would jeopardize the public policy;

3.   **causation**: the employee must prove that the public policy-linked conduct caused the dismissal; and

4.   **absence of justification**: the **employer** must not be able to show an overriding justification for the dismissal.

See Gardner v. Loomis Armored Inc., 913 P.2d 377, 941 (Wash. 1996) (quoting Henry H. Perritt, Jr., <u>Workplace Torts: Rights and Liabilities</u> §§ 3.7, 3.14, 3.19, 3.21 [1991]); *Collins v. Rizkana*, 652 N.E.2d 653 (Ohio 1995). The United States Supreme Court was faced with the case where an arbitrator ordered a truck driver who twice tested positive for use of marijuana to be reinstated to his job with restrictions. The employer appealed contending that the federal government required drug testing and reinstating this driver violated the public policy of the federal government. The Supreme Court said that in order to establish such a public policy the court must look to the "positive law" which is "explicit," "well-defined," and "dominant." The court must look to established law and legal precedent. General considerations of what the policy "should be" are insufficient. In this case the Supreme Court reviewed the law from Congress and rules and regulations of the U.S. Department of Transportation. The rules allow for treatment and do not required dismissal of a driver. Based upon these rules, the Supreme Court said that it could not hold that the reinstatement violated the "public policy" of the United States. *Eastern Assoc. Coal Co. v. Mine Workers, 531 U.S. 57 (2000).*

The public policy exception will prevent an agency from enforcing its policy against a tenured or nontenured employee. The courts will not allow the agency to enforce a rule or policy which conflicts with the "public policy." Such exceptions include the dismissal of an employee who refused to violate federal safety regulations relating to the hours for driving a truck, *Coman v. Thomas Mfg. Co.*, 325 N.C. 172 (1989), and the dismissal of a nurse who refused to lie for a doctor during a malpractice trial, *Sides v. Duke Univ.*, 74 N.C. App. 331 (1985). Along this line, requiring an employee to choose between relinquishing a constitutional right or losing a job is prohibited and subjects the employer to a lawsuit. *See Garrity v. New Jersey*, 385 U.S. 493 (1967).

Contracts

The employment-at-will doctrine can also be modified by a contract. It can be an individual contract such a college coach or a teacher. It can also be a union contract which outlines the pay, terms, and conditions of employment for a group of employees, including limitations on dismissals. The law allows for these contracts as long as they do not violate the law or public policy.

Constitutional Limitations on Dismissal

The Fourteenth Amendment to the United States Constitution prohibits a government agency from depriving a person of property or liberty without due process of law. This amendment affects employment rights when a public employee has a recognizable property or liberty interest. Once this property of liberty or property interest is established, certain procedures must be followed when a government agency takes this interest away. The due process clause does not guarantee against incorrect or ill-advised personnel decisions, only that the employee will be given an opportunity to object to the taking of liberty or property. *Collins v. City of Harker Heights, Tex.*, 503 U.S. 115 (1992).

Property Interest

The United States Supreme Court has said that a public employee may have a property interest in the employment which cannot be taken away without affording the employee due process. There are two issues: First, when does an employee acquire a "property interest" in employment? And second, what process must be followed before an employee can have this property taken away?

Establishing a Property Interest

Property interests are not created by the Constitution, but by state law or local ordinance. *See Board of Regents v. Roth*, 408 U.S. 564 (1974). State laws such as those of the North Carolina State Personnel System give the "career" employee a property interest. If a state law or local ordinance grants protection against discharge except for "just cause," then an employee will be considered as having a property interest in employment. A state law that grants a fixed term of employment of a certain number of years gives a property interest. Statutes which say that employees serve at the pleasure of the employer do not grant a property interest.

Contracts also grant property interests. Usually, public employees do not sign written contracts. School teachers and football coaches are different and usually do sign contracts for a specified period. They cannot be terminated during the contract period without being afforded due process.

Employee handbooks or policy manuals may grant a property interest if they are adopted as a local ordinance. Unilaterally adopted handbooks that establish procedures required prior to dismissal do not grant a property interest. The courts will look to state law on contracts to decide if the employee has a legitimate claim to entitlement to the job.

The United States Supreme Court, in *Bishop v. Wood*, 426 U.S. 341 (1976), addressed the issue of property interest in a case involving a Marion, North Carolina, police officer. Officer Carl Bishop was employed on June 9, 1969, as a probationary officer. Under city ordinance, after six months he became a "permanent employee." On March 31, 1972, he was told that he was no longer needed as a police officer and was terminated. He was not told the reasons for his dismissal until he requested them, after filing the lawsuit. The local ordinance provided that "any discharged employee shall be given written notice of his discharge setting forth the effective date and the reasons for his discharge if he shall request such a notice." *Id.* at 344 n.5. There was no requirement for a hearing, but the ordinance did provide that if a "permanent employee fails to perform work up to the standard of the classification held, or continues to be negligent, inefficient, or unfit to perform his duties, he may be dismissed by the City Manager." *Id.* Despite this language, the United States Supreme Court held:

> On its face the ordinance . . . may fairly be read as conferring such a guarantee [of continued employment]. However, such a reading is not the only possible

interpretation; the ordinance may also be construed as granting no right to continued employment but merely conditioning an employees removal on compliance with certain specified procedures.

Id. at 345

The Court then held that North Carolina did not usually grant job protection. Since the state courts had not construed the ordinance, the Court would apply the usual rule and find no property interest. Officer Bishop, therefore, had no claim under the Fourteenth Amendment.

In the case of *Pittman v. Wilson County*, 839 F.2d 225 (4th Cir. 1988), the county adopted a personnel system by resolution of the county commissioners. All employees were given a copy of the resolution in an employee handbook. All employees agreed to be bound by the handbook. The handbook said that an employee could be dismissed only for causes related to poor job performance or personal conduct. Poor job performance required at least three prior warnings. Vickie Pittman, a dispatcher, resigned after a meeting with her superiors during which her resignation was demanded or she would be fired. Three days later, she asked for her job back, claiming that her resignation had been coerced. When she was not given her job back, she sued and claimed that her due process rights had been violated and that the county failed to follow its own procedures. The Fourth Circuit Court of Appeals was faced with the issue of whether Pittman had a property interest in her employment because of this handbook. After discussing the difference between a resolution and an ordinance, the court determined that the handbook was not adopted with sufficient formality to constitute a grant of a property interest in continued employment. Since there was no property interest in employment, the court held that the Due Process Clause did not apply and that Pittman had no claim.

Managers need to know the extent to which employees are protected from dismissal. If there is a statute, ordinance, or legally binding agreement between the government employer and the employee, then all procedures are established in the statute, ordinance, or contract. When there are no procedures established, then the constitutionally mandated procedures must be followed.

Procedures When Employee Has a Property Interest

When an employee does have a property interest in employment, the employer must grant the employee due process. The essence of due process is notice and an opportunity to be heard. Notice means the employee is given the reasons for the dismissal and told of any appeal rights. Notice should be in writing so that there are no questions as to the reasons for the dismissal and the procedures to follow to obtain a hearing. The timing and formality of the hearing under the Due Process Clause vary and depend upon a balancing of the citizen's interest and the government's interest. In the employment setting, an employee with a property interest in the job involves the balancing of the employee's interest in retaining his property, i.e., the job, versus the government's interest in removing an inefficient employee.

The Court also considers the risk of an erroneous deprivation of such property interest through the procedures used, and probable value, if any, of additional or substitute procedures. The Court adds into this evaluation the length and finality of the deprivation. Is it permanent or temporary? If temporary, how long does it last before a hearing or resolution of the matter? Under these circumstances, due process does not require an informal pre-suspension conference prior to suspension of an employee, even if the suspension is without pay. On the other hand, an informal, pre-dismissal conference is required prior to dismissal, as well as a full hearing after dismissal.

In *Gilbert v. Homar*, 520 U.S. 924 (1997), a police officer employed by a state university was charged with felony drug possession. University officials suspended the officer without pay pending their investigation. The officer sued claiming that the Due Process Clause required that he be given a pre-suspension conference prior to suspension, because he had a property interest in his job. The Supreme Court disagreed. The Court said that the Due Process Clause does not require a hearing, formal or informal, prior to a temporary deprivation of the officer's property interest in his job. The Court did say that the Due Process Clause requires some type of prompt post-suspension hearing and cited a case which provided a post-suspension hearing within 90 days. The Court did not decide the question of how long the suspension can last before the post-suspension hearing must be held.

In the case of *Cleveland Bd. of Education v. Loudermill*, 470 U.S. 532 (1985), the United States Supreme Court held that a state statute that established a civil service system created property interest in continued employment. The civil service system provided that employees were entitled to retain their positions during good behavior and efficient service, and prohibited dismissal except for misfeasance, malfeasance, or nonfeasance in office. The statute provided for a trial-type hearing **after** an employee was dismissed. The Court further said that due process requires an opportunity to present evidence of why the employee's property interest in the job should not be taken away, prior to the actual taking. This "predismissal conference" does not need to be elaborate. The Court does require:

> The essential requirements of due process . . . are notice and an opportunity to respond. The opportunity to present reasons, either in person or in writing, why proposed action should not be taken is a fundamental due process requirement. The tenured public employee is entitled to oral or written notice of the charges against him, an explanation of the employer's evidence, and an opportunity to present his side of the story. To require more than this prior to termination would intrude to an unwarranted extent on the government's interest in quickly removing an unsatisfactory employee.

> *Id.* at 546 (citations omitted)

At the predismissal conference, there is no requirement that an attorney be allowed into the room or that the employee be given an opportunity during the conference to consult with one. *Wallace v. Tilley*, 41 F.3d 296 (7th Cir. 1994). The exact parameters of such a hearing have not been settled by the United States Supreme Court. Due process does require that the employee be judged by an impartial decisionmaker. An "impartial decisionmaker" is some one who does not have a personal bias against the employee. The United States Supreme Court has held that there is no *per se* violation of due process when an administrative tribunal acts as both investigator and adjudicator on the same matter. *Withrow v. Larkin,* 421 U.S. 35, 58 (1975).

This author suggests that the employer always conduct an investigation in which the employee is informed of the complaint or charges and is given an opportunity to respond prior to any tentative decision on discipline. This investigation should inform the employee of the evidence known to the employer so that at the "predismissal conference," the employee should have nothing further to add. The employee should be given written notice of the proposed action and the reasons for it at least twenty-four hours in advance of the hearing. *Staples v. Milwaukee*, 142 F.3d 383 (7th Cir. 1998) (contemporaneous notice of reasons for dismissal is insufficient); *Panozzo v. Rhoads*, 905 F.2d 135 (7th Cir. 1998) (notice the night before is sufficient). If a written internal investigative report has been prepared, a copy should be made available to the employee. The employee then has the required information. *Harrison v. Wille*, 132 F.3d 679 (11th Cir. 1998) (reviewing the investigative file is sufficient). The representative(s) of the employer, preferably only one or two people, and the employee should sit in a room, and the evidence and the reasons should be outlined for the employee's response. The meeting can be recorded or notes transcribed if there is no recording. After the conference, all the additional information presented by the employee should be given to the final decision-maker, along with the original report. *Samuel v. Holmes*, 138 F.3d 173 (5th Cir. 1998) (employee must be given an opportunity to respond to evidence, even if the employee chooses to remain silent). The final decision should not be made until after an adequate time to consider the additional information.

After a dismissal, the employee must be given the opportunity for a full adversary hearing before an impartial decision-maker. The employee should have the right to an attorney and the right to cross-examine witnesses and present witnesses on his or her behalf. The final decision-maker should make a written decision stating the basis of the action taken.

Whether all this formality is necessary has not been finally decided. However, this procedure should be sufficient to meet any challenge.

Liberty Interest—What It Means

The Due Process Clause protects not only property, but also liberty. Within the employment context, liberty means the freedom to pursue other occupations. The United States Supreme Court has interpreted this term to include an employee's "good name, reputation, honor, or integrity." *Board of Regents v. Roth*, 408 U.S. 564, 573 (1972). An employer may not deprive the employee of his or her "good name, reputation, honor, or integrity" by publicly revealing charges against the employee that would stigmatize him or her so as to seriously damage the employee's standing and associations in the community or foreclose the employee's opportunity to take advantage of other employment opportunities. *Shands v. City of Kennett*, 993 F.2d 1337 (8th Cir. 1993). In order for a liberty interest to be affected, there must be defamation and a dismissal that foreclose future employment opportunity. The employee must allege and prove that the stigmatizing information contained in his or her personnel file was in fact false. True information in the file, no matter how negative, does not give rise to a liberty interest claim. *Codd v. Velger*, 429 U.S. 624 (1977).

The Eleventh Circuit Court of Appeals summarized the elements of a claim for a violation of liberty interest:

> In order to establish that a deprivation of a public employee's **liberty interest** has occurred without due process of law, the employee must prove that: (1) a false statement (2) of a stigmatizing nature (3) attending a governmental employee's

discharge (4) was made public (5) by the governmental employer (6) without a meaningful opportunity for employee name clearing.

Cannon v. City of West Palm Beach, 250 F.3d 1299 (11th Cir. 2001)

Placing false information in a file that is subject to inspection by the public amounts to making the information public. In Florida, personnel files of government employees can be viewed by the public. *Id.* at 1301.

Defamation means that the charges are, in fact, false. Stating true reasons for a dismissal does not deprive the former employee of liberty, but the employer must prove the truth of the allegations during a hearing of some kind. Also, the allegations must be of a serious character defect, such as dishonesty or immorality, in order to affect a person's liberty interest. Allegations of unsatisfactory job performance or general misconduct are insufficient to trigger a due process liberty interest. *Robinson v. City of Montgomery*, 809 F.2d 1355 (8th Cir. 1987). Allegations of writing false speeding tickets is sufficient to trigger liberty interest protection. *Palmer v. City of Monticello*, 31 F.3d 1499 (10th Cir. 1994). The defamation must be made in connection with a dismissal from employment. Merely having defamatory information in the file may allow for a state tort of defamation, but it is not a constitutional violation. *Seigert v. Gilley*, 500 U.S. 226, 233 (1991) ("Defamation, by itself, is a tort actionable under the laws of most States, but not a constitutional deprivation."). There must be a change or alteration in the legal status of the employee to establish a liberty interest claim. *See Paul v. Davis*, 424 U.S. 693, 701 (1976).

Consequently, employees without a property interest in employment, such as trainees, probationary employees, and deputy sheriffs, are usually dismissed without any reason being given. The "Dear John" letter will usually state that the employee's services are "no longer needed." This letter avoids creating a liberty interest and thus avoids the necessity for a hearing.

Procedures Required for Liberty Interest—"Name Clearing" Hearing

If a liberty interest is affected by a dismissal, the employee is entitled to a "name clearing" hearing. This hearing need not be as formal as one involving a property interest. It is not one in which the employee can get his job back, only one in which he can clear his name. In *Boston v. Webb*, 783 F.2d 1163 (4th Cir. 1986), Boston was a Washington, North Carolina, police officer. Allegations surfaced that he was taking bribes from known drug dealers. The State Bureau of Investigation (SBI) was called in to investigate. During the six-month investigation, the SBI gave a polygraph to a witness who claimed to have seen Boston accept the bribe. The witness passed the polygraph. Boston asked for the opportunity to take a polygraph and was given one. Although the results of Boston's polygraph were not introduced into evidence, after the police chief learned of the results, Boston was fired. Boston asked for a hearing. The hearing was held before Webb, the city manager. The chief stated that the reason for Boston's dismissal was the taking of a $1,000 bribe, but he admitted that he had no firsthand knowledge. Boston denied the charges, and the drug dealer who was alleged to have given the bribe appeared and denied giving the bribe. The hearing was recessed so that

Webb could talk with the SBI agent who gave the polygraph and to the witness. Boston was not allowed at this "investigatory hearing," although his attorney was given the right to submit written questions, which he did not do. A tape recording of the witness denying he ever made charges of bribe-taking was presented. Boston was told he would be given an opportunity to "rebut" the allegation in a final hearing. The hearing was held, and Boston and his counsel appeared and denied the allegations. No other evidence or witnesses were presented. Webb wrote to Boston, stating that his dismissal was upheld. A news release was issued by Webb stating that Boston was warned of the allegations, was given an opportunity to disprove the allegations, and was unable to do so.

Boston sued, claiming a violation of his due process rights under the Fourteenth Amendment. The federal court dismissed the lawsuit and said that the procedure employed was constitutional. The court said that a "liberty interest" or "name clearing" hearing need not be as formal as a property interest hearing. The balancing of competing interests of the government's need to remove inappropriate employees versus the employee's right to clear his name has been met under these procedures. The right to cross-examine witnesses is not essential to due process, and the city manager was sufficiently impartial to meet due process despite the fact that he knew of the investigation and allegations prior to holding the hearing.

This case emphasizes that due process is a balancing of competing interests. It also shows that care must be taken in releasing personnel information if a hearing is not provided. Most personnel information is not public but can be released in limited circumstances. The agency has an interest in assuring the public that employees are treated appropriately and also that employees who commit improper acts are removed. In many cases, the public will rightly demand to know what the public manager did and why. The manager will be compelled to release some information. The agency, however, must provide for a procedure to allow the dismissed employee an opportunity to clear his name.

CONCLUSION

Most employees have some protection from job actions. The public manager must be familiar with agency policy. In our litigious society and with jobs being so important, civil litigation over job action drains needed resources and disrupts the proper functioning of an agency. Personnel decisions concerning demotions and dismissals must be made only after a thorough investigation and in strict compliance with agency policies and applicable laws.

CHAPTER 4

DISCRIMINATION IN EMPLOYMENT

(TITLE VII OF THE CIVIL RIGHTS ACT)

INTRODUCTION

This chapter will provide an overview of the federal Equal Employment Opportunity Act found at 42 U.S.C. §§ 2000e-1 to -13 and 42 U.S.C. §§ 1981 and 1981a. In addition to these statutes, there are other laws which affect employment, including the Americans With Disabilities Act, 42 U.S.C. § 12101; the Age Discrimination in Employment Act, 28 U.S.C. § 623; and other federal and state laws that are too extensive to be discussed here.

BACKGROUND

Prior to the 1964 Civil Rights Act, there existed in many parts of the country, particularly the South, government-enforced racial segregation in public facilities and employment. The first attempt to dismantle government-authorized segregation was in public accommodations and transportation. In 1964, Titles I and II of the Civil Rights Act were enacted; they outlawed discrimination based upon certain criteria including race, color, religion, sex, or national origin. Congress next turned to employment discrimination. In 1968, Title VII was added to the Civil Rights Act, prohibiting discrimination in the private sector by any company employing twenty or more employees. The Equal Employment Opportunity Commission (EEOC) was also created to investigate and attempt to resolve complaints prior to the filing of a lawsuit. States, counties, and municipalities were exempted from the definition of employer.

Title VII was amended in 1972, and state and local governments were added to the definition of employer. As a result, the federal government began investigating complaints of discrimination involving state and local police agencies. The 1972 amendments prohibited the EEOC from suing a state or local government agency. Such a lawsuit must be initiated by the United States Department of Justice. The United States Department of Justice began investigating state police agencies and the larger county and municipal agencies. Numerous lawsuits were filed and resulted in consent decrees mandating affirmative action in hiring and the abolition of many preemployment requirements. Most of such preemployment requirements were based upon the practices of the military or the Federal Bureau of Investigation. The decision-making process for employing law enforcement officers was forever changed. The makeup of the law enforcement agencies' workforce was also changed with the addition of many more women and minorities.

Title VII was not substantially changed from 1972 until 1991. During this time, the courts made many decisions that had a substantial effect on hiring and promotion policies. In 1990, certain members of Congress became concerned with the "conservative" interpretations that the United States Supreme Court had given to Title VII. In 1990, amendments were passed by Congress to "restore" certain provisions to Title VII. President Bush vetoed these amendments. In 1991, a second bill was passed; this bill was signed by President Bush. The 1991 Civil Rights Act was a compromise, and members of Congress disagreed among themselves about what it meant and also disagreed with the President. The full effect of these amendments will not be known for years to come.

In addition to Title VII, a statute enacted after the Civil War, 42 U.S.C. § 1981, prohibited discriminating on the basis of race in the making of any contract. This law was not originally used to prohibit employment discrimination but by its plain language made intentional discrimination in employment unlawful. The United States Supreme Court interpreted this statute to prohibit racial and ethnic discrimination, but not discrimination on the basis of sex or religion. The Court also strictly interpreted this to the "making" of a contract and not to on-the-job harassment. The 1991 Civil Rights Act amended this statute to prohibit discrimination in the "formation and enforcement" of a contract. Also, the 1991 act added Section 1981a, which is used in conjunction with Title VII when there is an issue of "intentional" discrimination.

STATUTORY SCHEME

Title VII establishes a statutory framework for analysis of claims of discrimination. It also establishes a mandatory administrative procedure for reviewing such claims prior to filing lawsuits. Title VII prohibits consideration of certain characteristics when making employment decisions. Consideration of race, color, religion, sex, or national origin is made an unlawful employment practice. There are some exceptions to the prohibition if the employer can show that the particular characteristic is essential to the business. Title VII was not intended to interfere with legitimate business decisions, but only to treat persons fairly.

§ 2000e-2. Unlawful Employment Practices

(a)   Employer practices. It shall be an unlawful employment practice for an employer:

(1)   to fail or refuse to hire or to discharge any individual, or otherwise to discriminate against any person with respect to his compensation, terms, conditions, or privileges of employment because of the individual's race, color, religion, sex, or national origin; or

(2)   to limit, segregate, or classify his employees or applicants for employment in any way which would deprive or tend to deprive any individual of employment opportunities or otherwise adversely affect his status as an employee, because of such individual's race, color, religion, sex, or national origin.

42 U.S.C. § 2000e-2(a)

DISPARATE IMPACT

Title VII prohibits unlawful employment practices that are unintentional as well as intentional. Unintentional discrimination is shown by demonstrating that a selection device has the **effect** of disqualifying substantially more people possessing the identified criteria (e.g., race, sex, etc.) than others not possessing this criteria. This type of discrimination is referred to as "disparate impact" or "adverse impact." This employment practice has an effect or impact that results in discrimination, even if there was no intent to have such a result.

In order to show an unintentional violation of Title VII, or disparate impact, the complaining party must show that a neutral employment practice that is applied to all persons has an unintended effect of excluding persons based upon race, color, religion, sex, or national origin. If this is done, the employer must demonstrate that the challenged practice is job-related for the position in question and consistent with business necessity. The complaining party can still prevail if the complaining party demonstrates that there is an alternative employment practice that does not have disparate impact, and the employer refuses to adopt such alternative. *See* 42 U.S.C. § 2000e-2(k)(1)(A).

Disparate impact is shown if the requirement for a job or promotion results in selection or promotion in a racial, sexual, or ethnic pattern significantly different from the pool of applicants. The term "significantly different" has been defined by EEOC regulations as the "four-fifths" or the "eighty percent" rule. This rule reads as follows:

> A selection rate for any race, sex, or ethnic group which is less than four-fifths (4/5) (or eighty percent) of the rate for the group with the highest rate will generally be regarded by Federal enforcement agencies as evidence of adverse impact.

29 C.F.R. § 1607.4

This rule requires the agency to determine the passing rate or percentage for the most successful group and compare it to the other group. If the less successful group does not pass at eighty percent of the more successful group, then disparate impact has been shown. For example, assume your agency gives a physical agility test to applicants in order to test strength. If forty males take the test and twenty pass, the passing rate is fifty percent (20/40 = .5 or 50%). This means that the passing rate for females must be at least forty percent (50% x 80% = 40%). If twenty females take the same test, then at least eight must pass (20 x 40% = 8). The number of persons taking the test and used for the analysis must be sufficiently large so that the results are not cause by mere chance. The number needed is subject to debate by statisticians and is beyond the scope of this book.

This analysis must be performed for each selection device, even if the overall or bottom line does not result in a disparate impact. *Connecticut v. Teal*, 457 U.S. 440 (1982). An applicant can show disparate impact if a particular selection device resulted in his or her elimination and that device had an adverse impact. The 1991 Civil Rights Act added a proviso that if the employer can show that the elements of "the decision making process are not capable of separation for analysis, the decision making process may be analyzed as one employment practice." 42 U.S.C. § 2000e-2(k)(1)(B)(i). Most agencies will have selection devices that can be separated. Also, this analysis applies to subjective criteria, such as background investigations and applicant review boards, as well as objective ones. *Watson v. Fort Worth Bank & Trust Co.*, 487 U.S. 977 (1988).

By performing an analysis of this type for each step in the selection process, the agency can save itself substantial time and money. The 1991 Civil Rights Act added the following:

> If the respondent [employer] demonstrates that a specific employment practice does not cause disparate impact, the respondent shall not be required to demonstrate that such practice is required by business necessity.

> 42 U.S.C. § 2000e-2(k)(1)(B)(ii)

This means that the practice can be used without the necessity of a validation study or any other justification.

JOB-RELATED AND BUSINESS NECESSITY

If the applicant or employee, referred to as the "complaining party," demonstrates adverse or disparate impact as shown above, then the burden falls on the employer to "demonstrate that the challenged practice is job related for the position in question and consistent with business necessity." 42 U.S.C. Э 2000e-2(k)(1)(A)(i). The word "demonstrates" is defined to mean that the employer "meets the burden of production and persuasion." 42 U.S.C. Э 2000e-2(m). It is no longer sufficient to produce some evidence of job-relatedness; the employer must also persuade the judge that the selection device is related to the particular job sought by the applicant.

Most preemployment tests will demonstrate an ability to read and write or some general intelligence, all of which are required for any job. The question is how closely related the device must be to the job. This relationship is unclear, and the 1991 Civil Rights Act did not add much clarity. The Interpretive Memorandum that Congress adopted as legislative history provides:

> The terms "business necessity" and "job related" are intended to reflect the concepts enunciated by the Supreme Court in *Griggs v. Duke Power Co.*, 401 U.S. 424 (1971), and other Supreme Court decisions prior to *Wards Cove Packing Co. v. Atonio*, 490 U.S. 642 (1989).

> 137 Cong. Rec. § 15276.

In the *Griggs* case, the United States Supreme Court said the device "must have a manifest relationship to the employment in question." 401 U.S. at 432. The other cases included *New York City Transit Auth. v. Beazer*, 440 U.S. 568 (1979), which involved the prohibition in hiring anyone who had used narcotic drugs, including methadone. The Court held that the selection device was required by the employer's "legitimate employment goals of safety and efficiency." *Id.* at 587 n.31. The *Wards Cove* case even requires a showing that the selection device "serves, in a significant way, the legitimate employment goals of the employer." 490 U.S. at 659. The question is, do such legitimate employer goals include customer preference, morale, or company image? Or, is the legitimate goal limited to performing the essential functions of the job? The law does not say, but it is most likely that any selection device that has a substantial adverse impact must be shown to be directly related to the applicant's ability to perform the essential functions of the job or be related to the safety of co-workers or the public.

The best method of demonstrating that a selection device is job-related is to have it "validated." This means that an outside expert determines that the selection device is job-related and consistent with business necessity. A selection device, however, is not "validated" until the employer is sued, and some court determines that it is "validated." Public agencies have spent hundreds of thousands of dollars on selection devices, only to have a court determine that the device is not sufficiently job-related. A professionally developed selection device is the best way to assure that Title VII is not violated, but there are no guarantees.

Each such validation study starts with a job task analysis. This analysis is usually conducted by a survey of the members holding the particular job to determine the essential and nonessential functions of the job. This will be weighed according to the harm that will occur to the agency or the public if the employee cannot perform the task. After the essential functions are determined, selection criteria will be developed to measure an applicant's ability to perform these functions. Of course, if an essential function requires training to perform, then a preemployment selection device may not be appropriate. For example, it may be extremely important for an officer to be able to use a tear-gas gun. This is not the kind of skill that an applicant will acquire except through training and to require an applicant to demonstrate proficiency is not reasonable. Cutoff scores must then be established. The EEOC regulations refer to cutoff scores as follows:

> H.   Where cutoff scores are used, they should normally be set so as to be reasonable and consistent with normal expectations of acceptable proficiency within the work force. Where applicants are ranked on the basis of properly validated selection procedures and those applicants scoring below a higher cutoff score than appropriate in light of such expectations have little or no chance of being selected for employment, the higher cutoff score may be appropriate, but the degree of adverse impact should be considered.

29 C.F.R. § 1607.5

The cutoff score must be reasonable. This means that it cannot be higher than what existing employees who perform adequately can make. This does not mean, however, that the cutoff score must be the same as the lowest score of all current employees. The agency must look at the ability of the existing workforce and the adverse impact that the cutoff score has and select a reasonable score. This determination is subject to second-guessing by the courts.

If applicants are to receive a rank for the test, rather than just pass-fail, the correlation between the test score and job performance must be high. In other words, an applicant making ninety on the test will perform the job substantially better than an applicant making eighty-five. If challenged, a court may find that the test is sufficiently job-related to allow pass-fail, but find that there is no correlation between a higher score and job performance.

The agency may want to hire only people who will be sufficiently qualified so they can be promoted within a specified period of time. Does Title VII require that the selection criteria apply only to the entry level job, or can it relate to the first promotion? The EEOC regulations allow the use of such selection procedures that consider whether the applicant is capable of being promoted and do not limit inquiry to the entry level job if the job progression structures provide for the majority of employees to be promoted to a higher job within a reasonable time. The progress needs to be almost automatic, and a reasonable period cannot exceed five years. Also, the selection device may not measure knowledge, skills, or ability for the higher job, which the employee will be expected to develop principally from the training or experience on the job. 29 C.F.R. § 1607.5.

Validation studies that are performed must also be updated from time to time. This is especially true if the essential tasks change.

There are tests available that have been validated for particular law enforcement or other jobs. An agency is authorized to either purchase a test that is valid or borrow a validation study from another agency. This procedure can be used if the agency can show that its job is substantially the same as the other job for which the study or test was developed. 29 C.F.R. § 1607.7. Purchasing of such a test may be the least expensive method of obtaining a valid test.

ALTERNATIVE PRACTICE WITH LESS ADVERSE IMPACT

Even if the test is validated, the complaining party can still prevent its use and win if the complaining party can show that there is an alternative selection device that has less adverse impact and that can still serve the agency's legitimate goals. This procedure will be difficult to anticipate. It is clear that, in validating a test, alternative devices must be considered. 29 C.F.R. § 1607.3(B). A comparison of two tests to determine if they are equally effective will be difficult. The agency should, at least, explore alternatives and document the reasons for choosing a particular selection device.

ADVERSE TREATMENT

Title VII also prohibits intentional discrimination on the basis of race, color, religion, sex, or national origin. Intentional discrimination is referred to as "adverse" or "disparate" treatment. The statutory framework for an adverse treatment case involving the hiring of an employee is as follows:

1. The complaining party establishes a *prima facie* case by showing:
    a. the complaining party is from a protected class[race, sex, religion, etc.];
    b. the complaining party is qualified for and applied for the position;
    c. the complaining party was denied the position; and
    d. after the denial, the position remained open to persons of the complaining party's qualifications.
2. The employer must show a nondiscriminatory reason for the decision.

3.   The complaining party can show that the reason is a pretext to hide discrimination.

McDonald-Douglas v. Green, 411 U.S. 792 (1973).

A *prima facie* case means the applicant suing has proved sufficient facts to win the case. If the employer fails to come forward with a nondiscriminatory reason for the decision not to hire, the applicant has introduced sufficient evidence to prevail. The ultimate burden of proof of discrimination is on the applicant so the court is not required to rule in favor of the applicant. *St. Mary's Honor Center v. Hicks*, 509 U.S. 502 (1993) (Mere fact that the employer's reason was rejected does not mean that the person suing must prevail). The fact that the employer introduces evidence of a nondiscriminatory reason does not mean that the employer will win. The judge or jury can reject the employer's reason and can rule in the applicant's favor based solely upon the applicant's *prima facie* case. *Reeves v. Sanderson Plumbing Products, Inc.*, 530 U.S. 133 (2000).

Unlike unintentional discrimination, where the agency can defend its actions by showing they are required by "business necessity," there is no such defense to intentional discrimination. Even if a practice is required by business necessity, the requirement cannot be justification for intentional discrimination against a person. 42 U.S.C. § 2000e-2(k)(2). In other words, if the practice is necessary, it must be applied to all candidates and not applied to some and not to others.

The agency must be very careful to be consistent in the application of preemployment and promotion requirements to prevent intentional discrimination claims. An applicant or employee who is passed over and who can show favorable treatment for a person of another race, color, religion, sex, or national origin can most likely establish a *prima facie* case for discrimination. The agency must then demonstrate a nondiscriminatory reason for treating either the complaining party or the other person differently. As long as the reason for the different treatment is not based upon race, color, religion, sex, or national origin, the complainant cannot prevail. Even such reasons as political connections or familial relations are defenses to a discrimination claim under Title VII.

When investigating such a claim of intentional discrimination, the EEOC or the complainant will look at the files of the other employees or applicants of another race, sex, etc., who passed the test and compare them to the complaining party and others of the complaining party's race, sex, etc. The complaining party will then attempt to show that the agency holds the complainant and others of his or her race, sex, etc., to a higher standard. For example, assume the complainant is alleging discrimination based upon sex in hiring. The complainant will determine if there are any **automatic disqualifiers**, such as a felony conviction. If a male applicant with a felony conviction is hired, then this will be evidence of discrimination on the basis of sex.

The complainant will review all subjective selection criteria, such as background investigations or applicant review boards. The complainant will then compare the number of negative factors for males who are hired to the negative factors for females who are rejected. If a male has a child out of wedlock and is hired but a female has a child out of wedlock and is not hired, this is evidence of discrimination. This procedure will be followed for all applicants and all selection criteria.

The agency can protect itself by having one person review all minority and female applicants who are rejected because of subjective criteria and compare them to the majority and male applicants who are accepted in order to ensure consistency. If this is not done, then a complainant may find evidence to argue that your reason for rejection was a pretext for discrimination.

The same type of investigation will be used when the issue is a discriminatory discharge because there is a similar statutory procedure for proving intentional discrimination in imposing discipline on an employee. The analysis is:

1. The complaining party establishes a *prima facie* case by showing:
   a. the complaining party is from a protected class (race, sex, etc.);
   b. the prohibited conduct in which he engaged was comparable in seriousness to misconduct of employees outside his class (another race, sex, etc.); and
   c. that the disciplinary measures enforced against him were more severe than those enforced against employees outside his class.
2. The employer must show a nondiscriminatory reason for the decision.
3. The complaining party can show that the reason is a pretext to hide discrimination.

Cook v. CSX Trans. Corp., 988 F.2d 507, 510 (4th Cir. 1993)

The person suing will attempt to show that the discipline imposed on him is more severe than other employees of another race, sex, color, religion or national origin. If there is not a nondiscriminatory reason for the severity of the punishment, then the court could conclude that the real reason is unlawful discrimination. For example, a female who is discharged will compare her record to the records of male employees who were charged with similar violations of policy. If she was treated more severely, then this will be evidence that an unlawful characteristic, "sex," was the basis of the decision to terminate the female employee. Consistency in application of policies is essential. If a male employee who has a child out of wedlock is merely required to support that child, then the female employee cannot be disciplined for having a child out of wedlock.

MIXED MOTIVE DECISIONS

There are many factors that enter into an employment decision. One issue is, what is the appropriate remedy when a complaining party can prove the existence of a discriminatory motive, and the employer can prove it would have taken the same action even absent that motive? The Supreme Court in *Price Waterhouse v. Hopkins*, 490 U.S. 228 (1989), held that the complaining party was not entitled to relief since the discriminatory motive could not be shown to be the cause. Congress specifically overruled this decision when it passed the 1991 Civil Rights Act.

> An unlawful employment practice is established when the complaining party demonstrates that race, color, religion, sex, or national origin was a motivating factor for any employment practice, even though other factors also motivated the practice.

> 42 U.S.C. § 2000e-2(m)

However, Congress did limit what a court can award to the complaining party.

> On a claim in which an individual proves a violation of section 703(m) [42 U.S.C. § 2000e-2(m)] and a respondent [employer] demonstrates that the respondent would have taken the same action in the absence of the impermissible motivating factor, the court --
> (i)   may grant declaratory relief, injunctive relief (except as provided in clause (ii)), and attorney's fees and cost demonstrated to be directly attributable only to the pursuit of a claim under section 703(m) [42 U.S.C. § 2000e-2(m)]; and
> (ii) shall not award damages or issue an order requiring reinstatement, hiring, promotion, or payment of back pay.
>
> 42 U.S.C. § 2000e-5(g)(2)(B)

The employee can get an injunction prohibiting discrimination in the future and the employer will be required to pay the employee's attorney's fees, but not back pay or reinstatement.

RETALIATION

Title VII also prohibits an employer from taking adverse action against an employee who files an Title VII complaint, testifies against the employer about Title VII violations or even merely complains to supervisors about violations of Title VII. Even if the employer did not discriminate against the employee, if the employer retaliates against the employee, Title VII is violated. The statutory analysis is as follows:

1.   The complaining party establishes a *prima facie* case by showing:
   a.   the complaining party engaged protected activity [filed Title VII complaint, etc];
   b.   her employer took adverse employment action against her; and
   c.   a sufficient causal connection exists between her protected activity and her employer's adverse employment action.
2.   The employer must show a nondiscriminatory reason for the decision.
3.   The complaining party can show that the reason is a pretext to hide discrimination.

McNair v. Sullivan, 929 F.2d 974, 980 (4th Cir. 1991)

If an employee files a Title VII complaint or openly complains about discrimination, then the employer must be cognizant of the fact that the employee can allege retaliation. An employee may file a discrimination complaint in order to discourage an investigation or discipline. There is no way to avoid a complaint of retaliation when an investigation or discipline is necessary. The more compelling the reason for the investigation or discipline the stronger the employer's position.

EEOC PROCEDURES

When Title VII was passed in 1968, Congress realized that thousands of complaints of discrimination could be filed. In order to reduce the number of lawsuits and to attempt to resolve these matters as quickly and as inexpensively as possible, the Equal Employment Opportunity Commission (EEOC) was established. This Commission was charged with investigating and attempting to settle all claims. To assure that this administrative procedure was used, Congress prohibited a lawsuit being brought pursuant to Title VII until it was investigated by the Commission, and if not resolved, the complaining party received a "right to sue" letter. Failure to file with the EEOC or follow its rules prohibited a complaining party from bringing a claim under this statute. The EEOC procedures are as follows:

1.   The complaining party must file a complaint with the EEOC within 180 days of the last act of discrimination. The complaint must be under oath and specify the type or types of discrimination. (In some cases, the EEOC has a Section 706 deferral agreement with a state or local agency. This means that instead of the investigation being conducted by the EEOC, the state or local agency will investigate and report its findings back to the EEOC.)

2.   A copy of the complaint will be sent to the employing agency or the agency to which the complainant applied for employment. This form contains the statutory language prohibiting retaliation against the complaining party. (Note: The employer should immediately conduct its own investigation and if there is a problem, settle it as soon as possible. The longer the wait, the more expensive it becomes.)

3.   The EEOC sends a detailed questionnaire to the agency asking about the complainant and other issues. This questionnaire may ask for personnel files of other employees when the complaint involves disparate treatment. This document will also ask for the agency's position on the complaint. (The employer's legal counsel should assist the employer in responding. This questionnaire must be answered, or the EEOC will issue a subpoena for the information. The employer should limit the response to the facts of the complaint and nothing else.)

4.   In some cases, the EEOC will hold a fact-finding conference to ask questions about the information and to discuss the case. (The agency's legal counsel should be present. If individual employees are named in the complaint as personally discriminating, there is a potential for individual liability and a conflict between the agency and the named individuals. Each named individual may need a separate attorney.)

5.   The EEOC will push hard for a settlement or compromise. (Now is the time to settle if you are going to settle.)

6.   If no settlement, the EEOC will determine if there is "cause" or "no cause" to believe discrimination occurred. If cause is found, the attorney for the agency should draft an objection to the finding and send it to the EEOC to be included in the file.

7.   The EEOC will then issue the right-to-sue letter to the complainant, even if no cause is found. The complainant has ninety days to sue in federal court.

8.   The EEOC can sue a private employer on behalf of a complainant. However, lawsuits are usually limited to large employers. The EEOC cannot sue a state or local agency; it must

refer the matter to the United States Department of Justice, which can sue on behalf of the complainant.

The EEOC procedures give the agency several opportunities to resolve the complaint, either because of mistakes made or because the costs of fighting the complaint are too high. Many cases can be won or lost during the EEOC investigation.

REMEDIES

The remedies available to a complainant have changed since the 1991 Civil Rights Act. A successful complainant under Title VII may obtain an injunction against the agency to prohibit the use of a particular selection device or promotion procedure. The complainant can obtain an order requiring that he or she be hired or promoted. In addition to an injunction, the complainant can recover in court compensatory damages that include back wages from the time the complainant should have been hired or promoted. Also, if the complainant can show intentional discrimination (as opposed to only disparate impact), part of the compensatory damages may include "front pay." This is money to compensate the complainant for what he or she would have earned had the complainant been hired. Front pay is usually awarded when there is not an order for the agency to hire the person, but compensation is given in lieu of an order to hire. Emotional pain and suffering, inconvenience, mental anguish, loss of enjoyment of life, and other nonpecuniary losses may be recovered. This means that the case has the potential for becoming very costly.

A complainant may be entitled to punitive damages from a person who "engaged in a discriminatory practice or discriminatory practices with malice or with reckless indifference to the federally protected right." 42 U.S.C. § 1981a. Punitive damages may not be awarded against a government agency but can be awarded against employees of the agency. The amount of such damages is limited according to the number of employees, with the maximum being $300,000. (This limitation applies to lawsuits under Title VII and not to those brought pursuant to 42 U.S.C. § 1981. See below.)

Either party can request a jury trial when damages are sought for intentional discrimination. The prevailing party can also be awarded "reasonable" attorney's fees and expert witness fees. In order for the agency to recover attorney's fees, the agency must show that the complainant did not have probable cause to bring the lawsuit or brought it in bad faith. 42 U.S.C. § 1981

This statute was enacted just after the Civil War and is not part of Title VII. It is used in conjunction with Title VII and does not contain many of the procedures and limitations of Title VII. Under 42 U.S.C. § 1981, all persons within the jurisdiction of the United States have the right "to make and enforce contracts" as is enjoyed by "white citizens." This statute is limited to "intentional discrimination" and not adverse impact.

The Supreme Court interpreted this statute in *Patterson v. McLean Credit Union*, 491 U.S. 164 (1989), to be limited to the formation and enforcement of a contract and not to any other conduct occurring on the jobs, such as harassment. Congress overruled this decision in the 1991 Civil Rights Act by defining "make and enforce contracts" to include "making, performance, modification, and termination of contracts, and the enjoyment of all benefits, privileges, terms, and conditions of the contractual relationship." 42 U.S.C. § 1981(b).

This statute outlaws intentional discrimination in employment on account of race. It applies to white persons as well as black, *McDonald v. Santa Fe Trail Transp. Co.*, 427 U.S. 273 (1976), and on the basis of ancestry, *St. Francis College v. Al-Khazraji*, 481 U.S. 604 (1987). It does not prohibit sexual or religious discrimination. *Runyon v. McCrary*, 427 U.S. 160 (1976).

Although limited to intentional discrimination, this statute does not require filing of an EEOC complaint and waiting for a right-to-sue letter. This also means that the 180-day requirement for filing a complaint with the EEOC does not apply, and a person may have three years to file a lawsuit. The limitations on damages do not apply, and the complainant can still recover attorney's fees and expert witness costs. This statute is an additional remedy for intentional discrimination.

CONCLUSION

Discrimination in employment is a significant issue facing a public manager. These statutes limit discretion in hiring, promotion, and dismissal decisions. They also mandate an objective review of all personnel policies and procedures.

CHAPTER 5

SEXUAL HARASSMENT

INTRODUCTION

Sexual harassment has become one of the most difficult but potentially damaging problems faced by a supervisor. Failure to react appropriately not only has adverse effects for the agency, but also may result in personal liability and disciplinary action.

The supervisor must be able to determine when interaction between persons of the opposite sex changes from "fun" to "sexual harassment." Sexual harassment may be difficult to recognize because it is not sexual harassment unless the recipient perceives it as sexual harassment. In other words, sexual harassment to a great extent is in the eyes of the beholder. The beholder may, however, be either the intended recipient or another nearby employee. The second employee may perceive the "playful" conduct of the other employees as demeaning and creating a work environment that is hostile to a person of that employee's sex.

There are ways to reduce the potential for sexual harassment and also ways to react once conduct is determined to be inappropriate. This chapter will discuss the legal underpinnings of a claim of sexual harassment and suggest ways to reduce the adverse effect on the agency.

LEGAL FRAMEWORK

Title VII of the Civil Rights Act of 1964 prohibits the use of five criteria to discriminate among employees in the "terms and conditions, or privileges of employment." *See* 42 U.S.C. § 2000e-2(a)(1). These criteria are race, color, religion, sex, or national origin. Harassment or abuse of an employee because of the employee's race, color, religion, sex or national origin amounts to discrimination in the "terms and conditions or privileges of employment" and is an unlawful employment practice under Title VII. While a legal claim of harassment may be based upon any of the five criteria, and cases have been, this chapter is limited to harassment based upon sex.

Discrimination or harassment based a person's "sex" violates Title VII even if the harassment is a person of the same sex. *Oncale v. Sundowner Offshore Services, Inc.*, 523 U.S. 75 (1998) (male workers sexually assaulted another male worker). There are two distinct theories of sexual harassment: (1) hostile work environment, and (2) *quid pro quo*.

Hostile Work Environment

A claim for sexual harassment requires the employee to show under all the circumstances:

1. that the workplace was permeated with discriminatory intimidation, ridicule, and insult;
2. that the employee subjectively perceived that the workplace was abusive;
3. that the abuse interfered with the employee's work performance or altered the terms, conditions, or privileges of employment; and
4. that the discriminatory abuse was based upon the employee's gender.

Whether the workplace was "permeated" with discriminatory intimidation, ridicule, and insult so as to be abusive can only be determined by looking at all the circumstances. These circumstances include: (1) frequency, (2) severity, (3) whether physically threatening or humiliating or merely an offensive utterance, (4) the effect the conduct had on the employee, (5) prior complaints from this employee and others, and (6) whether the employee voluntarily participated in similar conduct. (This last factor is not a complete defense but is one factor.)

The United States Supreme Court in *Harris v. Forklift Systems, Inc.*, 510 U.S. 17 (1993), addressed the issues of the effect the abuse must have on an employee. Teresa Harris worked as a manager at Forklift Systems, Inc., an equipment rental company, from April 1985 until October 1987. Charles Hardy was Forklift's president and, according to testimony, was insulting to Harris because of her gender and often made her the target of unwanted sexual innuendoes. Hardy told Harris on several occasions, in the presence of others, "You're a woman, what do you know?" and "We need a man as a rental manager." At least once, he called her "a dumb ass woman." He suggested that she go with him to the Holiday Inn to negotiate a raise. He asked Harris and other women to get coins out of his pants pocket, threw down objects for them to pick up, and made comments about her and other women's clothing.

Harris complained to Hardy in mid-August 1987. Hardy was surprised that Harris was offended, said he was joking, and apologized. He promised to stop, so Harris stayed on the job. While Harris was talking with a customer about a rental, he asked in front of other employees, "What did you do, promise the guy some [sex] Saturday night?" Harris quit and sued.

The lower courts held that Harris must show not only an effect upon her job, but that the sexual harassment had an effect on her "psychological well-being." The Supreme Court disagreed and said that the employee must "subjectively perceive the environment to be hostile" but that Title VII "comes into play before harassing conduct leads to a nervous breakdown."

A hostile work environment may sneak up on a supervisor if no one is complaining. Offensive comments may be perceived by some as abusive, but not so perceived by others. Nonparticipating employees who overhear offensive utterances that do not offend the participants may have a claim. To prevent a hostile work environment and avoid potential claims, sexually graphic or degrading pictures, cartoons, drawings, and conversation need to be kept to a minimum and the workplace run on a "fairly" professional level.

Quid Pro Quo

The term *quid pro quo* is Latin and means something for something. That is, one employee conditions certain privileges of employment upon receipt of something else. If the "something else" is sexual in nature, then there is sexual harassment.

To prove a claim of *quid pro quo* sexual harassment, the employee must show that a term, condition, or privilege of employment was conditioned upon submission to a sexual demand. Sexual demands can range from touching to sexual intercourse. The terms and conditions of employment include continued employment, pay raises, good evaluations, etc. It is, in essence, sexual blackmail.

Such a claim can be proved if the employee turns down the demand. If a supervisor demands a sexual favor and is turned down and the employee can show that he or she is fired, denied promotion, assigned a different shift, or any other change in condition of the employment, a claim is made

LIABILITY

Liability will attach to the employer who condones sexual harassment. Liability depends upon who is the harasser. If the harassment is by co-workers, then the employer will not be held liable absent prior complaints to any supervisor and failure to take action to stop the conduct. The complaints need not be by this particular employee. Complaints of a similar nature and the failure to take action will be viewed as the employer condoning the harassment. Since a co-worker cannot promote, demote, etc., the conduct must amount to a hostile work environment.

Sexual harassment by a supervisor will result in liability for the agency if tangible job action is taken against the complaining party. This is true even if the supervisor was a first line supervisor and there is no prior knowledge on the part of management level employees. Tangible job action means that if the employee is dismissed (including being forced to resign), demoted, not promoted, or transferred to a less favorable position. On the other hand, if the employer has not taken tangible job action against the employee, then the employer has a defense to liability. If the employer can prove that it has (1) made reasonable efforts to prevent harassment or correct promptly and (2) the employee unreasonably failed to take advantage of this corrective opportunity. In other words, the employer must prove no tangible job action and that it had a policy prohibiting sexual harassment and that this employee failed to allow the employer an opportunity to correct the harassment. *Faragher v. City of Raton*, 524 U.S. 775 (1998); *Burlington Industries, Inc. v. Ellerth*, 524 U.S 742 (1998). Liability for harassment by a supervisor applies to both *quid pro quo* and hostile work environment theories. EEOC suggests that an employer (1) affirmatively raise the subject of sexual harassment, (2) express strong disapproval, (3) develop appropriate sanctions for violating the policy, up to and including dismissal, (4) inform employees of their right to raise this issue, including a method of complaining without going through their immediate supervisor who may be the harasser, and (5) develop methods to sensitize all employees and supervisors on sexual harassment. Following these suggestions will help in proving that the employer did everything possible to prevent the harassment. Title VII prohibits an employer from allowing sexual harassment and does not compel an employee to accept sexual harassment or lose his or her job.

CONCLUSION

Sexual harassment is a form of discrimination based upon the sex or gender of the person. It does not matter if the harasser and the victim are the same sex or not. The issue is whether the harassment is based upon the gender of the victim. Sexual harassment has the potential to disrupt the effective and efficient operation of the agency. It also has the potential for substantial liability. Strict policies prohibiting sexual harassment, an open procedure for reporting the harassment to someone other than the victim's immediate supervisor and training on recognizing and dealing with the harassment should reduce the risk of sexual harassment occurring.

CHAPTER 6

AMERICANS WITH DISABILITIES ACT OF 1990

(42 U.S.C. §§ 12101 - 12213)

INTRODUCTION

The Americans With Disabilities Act of 1990 (ADA) was signed into law on July 26, 1990, before over 2,000 people. The purpose of the ADA is to provide a clear and comprehensive national mandate for the elimination of discrimination against individuals with disabilities. 42 U.S.C. § 12101(b)(1). The ADA may not require as many basic changes in selection procedures and employment decisions as Title VII of the Civil Rights Act of 1964, as amended, which outlawed discrimination based upon race, color, religion, sex, or national origin. It will require the same review and analysis of selection procedures to determine if they measure the intended attribute. "Reasonable accommodation" or changes in existing conditions of employment may also be required.

The ADA did not repeal Title V of the Rehabilitation Act of 1973 (29 U.S.C. §§ 790-794a). The Rehabilitation Act previously applied only to agencies receiving certain federal funds. The ADA changed this, and effective January 26, 1992, the Rehabilitation Act applies to all employers. Compliance with the Rehabilitation Act will not assure lawful conduct since the ADA **does not** apply a lesser standard than the standards applied by the Rehabilitation Act. 42 U.S.C. § 12201(a); *56 C.F.R. § 1630.1(c)*. Generally, the ADA applies a higher standard. (The cases cited in this chapter interpret the Rehabilitation Act, not the ADA.)

The Rules and Interpretive Guidance, Title I of the ADA (Interpretive Guidance), adopted by the EEOC became effective July 26, 1991. *See 56 C.F.R. part 1630.*

The ADA does not preempt any state or federal law that establishes a higher standard of protection, and individuals may pursue any remedy available. *See, e.g.*, N.C. Gen. Stat. ch. 168.

OVERVIEW

The ADA requires that employers **not** judge a person on disability, but judge a person on ability to perform essential functions of the job. A person who is blind should not be told that blindness prevents employment as an officer but that the essential functions of a law enforcement officer's job includes driving and shooting a gun. If the applicant cannot demonstrate how those functions will be performed, then employment will be denied not on disability, but on the fact that the applicant cannot perform essential functions of the job.

Preemployment tests must be given to a disabled applicant in the most effective manner to assure that the disabled person will be able to demonstrate his or her ability. This may require extra time or increased lighting or that a written test be given orally. The employer should prepare a written job description containing the essential functions of the job and judge applicants against it.

The ADA also prohibits medical examinations from being given until the applicant has been determined to be able or unable to pass other preemployment requirements. The applicant must be given a "conditional offer of employment" prior to any medical examination.

Finally, the ADA requires that "reasonable accommodation" be given to any person with a disability who requests such accommodation and will then be able to perform the essential functions of the job. Reasonable accommodation includes reasonable changes in shifts, modifications to work stations, and changes in job duties if necessary to allow the disabled person to perform the job. The types of accommodation must be reasonable and are a matter of negotiation between the employer and the employee.

The Supreme Court in the case of *Board of Trustees v. Garrett* , 531 U.S. 356 (2001) ruled that the ADA cannot be used to sue state agencies under the Eleventh Amendment to the Constitution. States can waive their sovereign immunity and Eleventh Amendment immunity. *See* N.C.Gen. Stat. § 143-300.35.

EFFECTIVE DATES

The ADA is effective July 26, **1992**, for all employers with twenty-five or more employees and July 26, **1994**, for all employers with at least fifteen employees. 42 U.S.C. § 12111(5); *56 C.F.R. § 1630.2(e).*

PROHIBITED ACTS

A. It shall be unlawful for an employer to discriminate on the basis of *disability* against a *qualified individual with a disability* in regard to:
1. recruitment, advertising, or job application procedures;
2. hiring, promotion, demotion, transfer, or layoff;
3. rates of pay or other forms of compensation;
4. job assignment, job classification, or lines of progression;
5. leaves of absence, sick leave, or other leave;
6. fringe benefits;
7. selection and financial support for training;
8. activities sponsored by the employer, including social and recreational programs;
9. any term, condition, or privilege of employment. *56 C.F.R. § 1630.4.*

B. It is unlawful for an employer to limit, segregate, or classify persons on the basis of a *disability. 56 C.F.R. § 1630.5.*

C. It is unlawful for an employer to participate in a contractual arrangement with another who discriminates on the basis of *disability. 56 C.F.R. § 1630.6.*

D.   It is unlawful to use standards, criteria, or methods of administration that are not job-related, consistent with business necessity, and
      1.   have the effect of discriminating on the basis of *disability*, or
      2.   perpetuate the discrimination of others. *56 C.F.R. § 1630.7.*

E.   It is unlawful to exclude or deny equal job benefits to an individual because of a known *disability* of an individual with whom the qualified individual is known to have a family, business, social, or other relationship or association. *56 C.F.R. § 1630.8.* Refusal to hire an applicant because of marriage to a disabled person and the employer's belief that the applicant will be required to miss work frequently violates the ADA. *See Interpretive Guidance, 56 C.F.R. § 1630.8.*

F.   It is unlawful for an employer not to make *reasonable accommodation* to the known physical or mental limitations of an otherwise qualified applicant or employee with a *disability* unless the employer can demonstrate the accommodation would impose an *undue hardship* on the operation of the business. (A qualified individual with a disability is not required to accept an accommodation.) *56 C.F.R. § 1630.9.* Modification of preemployment tests and training materials may be required. An employer is not required to provide accommodation unless the employer is informed of the need or the need is obvious. It is unlawful to select a person who will not need accommodation over someone who will if the decision is based upon the need for accommodation. *Interpretive Guidance, 56 C.F.R. 1630.9.*

G.   It is unlawful to use *qualification standards*, employment tests, or other selection criteria that screen out or tend to screen out an individual with a *disability*, unless the standard test or selection criteria are shown to be job-related for the position in question and consistent with business necessity. *56 C.F.R. § 1630.10.*

H.   It is unlawful for an employer to fail to select and administer tests concerning employment in the **most effective manner** to ensure that when a test is administered to a job applicant or an employee who has a *disability*, the test results accurately reflect the job skills, aptitude, or whatever other factor the test purports to measure. *56 C.F.R. § 1630.11.*

I.   It is unlawful to retaliate against a person who opposes an act of discrimination or to coerce, harass, or interfere with an individual who exercises any right granted by the ADA. *56 C.F.R. § 1630.12.*

DEFINITIONS

A.   *Disability* means, with respect to an individual:
      1.   a *physical* or *mental impairment* that *substantially limits* one or more *major life activities* of such individual;
      2.   *a record of such an impairment*; or

3.   *being regarded as having such an impairment.* 42 U.S.C. § 12102(2)(A), (B), (C*);* 56 C.F.R. § 1630.2(g).

B.   Disability exclusions:
1.   A disability does not include:
     a.   transvestitism, transsexualism, pedophilia, exhibitionism, voyeurism, gender identification disorders not resulting from physical impairments, or other sexual behavior disorders;
     b.   compulsive gambling, kleptomania, or pyromania; or
     c.   psychoactive substance use disorders resulting from *current* illegal drug use.
2.   Homosexuality and bisexuality are not impairments and so are not disabilities. 42 U.S.C. § 12211; *56 C.F.R. § 1630.16(d), (e).*
3.   Disability does not include individuals currently engaged in the illegal use of drugs. A person is disabled, however, who has successfully completed a supervised drug rehabilitation program and is no longer engaging in illegal use of drugs, or is participating in a supervised rehabilitation program and is no longer engaging in such use, or is erroneously regarded as engaging in such use but is not engaging in such use. *56 C.F.R. § 1630.3(a), (b).*
4.   A law enforcement agency may be able to impose a *qualification standard* that excludes individuals with a history of illegal use of drugs if it can show that the standard is job-related and consistent with business necessity. *See Interpretive Guidance, 56 C.F.R. ∋ 1630.4; Huff v. Israel,* 573 F. Supp. 107 (M.D. Ga. 1983) (officer with convictions for DWI can be dismissed even if an alcoholic; convictions show officer cannot perform duties).
5.   From the moment of infection and throughout every stage of the disease, HIV infection satisfies the statutory and regulatory definition of a "physical impairment" which "substantially limits a "major life activity," *e.g.* ability to reproduce and to bear children. A person who is HIV positive, even if there are no symptoms of AIDS, is disabled within the meaning of the ADA. Whether a person with HIV is a "direct threat" was not decided, but this case was returned to the lower court for a factual determination. *Bragdon v. Abbott,* 524 U.S. 624 (1998).

C.   *Physical or Mental Impairment:*
1.   *Physical or mental impairment* means any physiological disorder, cosmetic disfigurement, or anatomical loss affecting one or more of the following body systems:
     a.   neurological, musculoskeletal, special sense organs, respiratory (including speech organs), cardiovascular, reproductive, digestive, genito-urinary, hemic and lymphatic, skin and endocrine; or

      b.   any mental or psychological disorder such as mental retardation, organic brain syndrome, emotional or mental illness, and specific learning disabilities. *56 C.F.R. 1630.3(h).*

    2.   An individual with epilepsy would be considered to have an impairment even if the symptoms were completely controlled by medicine. A personality trait of poor judgment or a quick temper is not an impairment unless it is the result of a mental or physical disorder. Hearing and eyesight loss may be impairments. *See Interpretive Guidance, 56 C.F.R. § 1630.2(h).*

D.   *Major life activities* means functions such as caring for oneself, performing manual tasks, walking, seeing, hearing, speaking, breathing, learning, and working. *56 C.F.R. § 1630.2(i).*

    When the "major life activity" is "working," the impairment must restrict a person's "ability to perform either a class of jobs or a broad range of jobs in various classes as compared to the average person have comparable training, skills, and abilities." *Murphy v. United Parcel Service,* 527 U.S. 516 (1999) (High blood pressure prevented employee from obtaining a commercial drivers license, so could not work as a mechanic on commercial motor vehicles does not restrict the major life activity of working).

E.   *Substantially Limits*:
    1.   *Substantially limits* means:
        a.   unable to perform a *major life activity* that the average person in a general population can perform; or
        b.   significantly restricted as to the condition, manner, or duration under which an individual can perform a *major life activity*.
    2.   The following factors should be considered in determining whether an individual is substantially limited:
        a.   the nature and severity of the impairment;
        b.   the duration or expected duration of the impairment; and
        c.   the permanent or long-term impact, or the expected permanent or long-term impact, resulting from the impairment.
    3.   With respect to *major life activity* of working, the term *substantially limits* means significantly restricted in ability to perform either a class of jobs or a broad range of jobs in various classes as compared to the average person having comparable training skills and ability. The inability to perform a single, particular job does not constitute a substantial limitation in the major life activity of working. *56 C.F.R. § 1630.2(j).*
    4.   *Substantially limits* requires that the impairment "prevented or severely restricted the individual from doing activities that were of central importance to most peoples' daily lives and the impacts were required to be permanent or long-term." *Toyota Motor Mfg., Ky. v. Williams,* 534 U.S. 184 (2002) (Carpal tunnel syndrome does not substantially limit the major life activity of performing manual tasks).
    5.   When determining if an impairment "substantially limits" a major life activity, a

person's impairment must be considered after it has been corrected or mitigated by medication, the body itself or other measures. *Sutton v. United Air Lines, Inc.*, 527 U.S. 471 (1999) (Uncorrected vision 20/200 not considered, only corrected vision).

6. "Being declared unsuitable for the particular position of police officer is not a substantial limitation of a *major life activity.*" *Daley v. Koch*, 892 F.2d 212, 215 (2d Cir. 1989); *see also Forrissi v. Bowen*, 794 F.2d 931 (4th Cir. 1986).

F. *Has a record of such impairment* means an individual has a history of or has been misclassified as having a *physical* or *mental impairment* that *substantially limits* one of the *major life activities. 56 C.F.R. § 1630.2(k).*

G. *Is Regarded as Having Such an Impairment*:
1. *Is regarded as having such an impairment* means:
    a. has a *physical* or *mental impairment* that does not *substantially limit major life activities* but is treated by an employer as having such an impairment,
    b. has a *physical* or *mental impairment* that *substantially limits major life activities* only as a result of the attitudes of others toward such impairment, or
    c. does not have a *physical* or *mental impairment* but is treated by an employer as having a substantially limiting impairment.
2. There are two apparent ways in which individuals may fall within this statutory definition: (1) a covered entity mistakenly believes that a person has a physical impairment that substantially limits one or more major life activities, or (2) a covered entity mistakenly believes that an actual, nonlimiting impairment substantially limits one or more major life activities. *Sutton v. United Air Lines, Inc.*, 527 U.S. 471 (1999).
3. For example, if an employee has a facial scar or other disfigurement and the employer discriminates against him due to the reaction of others, then the ADA treats this as an impairment. Also, discharging someone suspected of being infected with HIV, even though unfounded, violates the ADA. *Interpretive Guidance, 56 C.F.R. § 1630.2(l); see School Board of Nassau County v. Airline*, 480 U.S. 273 (1987) (co-workers believed employee's tuberculosis was contagious). *56 C.F.R. § 1630.2(l).*

H. A *qualified individual with a disability* is an individual with a *disability* who satisfies the requisite skill, experience, education, and other job-related requirements of the employment position such individual holds or desires and who, with or without *reasonable accommodation*, can perform the *essential functions* of such position. *56 C.F.R. § 1630.2(m).*

I.   *Essential function* means the fundamental job duties of the employment position the individual with the disability holds or desires.

1.   The term "essential function" does not include the marginal functions of the position.

2.   A job function may be considered essential for any of several reasons, including but not limited to the following:

a.   the function may be essential because the reason the position exists is to perform that function;

b.   it may be essential because of the limited number of employees available to whom the performance of that function can be distributed; and/or

c.   the function may be highly specialized so that the incumbent in the position is hired for his or her expertise or ability to perform the particular function.

3.   Evidence of whether a particular function is essential includes but is not limited to:

a.   the employer's judgment,

b.   a written job description prepared before advertising or interviewing applicants,

c.   the amount of time spent in the job performing the function,

d.   the consequence of not requiring the incumbent to perform the function,

e.   the terms of a collective bargaining agreement,

f.   the work experience of past incumbents in the job, and/or

g.   the current work experience of incumbents in similar jobs. *56 C.F.R. § 1630.2(n)*

5.   Ability to fire a gun and to make a forcible arrest are *essential functions* of the job of police officer. *Coski v. City & County of Denver,* 795 P.2d 1364 (Colo. Ct. App. 1990).

J.   *Reasonable Accommodation*:

1.   Reasonable accommodation means:

a.   modifications or adjustments to a job-application process that enable a qualified applicant with a disability to be considered for a particular position,

b.   modifications or adjustments to work environment to enable a *qualified individual with a disability* to perform the *essential functions* of that position, or

c.   modifications that enable an employee with a disability to enjoy equal benefits and privileges of employment.

2.   Reasonable accommodation may include, but is not limited to:

a.   making existing facilities used by employees accessible to individuals with disabilities; and

b.   restructuring; part-time or modified work schedules; reassignment to vacant positions; acquisition or modification of equipment or devices; appropriate adjustments or modifications of examinations, training material, or policies; or providing qualified readers or interpreters and similar accommodations for individuals with disabilities.

3. To determine appropriate *reasonable accommodations*, it may be necessary to discuss the matter with the individual involved to reach an agreement. *56 C.F.R. § 1630.2(o)*

4. Accommodation is not reasonable if it imposes undue financial or administrative burdens or requires a fundamental change in the nature of the job. *Southeastern Community College v. Davis*, 442 U.S. 397 (1979). *Reasonable accommodation* may require offering the employee alternative employment available with the employer. *School Board of Nassau County v. Airline*, 480 U.S. 273 (1987). Providing a personal assistant to a disabled individual may be required. *See Interpretive Guidance, 56 C.F.R. § 1630.2(o)*.

K. *Undue Hardship:*

1. *Undue hardship* means that a provision for a *reasonable accommodation* is difficult or expensive.

2. Factors to be considered in determining whether an accommodation will impose an *undue hardship* on an employer include:
    a. the nature and net cost of the accommodation needed, taking into consideration the availability of tax credit and other deductions;
    b. overall financial resources of the facility involved in the accommodation;
    c. overall financial resources of the employer, including the size of the business, number of employees, and type and location of facilities;
    d. the type of operation, including the composition, structure, and functions of the workforce;
    e. the impact of the accommodation upon the ability of the other employees to perform their duties and the agency's ability to conduct business. *56 C.F.R. § 1630.2(p)*

3. *Undue hardship* refers to an accommodation that would be unduly costly, extensive, substantial, or disruptive, or that would alter the operation of the business. Vocational rehabilitation agencies of state and local governments may provide some funds to defray the costs. *Interpretive Guidance, 56 C.F.R. § 1630.2.*

L. *Qualification standard* means the personal and professional attributes established by the employer, including the skill, experience, education, physical, medical, safety, and other requirements, that an individual must have or meet in order to be eligible for a particular position. *56 C.F.R. § 1630.2(q)*.

M. *Direct Threat:*

1. A *direct threat* means that a significant risk of substantial harm to the health or safety of the individual or others cannot be eliminated or reduced by a *reasonable accommodation*. The determination that an individual poses a direct threat must be based upon an individual assessment. Factors include the duration of the risk, the

nature and severity of the potential harm, the likelihood potential harm will occur, and the imminence of the potential harm. *56 C.F.R. § 1630.2(r)*

2. The agency must identify the specific risk involved and show that *reasonable accommodation* will not eliminate this risk. Generalized fears are insufficient. *Interpretive Guidance, 56 C.F.R. § 1630.2(r).*

3. The determination of a direct threat is a factual determination based upon the job and the disability. See *Bragdon v. Abbott,* 524 U.S. 624 (1998) (HIV infection may or may not be a direct threat; case remanded for facts to be developed).

4. Direct threat must be based upon medical or objective evidence. *Albertsons, Inc. v. Kirkingburg,* 527 U.S. 555 (1999) (Blood pressure too high to obtain commercial drivers license).

5. Direct threat includes a threat to the health or safety of the applicant or employee by the particular job. *Chevron, USA v. Echazabal,* 536 U.S. 73 (2002) (liver damage or abnormality caused by Hepatitis C which the employer's doctors said would be aggravated by continued exposure to toxins at employer's oil refinery can amount to a direct threat and justify not hiring an individual).

MEDICAL EXAMINATIONS

A. An employer may make a preemployment inquiry into the ability of an applicant to perform a job-related function and may ask an applicant to describe or demonstrate how, with or without *reasonable accommodation,* the applicant may be able to perform job-related functions. For example, an employer may ask if an applicant has a driver's license or can drive but may not ask if he or she has a visual impairment.

B. An employer may require a medical examination after making an offer of employment to the job applicant and may condition the offer of employment on the results of such examination if all entering employees in the same job category are subject to the same examination. Otherwise, it is unlawful for an employer to require a medical examination of an applicant or to make inquiries as to whether an applicant is an individual with a *disability* or as to the nature and severity of such *disability*. A physical agility test is *not* a medical exam and may be given at any time. If the test tends to screen out the disabled, the employer must show that the test is job-related and a business necessity and that performance cannot be achieved through *reasonable accommodation. 56 C.F.R. §§ 1630.13, 1630.14.*

C. A medical examination conducted after a conditional offer of employment need not be job-related and consistent with business necessity unless the examination results in excluding a *qualified individual with a disability. 56 C.F.R. § 1630.14(b)(3).*

DEFENSES

A. It is a defense to the charge of discrimination in the application of selection criteria that a *qualification standard* or selection device has been shown to be job-related and consistent with business necessity and that such performance cannot be accomplished with *reasonable accommodation.* If the disabled are being excluded by a preemployment test or *qualification standard,* the agency must show that the test or standard relates to the job and is necessary. The term "business necessity" has the same meaning as used in the Rehabilitation Act. The selection criteria or qualification standard must concern an *essential function* of the job. Even if the preemployment test measures *essential functions,* the agency has a responsibility to provide *reasonable accommodation.* If the applicant can pass the test or perform the function with *reasonable accommodation,* he or she must be hired. *Interpretive Guidance, 56 C.F.R. § 1630.10.* Accommodation is required for taking a preemployment test when the employer is informed of the need. *Interpretive Guidance, 56 C.F.R. 1630.11.*

B. The term *qualification standard* may include a requirement that an individual not pose a *direct threat* to the health or safety of the individual or to others in the workplace.

C. It may be a defense that the standard criteria or policy that has a disparate impact has been shown to be job-related and consistent with business necessity and that such performance cannot be accomplished with *reasonable accommodation.*

D. It is a defense to a charge of not making *reasonable accommodation* that the requested or necessary accommodation would pose an *undue hardship* on the operation of the covered entity's business.

E. It may be a defense to a charge of discrimination that the action is required or necessitated by another federal law or regulation. *56 C.F.R. § 1630.15.*

RECORD KEEPING

The record keeping requirements for Title VII, Civil Rights Act of 1964, 42 U.S.C. § 2000(e), now include disability. *See 29 C.F.R. §§ 1602.1 to 1602.56.*

POSTING OF NOTICES

Notices of nondiscrimination developed by the EEOC must be posted.

COMPLYING WITH THE ADA

A.   Analyze each job classification within the agency and reduce to writing all **essential functions** of each job.

B.   Reexamine all physical standards and hiring criteria to determine job-relatedness and effect on disabled persons.

C.   Reorder medical and psychological testing so that testing occurs, if at all, only after a conditional offer of employment has been made.

D.   Reevaluate medical standards and criteria to determine relationships to essential functions of the job and for their effect on disabled persons.

E.   Review application forms and remove any questions about the existence, nature, or severity of a **disability**. Any such inquiry should occur only after a conditional offer of employment has been made.

F.   Educate recruiters, background investigators, interview panels, and others who come in contact with potential applicants as to the requirements of the ADA and the prohibition on preoffer inquiries about disabilities.

G.   Assure that medical information is kept separate from other nonconfidential information.

H.   Inform medical services personnel of the requirements of the ADA.

I.   Review all mandatory wellness or fitness standards applied to incumbents to assure compliance with ADA.

CHAPTER 7

THE INJURED EMPLOYEE: THREE BITES OF THE APPLE

INTRODUCTION

Employees who are injured on the job may be entitled to job protections under three distinct laws: state workers' compensation laws, the federal Family and Medical Leave Act (FMLA), and the Americans with Disabilities Act (ADA). All three acts have distinct purposes, but they may all come together for an employee who is injured on the job. The employee injured off the job may still be entitled to two of the three, the FMLA and the ADA. An employer must be familiar with all three to avoid liability for violating them and to assure that all employees obtain the correct benefits.

WORKERS' COMPENSATION ACTS

Most states have mandatory workers' compensation for public employees. These laws generally provide for limited benefits to employees who sustain personal injuries or diseases "arising by accident out of and in the course and scope of employment." N.C. Gen. Stat. § 97-2(6). These acts cover only "accidents" and those accidents "arising out of and in the course of employment." Intentional injuries or those occurring off duty or while commuting to work are not covered.

This is no-fault coverage. In other words, the employer cannot refuse payment because of the negligence or fault of the employee, and the employee gives up the right to sue the employer for additional money. There are certain limitations on no-fault coverage. Unauthorized horseplay by one employee resulting in injury may not be compensated. On the other hand, the employer who creates an unreasonable risk of injury to employees, such as violating safety rules, may face a lawsuit by an injured employee. The injured employee also gives up any rights to sue another employee for injuries arising out of the job, absent outrageous conduct.

AMERICANS WITH DISABILITIES ACT

The ADA was passed by Congress in 1990 and was signed by President Bush before over 2,000 people. *See* 42 U.S.C. §§ 12101-12213. The ADA prohibits discrimination against the physically and mentally disabled. The prohibition against discrimination applies to applicants and current employees for employers with at least fifteen full-time employees. It prohibits discrimination in hiring; promotion; discharge; compensation; training; and all terms, conditions, and privileges of employment. The ADA requires the employer to take affirmative steps to accommodate an applicant or employee with a disability. This requirement applies to disabilities suffered both on and off the job and before and after employment.

FAMILY MEDICAL LEAVE ACT

The FMLA was passed in 1993 and establishes the minimum standards all employers must meet for the granting of leave to an employee for personal and family medical needs. *See* 29 U.S.C. §§ 2601-2654. The purpose of the FMLA is to allow employees up to twelve weeks per year of **unpaid** leave for personal medical reasons or family health reasons. These reasons include the birth, adoption, or foster care of a child (applies to mother and father); care of a spouse, son, daughter, or parent with a serious health condition; or if the employee suffers a serious health condition that prevents the employee from doing his or her job. During the leave, the employee cannot lose any benefit that accrued before the leave; the employer must maintain the employee's group health insurance; and at the end of the leave, the employee must be placed back in the same position or an equivalent position. An equivalent position is one having the same pay, benefits, and other terms and conditions of employment. The FMLA is considered as a minimum requirement. The employer can apply any vacation or sick leave toward the twelve weeks. For example, an employee who wants to take time off for a new child has two weeks of vacation and two weeks of sick leave that can be used for this purpose. The FMLA allows the employer to deduct these four weeks from the 12 granted by FLMA and the employee is only entitled to take an additional eight weeks of unpaid leave. On the other hand, the FMLA is a minimum guarantee. Any federal, state, or local law granting greater benefits is to be applied first.

COVERAGE OF THE LAWS

The three laws provide different coverage. They apply to different employers, different employees, and different medical conditions, as well as to how the medical conditions occurred. In certain cases, the laws will apply simultaneously, and other times, the employee has protection under one and then another or even all three. The following summary will attempt to guide employers through the maze.

1.   What employer is covered?

       Workers' Compensation: All state and local government agencies are covered. *See* N.C. Gen. Stat. § 97-2(1). This may vary from state to state.

       ADA: All state and local employers with at least fifteen full-time employees are covered.

       FMLA: All state and local employers with at least fifty employees are covered.

2.   What employees are covered?

       Workers' Compensation: Covers all employees (full- and part-time), but not applicants.

       ADA: Covers all employees and applicants who are "qualified" for the job.

FMLA: Covers employees who have worked at least one year, who have worked at least 1,250 hours in the preceding year, and who work for an employer who employs fifty or more workers within seventy-five miles of the work site.

3.   Is the medical condition covered?

Workers' Compensation: Any injury or disease occurring by accident and in the course and scope of employment is covered.

ADA: Medical condition must result in a disability. Disability means substantial impairment of a major life function, such as walking, seeing, hearing, speaking, breathing, learning, and working. Temporary disabilities are not covered if the employee is expected to heal within a few weeks. A person who has previously been disabled and has a record of a disability or is regarded as having a disability may be entitled to ADA protection even if the employee is not in fact disabled. The disability may arise either on or off the job.

FMLA: Medical condition must be considered a "serious health condition" that prevents performing essential job functions. It can arise on or off the job.

4.   What benefits are employees entitled to receive?

Workers' Compensation: Benefits vary from state to state. Payment of medical bills; a percentage of the employee's average weekly wage for a specified period of time; and a lump-sum payment for permanent disability, total or partial, are usually included. The average weekly wage is usually tax free.

ADA: "Reasonable accommodation" is required for any disabled employee unless it creates an undue hardship. Reasonable accommodation for a disabled employee may include job restructuring, part-time work, paid or unpaid leave, flexible hours, etc. Reasonable accommodation must be decided on a case-by-case basis.

FMLA: Employees may receive up to twelve weeks per year of unpaid leave. The twelve weeks can be "intermittent" and need not be taken all at once. A reduction in the employee's work schedule is also an option. FMLA leave can be counted simultaneously with workers' compensation leave or paid sick or vacation leave. For example, if an employee is out six weeks on workers' compensation leave, then the employee is only entitled to six weeks of FMLA leave that year. The employee must be informed that the paid leave will offset the FMLA leave.

5.   Are employees entitled to light duty?

Workers' Compensation: An employee is usually required to accept a light-duty assignment if capable of performing the function. Compensation payments are suspended during the time the employee refuses to accept light duty.

ADA: The ADA allows light duty as part of the reasonable accommodation.

FMLA: Light duty cannot be required in order to avoid the twelve weeks' unpaid leave benefit.

6. What reinstatement rights do employees have after leave?

Workers' Compensation: An employee is usually reinstated to the same or equivalent position, or the employer may face lawsuit for retaliation against the employee for filing a claim. Some state statutes do not require reinstatement at all if the employee is paid compensation for permanent total or partial disability.

ADA: The employer must give the employee the same position unless the employee is no longer qualified.

FMLA: The employee must be given the same or equivalent position with the same pay, benefits, and other terms and conditions.

7. Which law controls when there is a conflict?

The ADA and FMLA both include language that they are not to be interpreted to supersede any federal or state law guaranteeing more protection. The general rule is that the act providing the greatest protection or benefit to the employee is to be applied.

CHAPTER 8

FAIR LABOR STANDARDS ACT

INTRODUCTION

The Fair Labor Standards Act (FLSA) is composed of many provisions including minimum wage, overtime pay, and equal pay. *See* 29 U.S.C. §§ 201-217. This act is enforced by the United States Department of Labor's Wage and Hour Division. This federal agency has authority to enforce provisions of this act by filing claims in federal court. In addition, individuals may also sue in federal court after seeking relief through the Department of Labor.

BACKGROUND

A. The 1974 amendments to the FLSA extended the minimum wage and maximum hour provisions, including overtime, to all employees of states and their political subdivisions. In the landmark case *of National League of Cities v. Usery*, 426 U.S. 833 (1976), the United States Supreme Court in a 5-4 decision held that the Commerce Clause of the Constitution (Article I, Section 8, Clause 3) did not authorize Congress to displace the states' ability to structure employer-employee relationships in the area of traditional governmental functions such as fire prevention, police protection, sanitation, public health, parks, and recreation. The Tenth Amendment to the Constitution, which reserves all power not specifically granted to Congress, limited the authority of the Commerce Clause.

B. In 1985, however, the United States Supreme Court revisited this issue and in a 5-4 decision overruled *Usery* and held that the Commerce Clause **did** authorize the imposition of minimum wage and overtime provisions upon state government employees. *Garcia v. San Antonio Metro. Transit Auth.*, 469 U.S. 528 (1985).

C. As a result of the *Garcia* ruling, the states sought assistance from Congress. Public Law 99-150, effective April 15, 1986, gave the states relief from paying overtime compensation and allowed the use of compensatory time off in lieu of monetary payments. Congress, however, refused to legislatively reinstate the *Usery* decision.

D. The final chapter on this issue has not been written. The Supreme Court has subsequently ruled that a state employee may not sue its employer for violating the FLSA absent the state's consent. *Alden v. Maine*, 527 U.S. 706 (1999) (Congress lacks the authority under Article I of the Constitution to authorize a lawsuit against a state in either state or federal court). The result may be that local government employees may sue its employer in federal court and possibly in state court. A state employee may be limited to a grievance procedure with no right to sue in federal or state court. A state can waive its sovereign and Eleventh Amendment immunities.   *See* N.C. Gen.Stat. § 143-300.35.

OVERTIME

A.   The standard work week was set at forty hours per seven-day period, with any work time over forty hours required to be compensated at a rate of time and one-half.

B.   The section 7k overtime exemption applies to law enforcement personnel. This allows a law enforcement officer to be paid straight time for 171 hours worked in a 28-consecutive-day period or a proportionately shorter period down to seven days. Overtime pay will be owed only if the number of hours worked during that period exceeds 171 hours.

WORK TIME

A.   Hours worked are all hours an employee is engaged to work, waiting to be engaged to work, or actually at work, whether authorized or not.

B.   Work time includes:
1.   mandated medical and psychiatric evaluations—DOL Letter Ruling (8/2/89);
2.   washing and maintaining vehicle when required by employer—DOL Letter Ruling (9/27/90);
3.   care and feeding of a drug dog or police horse, but can pay at a lower rate—DOL Letter Ruling (6/13/89); DOL Letter Ruling (9/21/85);
4.   travel time from check-on to a place to work or travel on non-work days during normal work hours—DOL Letter Ruling (5/4/89);
5.   on-call time when unnecessarily restrictive:
    a.   requiring an employee to wear a pager and refrain from use of alcohol and mandating a twenty- to thirty-minute response time is **not** work time; *Bright v. Houston Northwest Med. Ctr.*, 934 F.2d 671 (5th Cir.) (*en banc*), *cert. denied*, 502 U.S. 1036 (1991);
    b.   if employee can leave home and leave word where he or she can be reached, it is **not** work time; if an immediate response in uniform is required, it **is** work time—DOL Letter Ruling (9/4/87);
    c.   a forty-five-minute response time after leaving home is **not** work time—DOL Letter Ruling (9/21/85);
    d.   can prohibit drinking—DOL Letter Ruling (9/21/85);
6.   nonsworn employees of an agency who volunteer to work as reserve officers—DOL Letter Ruling (April 10, 1990); *29 C.F.R. § 5553.103*;
7.   preparing for an employee grievance or hearings on vehicle accidents—DOL Letter Ruling (8/2/89);
8.   assignment to peer counseling committee occurring during regular duty hours—DOL Letter Ruling (6/8/89).

C.   Work time does **NOT** include:
1.   mealtime when uninterrupted and lasting at least one-half hour;
2.   voluntarily studying or preparing for work, such as firearms practice—DOL Letter Ruling (8/2/89), or maintaining physical fitness—DOL Letter Ruling (9/21/85);
3.   lectures and courses that are **not** mandated;
4.   employment with a third party to perform police work even though arranged through the police department, as long as it is voluntary—DOL Letter Ruling (3/22/89).

COMPENSATORY TIME

A.   Law enforcement officers may accumulate up to 480 hours of compensatory time at the rate of one and one-half hours compensatory time for each hour of overtime (320 hours straight time) in lieu of cash payment for overtime.

B.   This must be by a set policy or an individual agreement with employees or through a union labor agreement. If state law prohibits union contracts, then the employer need not enter into an agreement with the union. *Abbott v. City of Virginia Beach*, 879 F.2d 132 (4th Cir. 1989). However, if an employer representative is recognized, there must be an agreement with the union, or monetary compensation is required. *Nevada Highway Patrol Ass'n v. State of Nevada,* 899 F.2d 1549 (9th Cir. 1990).

C.   Cash must be paid when an employee is discharged or resigns. Compensatory time off must be allowed when the employee desires to take it as long as it will not unduly disrupt the employer's schedule.

D.   Nothing in the FLSA says that an employee may not use the bank of compensatory time to avoid disciplinary suspension without pay. DOL Letter Ruling (5/7/90).

EXEMPTIONS FROM OVERTIME PROVISIONS

The following categories of employees are exempted from the FLSA overtime provisions:

A.   A professional employee is an employee whose work requires knowledge of an advanced type in a field of science or learning requiring specialized intellectual instruction, or whose work involves teaching, and whose work consistently requires exercise of discretion and judgment and is predominately intellectual. *See 29 C.F.R. § 541.3.*

B.   An executive employer is an employee whose primary duty consists of managing an enterprise or a recognized subdivision thereof and who regularly directs the work of two or more other employees; who has the authority to make recommendations on hiring, firing, and promotions; and who does not devote more than twenty percent of his or her hours of work in the workweek to activities which are not directly related to the work described above. *See 29 C.F.R. § 541.1.*

C.   An administrative employee is an employee whose primary duty consists of either performance of office or nonmanual work related to management policies or general business operation and who customarily exercises discretion and independent judgment, regularly directly assists a bona fide executive, performs under only general supervision, and does not devote more than twenty percent of his or her hours of work in the workweek to activities which are not closely related to the work described above. *See 29 C.F.R. § 541.2.*

D.   A combination of exemptions is available. *29 C.F.R. § 541.600.*

E.   Working foremen are not exempt if twenty percent or more of their time is spent performing nonexempt functions. *29 C.F.R. Ə 541.115.*

F.   Exemptions vary, depending upon duties and the court.
1.   A first-line supervisor is exempt. *Clayton v. Oregon,* 925 F.2d 1469 (9th Cir. 1991) (unpublished).
2.   Criminal investigators are not exempt, DOL Letter Ruling (12/8/88), and state investigators cannot adopt an overtime system like the FBI's, DOL Letter Ruling (6/15/90).

ENFORCEMENT

A.   The United States Department of Labor may make a routine investigation or an investigation on the basis of a complaint. The fact that there is one complaint will not limit the Department of Labor to review of only one employee's file.

B.   The Department of Labor should divulge the scope of the investigation (overtime, record keeping, child labor), and the employer should avoid opening unrelated files. The employer should cooperate once the parameters of the investigation have been established and provide the records requested by the Department of Labor. The original request may be voluminous and can be pared down by providing representative samples.

C.   The employer's attorney should be notified immediately upon learning of an investigation. The attorney is allowed to be present at any interviews of management personnel since managers can bind the agency by their statements as to policy. The Department of Labor, however, may send surveys to employees to obtain information about their jobs without sharing this information with the employer.

D.   At the end of the investigation, the Department of Labor investigator will discuss the preliminary findings. This is a very important meeting to learn what the Department of Labor has discovered. If there are any disputes, a request to meet with the investigator's supervisor to resolve the disagreement should be pursued.

E.   If the Department of Labor determines that a violation has occurred, it will seek voluntary compliance, including back pay. There may be a willingness to compromise on back pay to assure future compliance. The failure of the Department of Labor to sue an employer will not prevent lawsuits by individuals.

F.   Before the Department of Labor will sue, the matter will be referred to the Office of the Solicitor in either a regional office or in Washington, DC.

SANCTION

A.   Back pay and injunctive relief are available. 29 U.S.C. § 217. In addition, liquidated damages in the same amount as back pay may be imposed for willful violations. Reasonable attorneys' fees can be awarded. 29 U.S.C. § 216(b).

B.   The statute of limitations for back pay is two years from the date the lawsuit is filed unless there is a willful violation, and then the statute is three years. 29 U.S.C. § 255.

C.   Criminal penalties are also available. 29 U.S.C. § 216(a).

CHAPTER 9

INTERNAL AFFAIRS PROCEDURES

INTRODUCTION

A code of conduct and internal affairs procedures are essential for a police agency to function properly. Members of the public believe, and rightly so, that law enforcement officers work for them. Even though members of the public do not always act in accordance with high standards, they demand that the police do so. Voluntary compliance with the law is the only way to protect the public, and public confidence in law enforcement agencies encourages voluntary compliance. Establishing high standards and enforcing them converts the position of a police officer from merely a vocation to an avocation. This chapter will discuss some of the legal issues in internal policy and procedures.

POLICY VIOLATIONS

All agencies should have written procedures to be followed in receiving complaints and investigating violations of policies, including employees' rights and responsibilities during investigations. Some states have officers' bills of rights. Any such bill of rights must be included in the written policy.

Internal investigatory policies have two purposes. First, they provide assurance to the public that there is a remedy to correct improper conduct by an officer. Second, they assure that officers are treated fairly during investigations.

ACCEPTANCE OF COMPLAINTS

Complaints involving improper conduct by an officer must be accepted to assure the public that officers will be held to high standards and to keep the agency informed of the conduct of its employees. The type of complaint which the agency will accept varies from anonymous complaints to requiring them to be in writing and signed under oath and acknowledging that a false complaint may result in a civil suit against the citizen. The more difficult it is for a citizen to file a complaint, the more likely it is that a supervisor will be held responsible for the actions of an officer without any complaints being filed. The courts will allow a person to present evidence of a complaint made to a supervisor even if the complaint was not accepted and/or investigated. Discouraging the filing of complaints merely results in no investigation being done until several years after the conduct occurred, when the lawsuit is filed. At that time, it may be impossible to show that the complaint was bogus. Also, some courts have held that the failure to have an effective complaint receipt and resolution system in place imposes liability on the supervisor or agency. *See Strauss v. City of Chicago*, 760 F.2d 765 (7th Cir. 1985).

Police officers can intimidate people. A person may not want to present a legitimate complaint because of the fear of retaliation. Adding to this fear the requirement for the complaint to be under oath, etc., may discourage legitimate complaints that could show a pattern of improper conduct before it escalates. Of course, an anonymous complaint need not be investigated like a written and signed one. It clearly has less credibility. An anonymous complaint may provide a supervisor with helpful information about an employee's conduct.

No matter what the agency policy is, the supervisor must accept all complaints that fall within the policy. Failure to follow this policy will not only result in discipline for the supervisor, but also liability for the actions of employees supervised.

INVESTIGATIONS

There are three categories of investigations: (1) violations of policy, (2) violations of policy that may also include criminal charges, and (3) critical incidents. A supervisor must be aware of the different legal issue involved in each category.

POLICY VIOLATION

This category involves an investigation into the conduct of an officer where the nature of the complaint shows only a violation of agency rules, code of conduct, or established procedures. Such investigations range from failing to meet job performance standards, e.g., reporting late, to on- or off-duty conduct that does not amount to a violation of the law, e.g., being rude to a motorist. In this type investigation, the established procedures should be followed and should include: (1) notifying the officer of the complaint; (2) interviewing all witnesses, including the officer and anyone the officer wants interviewed; and (3) preparing a written report to be submitted to the final decision-maker.

Right to Remain Silent

There is no right to remain silent in an internal/administrative investigation. The officer is required to answer questions relating to his or her fitness for the job. In the case of *Gardner v. Broderick*, 392 U.S. 273 (1968), Robert Gardner, a New York City police officer, was subpoenaed to appear before the grand jury, which was investigating allegations of an unlawful gambling operation. He was told that the grand jury proposed to examine him about his official duties. He was further told that under New York law, an officer called before a grand jury is required to answer questions concerning his or her official duties and to sign a waiver of immunity from indictment or prosecution relating to his or her official duties. If the officer refused to answer questions or sign the waiver, the officer would be removed from office. Gardner refused to sign the waiver of immunity and after an administrative hearing was fired. He sued, claiming a violation of his Fifth Amendment rights.

The United States Supreme Court held that Gardner was discharged for refusal to waive his constitutional rights and permit prosecution of himself. He was reinstated. The Court said:

> If [Gardner], a policeman, had refused to answer questions specifically, directly, and narrowly relating to the performance of his official duties, without being required to waive his immunity with respect to the use of his answers or the fruits thereof in a criminal prosecution of himself, the privilege of self-incrimination would not have been a bar to his dismissal.

Id. at 278 (footnote omitted) (citation omitted)

Consequently, in a noncriminal internal investigation, an officer has no right to remain silent and may be disciplined, including being dismissed for refusing to answer questions.

Right to Counsel

During an investigation, an officer is not entitled by the Constitution to an attorney. Some states may have a statute guaranteeing the right to counsel, either at the agency's expense or at the officer's expense. Also, the agency may have a policy concerning counsel, or there may be a union or association contract. Absent such a requirement, if the officer wants an attorney, then the officer must make the arrangements. No matter how counsel is obtained, when the officer appears with his attorney, the investigator must control the investigation and not be reluctant to establish the rules for the interview of the officer. In order to avoid complaints of unfairness, the investigator may choose to allow the attorney in the room to listen to the interview with his or her client. The attorney should not be allowed to object to questions or to stop the interview. If the officer under investigation wants to consult with his or her attorney during the interview, a reasonable number of consultations should be allowed. Consulting with the attorney after each question is unreasonable. The officer must answer the questions, not the attorney. If the attorney or the officer under investigation refuses to abide by these rules, then the officer should be warned that agency policy requires cooperation and that the officer can be disciplined for being uncooperative, even if innocent of the complaint under investigation.

Once the investigator has completed the interview, the officer should be asked to make any additional statement he or she cares to make. The attorney should be allowed to question his or her client and to make a statement upon the client's behalf. This procedure will prevent the attorney from later arguing that the procedure was unfair or that the officer's statement was incomplete.

Some police associations or unions may have a nonlawyer accompany the officer to the interview. The courts do not find unfairness as easily when the counselor is not an attorney. The investigator should be familiar with any policies or association or union contract covering this issue. These should be followed.

Nontestimonial Evidence

An investigation may require that the investigator obtain nontestimonial evidence from the officer under investigation. This evidence includes polygraphs, blood or breath tests for alcohol, blood or urine tests for drugs, lineups, hair, or bodily fluids. The same kind of evidence that is used in a criminal case may be needed in a noncriminal internal investigation. This evidence is necessary if: (1) the search for truth requires such evidence, and (2) agency written policy allows such nontestimonial procedures. If the agency procedures do not address this, the courts many times will not allow the dismissal of an officer who refuses to cooperate.

For example, in *Jackson v. Gates*, 975 F.2d 648 (9th Cir. 1992), Jackson was employed as a Los Angeles police officer. Another officer named Leach was a good friend of his, and they visited while off duty. Leach was under investigation by the internal affairs division (IAD) for illegal drug use. On February 13, Jackson and Leach rode together to an apartment building known for the sale and use of narcotics. Leach went in while Jackson waited in the car. Leach came out with a woman, and the three went to another location known for narcotics sale and use. Leach and the woman went inside while Jackson stayed in the car. Leach came out alone, and he and Jackson, "driving in a manner to avoid being followed," went to Leach's residence. Surveillance ceased until February 20 when IAD officers saw Leach and Jackson leave work together and drive to Exposition Park, drink beer, and talk. Leach returned alone to one of the narcotics buildings and was arrested. A search of his car revealed a "tinfoil bindle which is the size and shape consistent with the packaging of cocaine."

Under orders from their captain, IAD officers went to Jackson's home on February 21 at 1:30 a.m. and ordered him to provide a urine specimen to analyze for drugs. Jackson refused. Jackson was not arrested but was ordered to go to headquarters, which he did. Once downtown, Jackson met with the union representative of the LAPD Protective League. He was then formally ordered to provide a urine sample. He refused and was suspended without pay pending a hearing on the charge of insubordination. An administrative panel found Jackson insubordinate and recommended to Chief Gates that Jackson be dismissed, which he was. Jackson appealed through the arbitration process, and a year and one-half later, an arbitrator determined that the labor agreement between the LAPD and the union did not authorized compulsory urinalysis in Jackson's case. Jackson was reinstated with all back pay and benefits. Jackson then sued Chief Gates and the city for violating his rights and won $157,747. The court on appeal held that Jackson's Fourth Amendment rights were violated. The court held that even though random suspicionless drug testing is allowed under the Supreme Court's decision in *National Treasury Employees Union v. Von Raab*, 489 U.S. 656 (1989), for hiring, promotion, or as part of an establish policy, the test required of Jackson was not pursuant to any policy of random drug tests, but was after an incident. The court further said that drug tests are also allowed without a search warrant when the agency has compelling needs beyond law enforcement, such as public safety, and when there is particularized suspicion. *See Skinner v. Railway Labor Executive*, 489 U.S. 602 (1989) (a written policy providing for warrantless drug test of all railroad engineers after a train wreck is constitutional). The court of appeals said there was not sufficient compelling interest in this case or even sufficient suspicion to require the test, absent a search warrant. Jackson got his job back and got to keep the money also.

Agency written policy needs to be broadly written to allow nontestimonial procedures. Investigators must follow the policy as written.

Search during Investigation

The Fourth Amendment restrict searches by government employees whether the purpose of the search is criminal or administrative. The Fourth Amendment does not apply unless the employee has an expectation of privacy. A person usually does not have an expectation of privacy in property owned by another. An employer can give an employee an expectation of privacy in the employer's property by granting the employee a right to control access to the property. In other words, if the employer gives the employee the only key to a desk or cabinet and does not have a written policy allowing searches by investigators, then the employee may acquire a right of privacy in the property, and the usual Fourth Amendment limitations on searches will apply. If the policy allows searches at any time, then there is no privacy interest, and searches are allowed. The policy must specify that an employee's personal property brought onto the employer's premises or placed into a police car can be searched. Otherwise, the investigator cannot search an employee's personal briefcase or other personal property brought to work, at least without consent or a search warrant.

When the employee has a reasonable expectation of privacy in the employee's or employer's property, then a Fourth Amendment requires justification for the investigation. Work place searches can be divided into three categories; (1) work related, (2) internal investigations, and (3) criminal investigations. A work-related purpose means that the search was directly related to the duties of the job, such as looking for a file, trying to find a pencil, etc. No justification is required for this type of search except a work-related reason and the scope of the search only involves looking for the work-related item. An internal investigation requires reasonable suspicion that the search will reveal evidence of policy violation. No warrant is required. The search must be limited in scope to evidence of the policy violation. A criminal investigation must comply with the criminal rules and have probable cause and a search warrant unless there is an exception to the search warrant requirement. *See O'Connor v. Ortega,* 480 U.S. 709 (1987); *Kirkpatrick v. City of Los Angeles,* 803 F.2d 485 (9th Cir. 1986)(Strip search of employee for administrative purposes must be based upon reasonable suspicion).

The term reasonable suspicion has the same meaning as in the criminal context. One court has noted that factors that may affect the reasonableness of the suspicion are "(1) the nature of the tip or information; (2) the reliability of the informant; (3) the degree of corroboration; and (4) other facts contributing to suspicion or lack thereof." *Security & Law Enforcement Employees, Dist. Council 82 v. Carey,* 737 F.2d 187, 205 (2nd Cir. 1984) (in the context of strip searches of prison guards). *See also, Copeland v. Philadelphia Police Department,* 840 F.2d 1139 (3rd Cir. 1988), *cert. den.* 490 U.S. 1004 (1989)(Girlfriend's statement who was also a police officer that officer used illegal drugs in her presence, which statement was later withdrawn, amounted to the reasonable suspicion necessary to require officer to submit to a urinalysis); *DeMaine v. Samuels,* 2000 U.S. Dist. Lexis 16277 (2000) (Statements by two officers that DeMaine was taking notes on officers' comings and goings which would be relevant to an internal investigation into overtime abuses was sufficient to allow search of DeMaine's desk for the notes and to require DeMaine to remain in the room while the search took place); *Brambrink v. City of Philadelphia,* 1994 U.S. Dist. Lexis 16538 (E.D.Pa. 1994) (Search of 350 lockers of officers after illegal drugs found in heating duct in locker room was reasonable).

POTENTIAL CRIMINAL VIOLATIONS

Officers who violate policy may also be in violation of criminal statutes. When an agency receives information that an officer may have violated the law, the initial concern of the agency must be the criminal investigation. If the officer is being investigated by an outside agency, the employing agency must cooperate with the investigating agency. In addition to a potential charge of obstruction of justice, a criminal investigation involves society's rules of conduct, while an internal investigation involves agency rules.

When the employing agency is conducting an investigation, the priority must still be a criminal investigation. However, the agency must maintain a clear line between a criminal investigation and any internal investigation. This distinction also must be made clear to the officer under investigation. The officer has the obligation to cooperate with an internal investigation, but not a criminal investigation, even if his or her employer is conducting the investigation.

An officer under criminal investigation has the right to remain silent and the right to counsel, as does every other suspect. The fact that the suspect is sworn to uphold the law does not change this, and the officer cannot be disciplined for exercising these rights.

The initial decision that must be made is whether the investigation is criminal or administrative/internal. This decision is not always easy to make at the outset. The particular misconduct of the officer may not be known until the investigation has been partially completed. Sometimes, discussing the allegations with the local prosecutor, then letting the prosecutor decide that the allegations do not warrant criminal prosecution, settles the matter. On the other hand, if the investigation reveals more serious misconduct, the investigator may be required to go back to the prosecutor, and the investigation may change from an administrative/internal one to a criminal one.

Some agencies conduct both internal and criminal investigations, using the same investigators, with the officer being told when the investigation changes. Others use separate divisions within the agency. Finally, in significant cases, an outside agency such as the State Bureau of Investigation (SBI) may be brought in to do the criminal investigation, while the employing agency does the administrative/internal one. There is not a "correct" way to handle this situation. All of the procedures have advantages and disadvantages. The supervisor must follow established policy. If there is none, then the supervisor must select the procedure that will give the public confidence in the integrity of the investigation and will assure that the officer's constitutional rights are honored.

If the decision is for the agency to handle both the criminal and administrative/internal investigations, it is better for the criminal investigation to be completed first. In this way, the officer's constitutional rights will be honored. After that investigation is over, the administrative/internal investigator can then use all the evidence gathered from the criminal investigation.

The more difficult case is the one that could be criminal or administrative, depending upon the evidence. For example, a department vehicle driven by an officer is involved in a collision in which a citizen is killed. There is some evidence that the officer was exceeding the speed limit, and there is also evidence that the other vehicle turned in the officer's path. Is this a case of civil liability, or is it manslaughter? The agency has a compelling interest in knowing whether its officer knows how to drive, but the officer has a right not to answer questions if he or she is going to be charged with a felony. This is the kind of case where the evidence from the investigation, other than the officer's statement, may be presented to the prosecutor unless the officer specifically agrees to make a statement, knowing that he or she will not be dismissed for refusing to do so.

Garrity Rights

An officer under administrative investigation may be dismissed for refusing to answer questions narrowly and directly related to the job. *See Gardner v. Broderick*, 392 U.S. 273 (1968). The officer cannot, however, under threat of job loss be required to surrender his or her Fifth Amendment right to remain silent.

In the case of *Garrity v. New Jersey*, 385 U.S. 493 (1967), Edward Garrity was a police officer in New Jersey. The attorney general of New Jersey was investigating allegations of fixing traffic tickets. Garrity and others were told by the Attorney General (1) that anything they said might be used against them in state criminal proceedings; and (2) that they had the privilege to refuse to answer if the disclosure would tend to incriminate them; but (3) that if they refused to answer, they would be subject to removal from office as provided under New Jersey law.

The officers answered questions, no immunity was granted, and statements made by the officers were used to convict them of conspiracy to obstruct the administration of the traffic laws. They appealed, alleging that their statements were coerced. The Supreme Court said:

> The choice given [the officers] was either to forfeit their jobs or to incriminate themselves. The option to lose their means of livelihood or to pay the penalty of self-incrimination is the antithesis of free choice to speak out or to remain silent. . . .

> We conclude that policemen, like teachers and lawyers, are not relegated to a watered-down version of constitutional rights.

> There are rights of constitutional stature whose exercise a State may not condition by the exaction of a price. . . . We now hold the protection of the individual under the Fourteenth Amendment against coerced statements prohibits use in subsequent criminal proceedings of statements obtained under threat of removal from office, and that it extends to all, whether they are policemen or other members of our body politic.

> *Id.* at 497, 500

An officer can be required to answer questions about his or her job during an administrative noncriminal investigation. How is this done if the criminal investigation is not over or if a crime is discovered during the administrative investigation? The answer is to give the *Garrity* rights. The officer must be told that the investigation is an internal investigation and not a criminal investigation, that he or she is required to answer questions or face disciplinary action, and that any answers given will not be used against him or her in any subsequent criminal proceeding.

How does an investigator assure the officer under investigation that the answers will not be used against him or her? Some courts require that the prosecutor grant immunity. This is not usually necessary since the confession is involuntary. This is especially true in states that have a state law prohibiting personnel records from being released, except for limited purposes. In North Carolina, for example, state law prohibits the use of state and local government personnel records in criminal proceedings. *See* N.C. Gen. Stat. §§ 126-24, 153A-98, 160A-168. These statutes grant the necessary immunity.

If a evidence of a crime is discovered during the course of an administrative investigation, what can an investigator do? An employee should not be able to escape criminal punishment because there was an administrative investigation. The compelled statement of the employee is treated as a confession obtained in violation of *Miranda*. The employee is granted what is called "use" immunity. The statement and evidence discovered directly as a result of he statement cannot be used in criminal court against the employee. This is the "fruit of the poisonous tree" doctrine. The employee is **not** given "transactional" immunity or immunity from the crime or transaction identified in the statement. *Katisgar v. United States*, 406 U.S. 441, 452 (1972). The criminal investigator must be able to show that the evidence used to charge and try the employee for the crime was independently discovered or that some other established rule such as the "inevitable discovery rule," e.g. we would have found it anyway, applied. For example, during the course of an investigation into a patrol car crash resulting in a death, the officer involved states that he ran a stop sign without blue light and siren. If the officer claims that he was compelled to give this statement or be dismissed, the statement of the officer cannot be used in court. On the other hand, if there are other witnesses to the officer running the stop sign without blue light and siren, the officer can be prosecuted. The witnesses can testify. If the officer takes the witness stand in his own defense, then just like any other defendant, the prosecutor can use the officer's IA statement to cross examine him under *Harris v. New York*, 401 U.S. 222 (1971).

If there is a dispute as to whether an indictment was obtained in violation of *Garrity* or how the evidence was obtained, the court will hold what is called a *Katisgar* hearing. At this hearing the court will required the prosecutor to prove that the evidence presented to the grand jury for indictment or otherwise used to charge the officer or the evidence to be used in trial does not violate the immunity granted by *Garrity*. If the prosecution cannot show that the evidence was independently discovered, the charges against the officer will be dismissed. *See Katisgar v. United States*, 406 U.S. 441 (1972). Likewise, the *Garrity* evidence cannot be used in federal court either. A state or local agency cannot compel a statement and then turn it over to the FBI for use in a federal prosecution and vice versa. *Murphy v. Waterfront Commission*, 378 U.S. 52 (1964).

Right to Counsel

An officer under criminal investigation has the same right to counsel as any other criminal suspect. Also, *Miranda* warnings must be given when an officer is being subjected to a custodial interrogation concerning criminal charges.

Nontestimonial Evidence

In a criminal investigation, the investigator must follow established criminal procedures to obtain nontestimonial evidence. Criminal procedure statutes may require that the court issue a nontestimonial identification order before such evidence is obtained. Agency policy cannot be used to justify obtaining such evidence in violation of established criminal investigatory procedures.

Summary

An administrative/internal versus criminal investigation requires tact and knowledge of the law involving self-incrimination. The investigator must wear two hats, the one attempting to determine what occurred for the agency's benefit and the one attempting to determine what occurred for society's benefit. This tightrope becomes even more precarious when the investigation involves a critical incident.

CRITICAL INCIDENT

When a critical incident occurs, a supervisor is responsible to society, the agency, and the officer. A critical incident is defined as the use of substantial force resulting in serious injury or death to a citizen or serious injury to the officer, a patrol car collision involving death or serious injury to a citizen or serious injury to the officer, shootings involving death or serious injury, and other high-profile incidents, such as videotaped use of force or improper conduct where the employee may face criminal liability or where the public perception of the agency may be negatively effected because of the conduct of an officer. The supervisor must investigate these incidents in such a manner that society, the agency, and the officer believe that the truth was found, even if the action taken may be criticized. The worst thing a supervisor can do is to concentrate on the interests of one and ignore the interests of the others.

When a critical incident occurs and the supervisor is called to the scene, the supervisor must immediately realize that this is a "critical incident." Society will be watching, the effectiveness of the agency may be impacted, and the career of an employee is at risk. The supervisor must treat this situation as if criminal charges will be filed. The "crime scene" must be secured and evidence gathered. The extent of the investigation will depend upon the incident. For example, a supervisor called to an emergency room because an officer has just seriously injured a citizen during the course of an arrest must immediately determine what happened. The officer, the citizen, and witnesses must be interviewed. If the officer says that he struck the offender in the head with a flashlight because the offender was pulling on the officer's weapon or holster, the supervisor must decide whether to take the officer's holster and weapon to determine if fingerprints of the offender appear on them. The officer may view such action as indicating that the supervisor questions the truth of the officer's statement. However, a thorough investigation now will protect the officer in the future and assure that the agency cannot be accused of a cover-up because it had the opportunity to find such conclusive evidence and did not. Later will be too late.

These types of cases must be handled as any other incident where there is the potential for criminal charges. The only difference is that the high-profile cases will result in more public scrutiny, and the potential for criminal charges to be filed is much more likely.

The supervisor must also be prepared to handle the media. Statements to the media are essential, but they must be accurate. The policy of the agency in dealing with the media must be followed, and those persons charged with that responsibility must be contacted and consulted with prior to any release of information. When the media learn of a high-profile incident, the media are going to report it. To think that if you do not say anything, the media will go away is not only wrong, but may adversely affect the agency and the officer. The media may then report only one very negative side of the story. The supervisor must assure that the public views the agency as fairly investigating the incident. On the other hand, there is a potential for criminal charges, and the officer should not be denied a fair trial just because he or she is a public employee.

Accuracy in a statement to the media or statements made to groups are essential because they will be used in any subsequent legal proceeding. Supervisors must also be aware of public records laws. The media and the public have a lawful right to view public records, which may include police radio recordings, videotapes, and even investigative reports. *See, e.g.,* N.C. Gen. Stat. § 132-1. On the other hand, internal investigation files may be confidential under personal privacy acts. N.C. Gen. Stat. §§ 124-24, 153A-98, 160A-168. In critical incidents, the supervisor must work with the local prosecutor in determining what information should be released.

The supervisor must also be acutely aware of the impact the incident has on the officer from an emotional standpoint. The trauma of such an incident may affect the officer's ability to recall the events clearly. Physical injury may also affect the officer's recall. Extensive interviews made immediately after the incident may vary substantially from those given later, after time for reflection and thought.

The procedures employed in these cases may result in an officer giving several statements to several different persons. The supervisor on the scene may take a statement, an outside agency investigating the incident may take one, and a few days later, internal affairs may take one. Finally, the officer may be asked to compose his or her own statement. None of these will be the same. The statements given to the supervisor, the outside agency, and internal affairs will usually not be recorded but will be a summary taken from the investigators' notes. The officer will not be given an opportunity to review the statements to determine if they are accurate. The officer writing out a statement will have a tendency to put down what the officer views as "essential" details, may involve conclusory statements such as "I feared for my life" or "I used the force I believed was reasonable," and do not add any facts to the investigation. These conclusory statements should be included to show the officer's state of mind, but the facts that caused the officer to fear for his or her life or believe the force was reasonable must be clear. Invariably multiple statements result in inconsistent accounts which critics use against the agency or the officer.

The number of statements an officer gives should be kept to a minimum. The officer should not be told to compose his or her own statement. If the agency wants a signed statement, then the same procedures that followed with a criminal defendant should be employed. The investigator sits with the officer and asks questions. The responses are written down, and the officer signs the statement. This assures that the statement the officer gives is complete.

After many critical incidents, especially when the officer is seriously injured or a citizen has been killed, counseling for the officer will be essential. Many times, the officer's outward personality does not change, but his or her attitude toward the job or use of force will. Officers join police agencies to serve the public. An officer who kills someone will need counseling to assure that the officer will react appropriately when faced with a similar situation in the future.

CONCLUSION OF THE INVESTIGATION

At the conclusion of any category of investigation, a written report should be prepared. If no disciplinary action is warranted, the officer should be informed. If disciplinary action is indicated, then policies relating to implementation of the discipline must be followed. When a demotion or dismissal is to be imposed, then the due process procedures of a predemotion or dismissal conference must be followed for employees with a property interest in employment. If the reasons for a dismissal or other disciplinary action are going to be made public, then the agency must provide the employee with an opportunity for a name-clearing hearing or to challenge the report as inaccurate or misleading.

The complainant or the media many times will want to know the results of the investigation. The release of this information is usually controlled by state law relating to privacy of personnel files or the public records law. For example, the North Carolina State Personnel Act, N.C. Gen. Stat. § 126-23, -24, allows such release only if the head of the department determines in writing that the release is in the best interest of the department or if the officer consents. The unauthorized release of such information is a crime.

CONCLUSION

The internal investigation may involve the mixing of criminal and administrative/internal procedures with the need to assure the public that the agency is operating properly. The investigator must be familiar with agency policy and the laws relating to self-incrimination, public records, and privacy of personnel files.

CHAPTER 10

THE TEN (OR SO) WORST MISTAKES AN IA INVESTIGATOR CAN MAKE
—OR—
HOW TO BE SUED AND LOSE WITHOUT REALLY TRYING

Internal affairs (IA) investigators can assure that the department and the investigators will be subject to many lawsuits if the investigators will carefully follow the steps listed below. There is no guarantee the investigators will lose, but it is very likely they will be the lucky ones who do.

DO NOT ACCEPT CITIZENS' COMPLAINTS

IA investigators who do not accept citizens' complaints can assure themselves of not having to work very hard, and this will probably guarantee they will be named in several civil suits. For example, in *Spell v. McDaniel*, 824 F.2d 1380 (4th Cir. 1987), *cert. denied*, 484 U.S. 1027 (1988), the Fourth Circuit Court of Appeals upheld an award of $900,000 against the City of Fayetteville, North Carolina, based upon testimony of former officers that they were encouraged to use excessive force or to "take names and kick ass" by the chief of police. The court found the city responsible since there was no effective complaint receipt and investigation procedure. Also, in *Strauss v. City of Chicago*, 760 F.2d 765 (7th Cir. 1985), the court held that the lack of an effective complaint receipt and resolution system can, if proved, subject the supervisors and/or agency to civil liability.

DO NOT INVESTIGATE EVERY COMPLAINT, ONLY THE EASY ONES

IA investigators who believe that only certain types of complaints warrant the effort to investigate can be assured their names will be on file in the local district court. In *Harris v. City of Pagedale*, 821 F.2d 499 (8th Cir. 1987), *cert. denied*, 484 U.S. 986 (1988), the plaintiff established that the city had a custom of failing to investigate or act upon citizens' complaints of physical and sexual misconduct by officers. Several city officials testified they had personally received complaints of sexual misconduct by city police officers, that they contacted the police officials, and that nothing was done. A jury returned a verdict of $200,000 against the officer involved in the complaint and the City of Pagedale. *See Herrerer v. Valentine*, 653 F.2d 1220 (8th Cir. 1981) (city's liability for $300,000 in compensatory damages and $153,705 in attorneys' fees upheld when the plaintiff showed a pattern of police brutality against Indians that was known to municipal officials but that no action was taken); *see also Spell v. McDaniel*, 824 F.2d 1380.

DO NOT ADEQUATELY INVESTIGATE ANY COMPLAINT

IA investigators who are negligent in their investigations may subject themselves and others to lawsuits. Their failure to meet any reasonable standard for investigation will result in liability. For example, *in Harden v. San Francisco Transit Dist.*, 263 Cal. Rptr. 549 (Cal. Ct. App. 1989), a transit officer was awarded $531,000 compensatory damages and $11,000 punitive damages because of a negligent investigation. The officer was engaged in a part-time, off-duty typewriter repair business and used departmental computers to check typewriter serial numbers in order to avoid buying stolen equipment. The department adopted a rule forbidding the use of its computers for personal inquiries. An IA investigator assumed that the inquiries, some of which were for numbers belonging to stolen equipment, indicated that the officer knew the whereabouts of stolen typewriters and had them himself. The IA investigator did not make any attempt to find out if the officer engaged in receiving or selling stolen goods before reporting his suspicions and having the officer arrested. The IA investigator's failure to take such reasonable steps was the basis of the liability.

It is very important to interview all witnesses and to obtain a list of witnesses from the officer under investigation. The officer should always be allowed to respond to the original complaint and to any new charges learned during the investigation.

DO NOT KNOW WHAT *GARRITY v. NEW JERSEY* OR *GARDNER v. BRODERICK* MEAN, AND DO NOT FOLLOW THEM

In *Garrity v. New Jersey*, 385 U.S. 483 (1967), and *Gardner v. Broderick*, 392 U.S. 273 (1968), the United States Supreme Court discussed the use of compelled testimony in administrative and criminal proceedings. An officer may be disciplined if he refuses to answer questions about his conduct on the job or what he witnessed. *See Evangelista v. City of Rochester*, 535 N.Y.2d 928 (1988).

IA investigators who have never heard of these cases will clearly botch either a criminal investigation or an administrative investigation and may subject themselves to civil liability. Many states require that an employee be advised of the consequences of his refusal to answer questions in an IA investigation. The failure to inform the officer of the consequences may result in civil liability. *Lybarger v. Los Angeles*, 221 Cal. Rptr. 529 (Cal. 1985) (officer received reinstatement, $200,000 back pay and benefits, and $32,000 attorneys' fees).

DO NOT TELL THE OFFICER THE NATURE OF THE COMPLAINT

It is much easier to investigate when the officer under investigation is kept in the dark about the complaint. If this rule is followed, at least the agency will be required to hire the officer back, if not also pay for violation of the officer's rights. In *Zueck v. City of Nokomis*, 513 N.E.2d 125 (Ill. App. Ct. 1987), the officer was awarded $20,000 for stress and suffering, $24,000 for lost salary and benefits, $20,000 for loss of reputation, and $500.00 for miscellaneous damage, solely for failing to have been presented a copy of the written complaint prior to the termination hearing. The court found a violation of his due process rights.

DO NOT IMPOSE DISCIPLINE FOR CLEAR-CUT VIOLATIONS

An agency that investigates complaints adequately may not be subjected to civil liability merely for failing to take the most severe discipline. *See Stengel v. City of Hartford,* 652 F. Supp. 572 (D. Conn. 1987). On the other hand, many courts have held that the purpose of the internal investigation is to identify problems and to correct them. The standard for determining liability is whether a recurrence of the misconduct is prevented. If there is a recurrence of the misconduct, the prior investigation and discipline were inadequate, and the agency is responsible. *See Dobos v. Driscoll,* 537 N.E.2d 558 (Mass.) ($100,000 awarded against State of Massachusetts, the maximum allowed under state law), *cert. denied,* 493 U.S. 850 (1989); *see also Sims v. Adams,* 537 F.2d 829 (5th Cir. 1976); *Moon v. Winfield,* 383 F. Supp. 31 (N.D. Ill. 1974).

DO NOT TREAT EMPLOYEES FAIRLY; DISCRIMINATE WHENEVER POSSIBLE

An IA investigator who for inappropriate reasons chooses lesser disciplinary action against police officers may assure some legal attack. In *Moore v. City of Charlotte,* 754 F.2d 1100 (4th Cir.), *cert. denied,* 472 U.S. 1021 (1985), the federal District Court of the Western District of North Carolina ruled that a demoted officer could subpoena and review all IA files in order to compare the actions taken against minority police officers versus majority police officers. Based upon this analysis, the District Court determined discrimination on the part of the agency and ordered the demotion rescinded for the officer who had been charged with accepting bribes though acquitted at a criminal trial. On appeal, the Fourth Circuit Court of Appeals reversed the case, ruling there was inadequate evidence of discrimination.

DO NOT ALLOW THE OFFICER BEING INVESTIGATED TO CONSULT WITH AN ATTORNEY—THEY ARE ONLY TROUBLE

Unless there is a police officer's bill of rights or a departmental rule, there is no right to consult with an attorney during the course of an internal investigation. *See Wilson v. Swing,* 463 F. Supp. 555 (M.D. N.C. 1978). Even though there is no right, an IA investigator who wants to get sued should assure that this rule is enforced. Do not give any consideration to the officer's desires to determine his legal rights and responsibilities, and you will at least increase the likelihood of being sued.

SEARCH ALL PROPERTY OF THE OFFICER REGARDLESS OF THE REASON

IA investigators who want to be sued should remember that the officer has no rights and that the investigators have a right to search all the officer's personal and government property to see what else can be found. This will assure the investigators of being named as defendants in a lawsuit. For example, two IA investigators trespassed on property to determine that an officer was not living within city limits. The officer asked for $50,000—the jury awarded $100.00. *Riebesell v. Walker*, 187 Fire & Police Personnel Rptr. 86 (Jackson Co., Mo., 1990). In *O'Connor v. Ortega*, 480 U.S. 709 (1987), the United States Supreme Court held it was not a violation of the Fourth Amendment for an employer to search its own property over which it maintains control. A written policy should be adopted in advance stating what may be searched and under what circumstances the search may be conducted. The property can include not only the office, but the department vehicle and even a locked department brief case. *See Shields v. Burge,* 874 F.2d 1201 (7th Cir. 1989). Even **unlawfully** seized evidence may be used in a subsequent administrative investigation. *See Sheetz v. City of Baltimore*, 553 A.2d 1281 (Md. 1989); *People v. McGarth*, 385 N.E.2d 541 (N.Y. 1978), *cert. denied*, 440 U.S. 972 (1977). There are some contrary decisions on this issue. *See Rinderknecht v. Maricopa County*, 520 P.2d 332 (Ariz. Ct. App.), *cert. vacated*, 526 P.2d 713 (1974).

Search of a person, however, is different, and an officer may not be subjected to a strip search without the same type justification required in a criminal case. *See Kirkpatrick v. City of Los Angeles*, 803 F.2d 485 (9th Cir. 1986).

DO NOT GIVE AN OFFICER ANY OPPORTUNITY TO SAY ANYTHING—IT'S EASIER THAT WAY

Even if an IA investigator does an excellent job, do not worry. It is still possible to be sued by not providing any due process proceedings. First, for **nontenured** officers, be sure to announce to the world and place in the IA file the reasons the officer was not retained. Make it sound really bad, so that the officer can never get a job in law enforcement again. Then do not give the officer an opportunity to challenge it. After all, you did an excellent job!

A **nontenured** officer (not protected by contract, civil service, statute, or ordinance) is entitled to a "name-clearing" hearing if the reasons for the dismissal affect his good name, reputation, honor, or integrity. *Bishop v. Wood*, 426 U.S. 341, 348 (1976). Dismissal for inadequate performance does not entitle an officer to such a hearing, even if put in a news release. *Robinson v. City of Montgomery*, 809 F.2d 1355 (8th Cir. 1987). Allegations of dishonesty, such as bribery, do require such a hearing. *Boston v. Webb*, 783 F.2d 1163 (4th Cir. 1986). A name-clearing hearing must be made available and the officer informed of the procedure when stigmatizing information is placed in IA files. *Buxton v. City of Plant City*, 871 F.2d 1037 (11th Cir. 1989).

A hearing of this nature usually is held after the action is taken, but if the information is published to others, a hearing may be required before publication. *Willbanks v. Smith County*, 661 F. Supp. 212 (E.D. Tex. 1987). The name-clearing hearing is not required to be as formal as other hearings. *Boston v. Webb*, 783 F.2d 1163 (4th Cir. 1984).

The failure to give such a hearing may result in civil liability. *Willbanks v. Smith County*, 661 F. Supp. 212 (officer awarded $2,000 past mental anguish, $1,000 future mental anguish, $20,000 injury to reputation, and $2,000 punitive damages).

Next, for **tenured** officers, the easiest way to be sued is to go to the head of the agency with your report and convince the commander to fire the officer. If you do it right, a lawsuit will be filed. Walk into the room with the officer and announce that the commander has agreed with you that the officer must be dismissed. Hand the officer notice of the dismissal and demand the officer surrender all department equipment or face criminal charges. When the officer asks to speak, abruptly escort the officer off department premises. When we fire them, we make them know they are fired! The officer will be almost compelled to file a lawsuit.

A **tenured** officer must be given an informal hearing prior to termination, *Cleveland Bd. of Education v. Loudermill*, 470 U.S. 532 (1985). This **pretermination** hearing may be informal, between a representative of management and the officer. The officer must be told of the substance of the complaint and the proposed action. He must be allowed to respond prior to the final decision being made.

After **termination**, a tenured officer is entitled to a full due process hearing. *Board of Regents v. Roth*, 408 U.S. 564 (1972). The right to the names of witnesses, notice of the charges, and cross-examination of witnesses will be required.

CONCLUSION

If any or all of these procedures are followed, IA investigators can assure themselves of having a conference with the agency head and the attorneys for the department, as well as spending countless hours in depositions, hearings, and trials. Being sued is a sure way to advance a career (one way or the other).

CHAPTER 11

FREEDOM OF SPEECH

CONGRESS SHALL MAKE NO LAW . . . ABRIDGING THE FREEDOM OF SPEECH . . .

An employee does not give up the right to freedom of speech or expression by accepting public employment. Likewise, a public employer cannot condition employment upon surrender of the freedom of speech or expression. Like all other constitutionally protected rights, the right to freedom of speech and expression is not unlimited. The courts will weigh the interests of an employee in being free to speak against the interests of the government in providing efficient public services. In weighing the interests, the court will grant greater protection to matters of public concern or community interest than to matters of a private grievance. When the speech or expression involves a matter of public concern or community interest, the employer must produce evidence of substantial adverse impact upon the efficient operation of the agency. On the other hand, when the speech or expression involves only a private grievance, the courts usually defer to the opinion of the administrator that the efficiency of the agency has been or will be adversely affected.

PUBLIC CONCERN VS. PRIVATE GRIEVANCE

Every statement about government could be viewed as a matter of public concern. The focus of the inquiry must be on whether the "public" or "community" is likely to be truly concerned with or interested in the particular expression or whether it is more properly viewed as essentially a "private" matter between employer and employee. In making this determination, the courts will look at the content, form, and context of the statement as well as the time, place, and manner of the speech.

In *Pickering v. Board of Education*, 391 U.S. 563 (1968), the Board of Education, in February 1961, asked voters of the district to approve a $4,875,000 bond for two new schools. It was defeated. In December 1961, voters did approve a $5.5 million bond, and the schools were built. In May 1964, a proposed tax increase for educational purposes was defeated. In September 1964, a second proposed tax increase was likewise defeated. After the September defeat, Marvin Pickering, a teacher at Township High School in Will County, Illinois, sent a letter to the editor of a local newspaper in connection with a recent proposed tax increase that was critical of the way in which the board had handled past proposals to raise revenue for schools and its split of funds between academic and athletics.

The board determined after a full hearing that the publication of the letter "was detrimental to the efficient operation and administration of the schools of the district" and that the "interests of the schools required dismissal." Pickering was dismissed. Pickering sued, claiming his letter was protected by the First and Fourteenth Amendments. The Supreme Court ruled that teachers and other government employees cannot be compelled to relinquish their First Amendment rights as a condition of employment. On the other hand, the state as employer has an interest in promoting efficiency. The courts must arrive at a balance between these interests.

Statements of a public official on **matters of public concern** are protected by the First Amendment and cannot be the basis for dismissal unless there is proof of false statements, knowingly or recklessly made by him or her. Otherwise, the board, a public employer, must show that the statement interferes with the normal operation of the school. The Supreme Court said that was a matter of public concern, as evidenced by several letters from a teachers' organization and a principal written to the same newspaper urging passage of the taxes. The board could not show such interference with the operation of the school system. The Court ordered the teacher reinstated.

In the case of *Connick v. Myers*, 461 U.S. 138 (1983), the Supreme Court dealt with the issue of free speech on matters of **personal concern**. Sheila Myers was employed as an assistant district attorney (ADA) in New Orleans for five and one-half years, serving at the pleasure of the district attorney, Harry Connick. As an ADA, Myers was an employee-at-will. Myers adequately performed her duties. When Myers was transferred from one section to another, she strongly objected. As a result, she prepared a questionnaire soliciting the views of the fifteen other ADAs on office transfer policy, office morale, need for a grievance procedure, the level of confidence in supervisors, and whether persons were pressured to work in political campaigns. Connick ordered her fired.

Myers sued, claiming a violation of her First Amendment rights. The Supreme Court said that in a determination of whether a public employee's speech addresses a matter of public concern or merely a personal gripe, the Court will look to the **content, form,** and **context** of the statement revealed by all the circumstances including the **time, place,** and **manner** in which the statement is made. The Court found the questionnaire to be a personal gripe and not a matter of public concern. It then said that the federal courts are not the appropriate forum to review the wisdom of personal decisions for actions taken based upon an employee speaking out on matters of **personal concern**. The limited First Amendment interests involved in speaking out on a matter of personal concern do not require an employer to tolerate action that he or she reasonably believes would disrupt the office, undermine his or her authority, and destroy the close relationships within the office. Weight must be given to the employer's determination that the employee's actions threatened his or her authority.

For example, in the case of *Morris v. Crow*, 142 F.3d 1379 (11th Cir. 1998), Deputy sheriff David Morris from Polk County, Florida was assigned to investigate a vehicle crash where another deputy was traveling in an unmarked car to an emergency call for service. The deputy collided with a citizen's car , killing him instantly. In his crash report, Deputy Morris observed that the deputy was traveling 130 m.p.h. in a 50 m.p.h. zone without his blue light and siren activated in violation of department policy. The estate of the citizen sued the department for wrongful death. Deputy Morris was deposed in the lawsuit and reiterated what was in his report and also stated that in his opinion there was a "great possibility" the crash would not have happened if the deputy had the deputy been traveling the speed limit. The sheriff's department settled the case for $180,000.00 on September 1, 1991. Two days later Deputy Morris was suspended without pay. He was terminated on October 9, 1991, allegedly for two instances of misconduct. Deputy Morris sued claiming that he was dismissed for exercising his First Amendment rights on a matter of public concern, *e.g.* misconduct by the deputy, in his crash report and for testifying truthfully about the misconduct.

The Eleventh Circuit Court of Appeals said that any comment on police conduct are matters of "public interest," but that does not make the statement a matter of "public concern" within the meaning of the First Amendment. The court must determine "the purpose of the employees speech, that is , 'whether the speech at issue was made primarily in the employee's role citizen, or primarily in the role of employee.'" *Id.* At 1382 (quoting *Connick v. Myers*, 461 U.S. at 149). The Court concluded that since Morris' statements were generated in the normal course of his duties as an accident investigator and testify truthfully in response to a subpoena, Morris was speaking as an employee and not a citizen. The Court further said that Morris' testimony cannot be characterized as an attempt to make public comment on sheriff's office policies, the internal workings of the department, the quality of the employees or upon any issue at all. The court determined that Morris' report or deposition cannot transform them into constitutionally protected speech. The Court did note: "We cannot consider the unfairness that might have occurred if plaintiff was indeed fired for filing a truthful report and giving truthful testimony." *Id* at 1383. The Court said that unfairness does not create a First Amendment issue.

On the other hand, The mere fact that the employee has a personal interest in the subject matter does not automatically convert a matter of public concern to a matter of private concern. All of the *Connick* factors must be considered. It is a fact specific determination which is difficult to do as the following cases illustrate. *Azzaro v. Allegheny County*, 110 F.3d 968(3rd Cir. 1997) (A complaint of sexual harassment by a public official may be personal but still amounts to a matter of public concern); *Cromer v. Brown*, 88 F.3d 1315 (4th Cir. 1996) (A letter to the sheriff from the African-American deputies concerning discrimination in the department was a matter of public concern); *David v. City and County of Denver*, 101 F.3d 1344 (10th Cir.) *cert. den.* 522 U.S. 958 (1997) (Police officer suspended for tardiness after complaining about sexual harassment, not a matter of public concern since complaints related to personal harassment); *Tiltti v. Weise*, 115 F.3d 596 (2nd Cir. 1998)(Complaints about working conditions and pay are not matters of public concern); *Watters v. City of Philadelphia*, 55 F.3d 886 (3rd Cir. 1995)(Manager of Employee Assistance Program (EAP) for the police department complaints to the news media about the lack of a formal EAP policy is a matter of public concern).

BURDEN OF PROOF

In evaluating disciplinary action which the employee claims is based upon freedom of speech, the burden is on the employee to show that the conduct is protected and that it was a **substantial motivating factor**. "Substantial motivating factor" is also defined as: "but for" the speech, the employer would not have taken the action. The burden then shifts to the employer to show that the interests of the employer outweigh those of the employee or to show by a **preponderance** of the evidence that the employer would have taken the same action even without the protected conduct. *Mt. Healthy Bd. of Education v. Doyle*, 429 U.S. 274 (1977).

The Supreme Court in *Waters v. Churchill*, 511 U.S. 661 (1994), further refined this burden of proof when dismissing an employee for speech or expression on matters of public concern. The employer must show: (1) that the prediction of disruption because of the speech or expression is reasonable, (2) that the potential disruptiveness outweighs the value of the speech, and (3) that the employer disciplined the employee for the disruption caused by the speech or expression and not the content of the speech. *Id.* at 1889-91. If there is protected and unprotected speech, then the employer must show the discipline was for the unprotected speech, or it is presumed that it was based upon the protected speech.

In the case of *Hughes v. Bedsole*, 48 F.3d 1376 (4th Cir. 1995), Sandra Hughes was discharged as a shift supervisor with the Cumberland County Sheriff's Department. She sued and claimed that her discharge was based upon expression of concern for understaffing and improper training of jailers. She also said that some jail employees were making derogatory sexual slurs to female employees. The Fourth Circuit Court of Appeals held that the mere fact that the statements of Hughes to Bedsole occurred shortly before the dismissal was not sufficient evidence to establish that the speech was the cause of the dismissal. The court of appeals looked to the fact that Hughes accepted responsibility for leaving a jail door unlocked in one incident and that another unlocked door incident occurred while she was on duty a few days later. Also, the evidence was that Bedsole agreed with Hughes, and there was no evidence of any personal resentment toward Hughes. The court dismissed the case.

WEIGHING OF INTERESTS

The weighing test is very difficult to apply since administrators as well as the courts often disagree. On matters of public concern, a showing of "direct disruption of employment relationships, hence internal efficiency, naturally flowing from employee insubordination or disloyalty" is required. *Berger v. Battaglia*, 779 F.2d 992, 997 (4th Cir. 1985). The opinion of the supervisor that an employee's statement threatened the authority of the employer to run the office is to be given weight. *Connick*, 461 U.S. at 153. The courts have held that a public employer's interest in managing its personnel and internal operations is sufficiently weighty that a public employee's First Amendment rights to free speech relating to personal gripes are no greater than would be those of a private employee. Private gripes do not enjoy much protection from the Constitution. *Moore v. City of Wynnewood*, 57 F.3d 924 (10th Cir. 1995) (Deputy chief could be demoted for statements made at city council meeting while in uniform concerning role of police in exacerbating a riot-like incident).

The particular job that an employee holds also affects the interests of the employer. In the case of *Rankin v. McPherson*, 438 U.S. 378 (1987), a deputy county constable, who was a non-law enforcement employee and who had little public contact, was talking with a co-worker just after the assassination attempt on President Reagan. The constable said, "I hope the next time they try, they get him." This statement was overheard by another co-worker, who reported it to the boss. The constable was dismissed, and he sued for a violation of his First Amendment rights. The Supreme Court ordered the constable reinstated. The Court said that if an employee serves no **confidential, policy making, or public contact role**, then the danger to the agency's successful functioning from an employee's private speech is minimal. The Court considered whether the statement impaired discipline by superiors or harmony among co-workers or whether it had a detrimental impact on close working relationships for which personal loyalty and confidence are necessary. The weighing of the interest was in favor of the employee's freedom of speech. *See Campbell v. Towse*, 99 F.3d 820 (7th Cir.) *cert. den.* 520 U.S. 1120 (1997) (A lieutenant's criticism of the chief and his policy of being community-oriented was matter of public concern, but the interests of the agency outweigh the officer's because the chief had a right to expect loyalty of his immediate subordinates).

Whether the speech was made in public as opposed to private must be considered in determining the affect on the agency's efficiency. A principal at a school had an "open door" policy for all employees. He advertised that an employee with a problem could come in and talk. A teacher named Givhan took the principal up on this offer. Givhan sat in the principal's office and in a hostile, bad-mannered way, made petty demands and criticized the school board. After listening to this for a long period of time, the principal reported the teacher. Givhan was fired. Givhan sued and was reinstated. The Supreme Court held that a principal cannot invite employees in to talk and then fire them when they do. The private communication between the teacher and the principal could not disrupt the functioning of the school when the principal invited the speech. *Givhan v. Western Line Sch. Dist.*, 439 U.S. 410 (1979).

The type of agency makes a difference. The court will usually give more difference to management of a quasi-military organization in regulation of speech. Statements by officers will interfere with the confidentiality, *esprit de corps* and efficient operation of the police department. *Rogers v. Miller*, 57 F.3d 986 (11th Cir. 1995).

Even if the speech is a matter of public concern, the agency can restrict the use of the uniform. The agency cannot require the officer to conceal his employment, but on matters in which the agency must appear as neutral the officer can be prevented from using his job as an officer to undermine the agency's position. *Thomas v. Whalen*, 51 F.3d 1285 (6th Cir.) cert. den. 516 U.S. 989 (1995) (Police lieutenant who appeared in uniform on behalf of the National Rifle Association in opposition to gun control can be disciplined). On the other hand, the fact that the chief took a position on an issue cannot be used to restrict an officer's right to take a contrary position while off duty. *Edwards v. City of Goldsboro*, 78 F.3d 231 (4th Cir. 1999) (Agency could not prohibit officer from teaching in a concealed handgun safety course merely because the chief opposed the passage of the concealed handgun law).

Freedom of speech includes expressive conduct such as entertainment. The question of how to weigh off-duty entertainment that offended a segment of society was presented in *Berger v. Battaglia*, 779 F.2d 992 (4th Cir. 1985). In this case, Robert Berger was a Baltimore, Maryland, police officer. He and his brother performed music in the Baltimore area. They had been doing this since 1972. One part of the entertainment was for Berger to impersonate the late singer Al Jolson, which he performed, as Jolson had, in blackface makeup and a black wig. Berger did not identify himself as a police officer. Berger's superiors were aware of his secondary employment. In 1982, the Baltimore Hilton employed him to perform his act in the lounge. The advertisement by the Hilton showed a photograph of Berger in blackface makeup. There were protests from citizens offended by this part of the act. Some people demonstrated outside the hotel and threatened to disrupt the performance. The Hilton canceled the performance.

Berger was later instructed not to appear in blackface makeup, or he would be found in violation of a department policy that prohibited conduct "that tends to reflect discredit upon himself or upon the Department." *Id.* at 996. He was also denied permission to engage in secondary employment. Berger sued. During the lawsuit, the department could not produce any evidence of significant impairment of the Department's relations with the black community or internal disruption of departmental operations.

The court found that the artistic expression by Berger through his performance was the type of expression that had been accorded a great deal of weight, almost the same as social and political commentary. The fact that people paid to see the performance demonstrated that it was a matter of public interest. In the balancing of interests, the court found that there was no actual disruption of internal operations. The court then said that a public employer can consider in limited circumstances that "disruption by employee speech of a public employer's external operations and important external relationships might justify disciplinary actions." *Id.* at 1000-01. The court found that the perceived threat of disruption was insufficient to warrant the action taken by the department. In fact, the department had an obligation to protect Berger's right to free speech. The "heckler's veto" should not be allowed to prevent speech, even if the speech is found offensive. That is, a small group of very vocal opponents should not be able to intimidate the agency into prohibiting what is otherwise free speech. The court allowed the lawsuit to continue. Ultimately, the City of Baltimore settled the case by paying Berger $200,000.

The United States Supreme Court held that speeches made or articles written for publication by employees are matters of public concern and fall within the protection of the First Amendment. *United States v. National Treasury Employees Union*, 489 U.S. 656 (1989).

Off-duty shop talk among co-workers, even if personal gripes about the boss or the job, will usually be protected speech unless the agency can show actual disruption. As one court noted, the First Amendment protects "the American tradition of making passing allusion to the vicissitudes of the boss." *Yoggerst v. Stewart*, 623 F.2d 35, 40 (7th Cir. 1980).

DUTY TO INVESTIGATE

Many times, statements are verbal and not written or recorded. The question is, how sure of the content of the speech does the supervisor need to be before action can be taken? In other words, what if the employee denies saying what is reported? This was the very issue faced by the Supreme Court in *Waters v. Churchill*, 511 U.S. 661 (1994). Waters, the manager of a public hospital, learned that Churchill, a nurse, had spent twenty minutes during a dinner break criticizing the obstetrics (OB) section of the hospital to another nurse who had intended to transfer into that section. Churchill had allegedly said that Davis, the vice present for nursing, was ruining the hospital. Parts of this conversation were overheard by two other nurses and Dr. Thomas, the clinical head of the OB unit. As a result, the nurse decided not to transfer.

A few days later, one of the two nurses who overheard the conversation reported it to Waters, who was Churchill's supervisor. This nurse also reported that during the conversation, Churchill had said that Waters was looking for reasons to fire her. Waters and Davis met with the nurse who had intended to transfer to OB and asked what Churchill had said. She confirmed, at least in part, the report of the first nurse.

The hospital decided to fire Churchill. Waters and Davis met with Churchill, and at that time, Churchill told them her story. She said that she had criticized the policy of "cross-training" nurses, under which nurses from one department could work in another when their usual location was overstaffed. She admitted that she had stated that this policy threatened patient care and had criticized Davis for this policy and said that it would "ruin" the hospital. However, Churchill also contended that during this conversation, she had defended Waters and encouraged the nurse to transfer to OB. The other nurse who overheard the conversation and Dr. Thomas both remembered the conversation like Churchill did. Churchill also said that the nurse who reported the conversation to Waters has a personal grudge against her. The hospital fired her anyway, and Churchill filed a grievance. The president of the hospital reviewed the reports and denied the grievance.

Churchill sued, claiming a violation of her First Amendment rights. The Supreme Court first reiterated that for speech of a government employee to be protected speech, it must be of a matter of public concern, and the employee's interest in expressing herself must not be outweighed by any injury the speech could cause to the interest of the state, as an employer, in promoting the efficiency of the public service it performs through its employees. The question here was, how should the *Connick v. Myers* test be applied from a factual standpoint? Do we use the speech as the employer found it to be, or do we let the jury decide: (i) what was said, (ii) in what tone the speech was delivered, and (iii) what the listener's reaction was (*Connick* factors)? The Court said that the government as an employer has more authority to regulate the speech of its employees than the government as a sovereign has to regulate speech of the people in general. There is no general test for procedural safeguards, and the Court did not set one in this case. It is on a case-by-case basis. The Court did say that the government as an employer can restrict the First Amendment rights of an employee when necessary to deliver government services effectively and efficiently. The government as an employer is not required to consider only the information admissible in court under the rules of evidence in determining what was said and how it was said and received. In cases where the content or context of the speech is in dispute, the employer must conduct a reasonable investigation to determine what the speech actually was and must in good faith believe the facts upon which it purports to rely. The fact that the employer is wrong is not the key; whether the belief was reasonable is the only requirement.

A supervisor must make a reasonable, good-faith investigation to determine what was said, the tone, the manner, and the context before making a decision. If the investigation was reasonable and performed in good faith, without improper motive, then the court will defer to the employer in deciding what was said, the tone, the manner, and the context.

EXAMPLES

A.   Operation of the Agency/Personal Grievance

The Missouri Highway Patrol was required to apply the balancing test. In *Bartlett v. Fisher*, 972 F.2d 911 (8th Cir. 1992), Bartlett was employed as a trooper. From 1982-1986, he received high scores on his monthly and yearly evaluations. In 1987, Captain Davis decided to institute new "minimum work standards" to be used in monthly and annual evaluations. One of the work standards was "public contacts," which included tickets, warnings, and services provided to motorists. Bartlett's 1987 evaluation score was substantially less than his 1986 score. The weaknesses noted were "low contacts and spends too much time off the road." Bartlett complained to his superiors, including Captain Davis, that the work standards were in reality a "quota system." In 1988 during April, June, and July, Bartlett failed to meet the minimum standard for "public contacts." He again complained that this was a quota and said to his superiors that he intended to write the Governor, which he did. In his letter to the Governor, he said that all the troopers were writing more tickets just to meet the standard, and because the local people complained, they were targeting the tourists in the area. He told the Governor that he did not want anything personally, only that the quota system be stopped. He sent copies of the letter to three state senators. The letter was circulated to many others.

Captain Davis, in the meantime, had rescinded the new work standards two days after the meeting with Bartlett and, according to Davis, before he learned that Bartlett had written the Governor. Bartlett, however, claimed credit for this change in policy.

Bartlett's 1988 evaluation score was substantially less than his 1987 score. Bartlett filed a grievance. About that same time, an internal investigation was begun on Bartlett based upon allegations that he falsified seven reports. After a six-month investigation, Bartlett was given a thirty-day suspension. He appealed, and the suspension was later reduced to twenty-five days. Bartlett sued, claiming that the suspension was retaliation for speaking out on a matter of public concern, i.e., the quota system. The Patrol denied this was the reason.

The Eighth Circuit assumed that the letter to the Governor was the real reason for the suspension, but found that disciplinary action did not violate Bartlett's First Amendment rights. The court first determined that Bartlett's First Amendment interest as a citizen in commenting on matters of public concern was outweighed by his self interest in the matter, since he was subject to disciplinary action for failure to meet the standards he criticized. The court went on to say that the Highway Patrol, as a police agency, more so than the typical government employer, has a "significant governmental interest in regulating speech in order to promote efficiency, foster loyalty and obedience to superior officers, maintain morale, and instill public confidence in the law enforcement institution." *Id.* at 917 (quoting *Hughes v. Whitmer*, 714 F.2d 1407, 1419 (8th Cir.), *cert. denied*, 465 U.S. 1023 [1983]). The Patrol's determination that such speech has contributed to dissension within the ranks is entitled to considerable deference.

Determining whether speech is a matter of personal interest or one of public interest will many times determine whether discipline can be imposed. Some examples are as follows:

1. A female officer was awarded $75,000 for emotional distress after she was terminated following an interview with the media concerning the Department's bias against women. *Matulin v. Village of Lodi*, 862 F.2d 609 (6th Cir. 1989).

2. A Colorado police lieutenant's letter to the city council complaining of **mismanagement** was not protected. *McEvoy v. Shoemaker*, 882 F.2d 463 (10th Cir. 1989).

3. A Kansas police lieutenant's comments which alleged **serious misconduct** were a matter of public concern. *Wulf v. City of Wichita*, 883 F.2d 842 (10th Cir. 1989).

4. A former police officer's statements concerning working conditions were made to further personal interests and not to encourage public debate and were not protected. *Dunn v. Town of Emerald Isle*, 722 F. Supp. 1309 (E.D. N.C. 1989).

5. A captain's accusations against the chief, including that he stole liquor from the evidence locker seven years earlier, were so disruptive to the agency that First

Amendment considerations were outweighed. *Bryson v. City of Waycross*, 888 F.2d 1562 (11th Cir. 1989).

6. A captain's reference to the chief as an "SOB" and a "bastard" made while off duty to a co-worker he believed to be a friend and confidant is protected absent the agency showing actual disruption. *Waters v. Chaffin*, 684 F.2d 833 (11th Cir. 1982).

7. Sending an unsigned letter to the city council that a person promoted to major was involved in "unethical and illegal activities" was not protected speech. *Warner v. Town of Ocean City*, 567 A.2d 160 (Md. Ct. App. 1989).

8. A state trooper could not be transferred after becoming outspoken about taxes, school construction, and other such issues concerning the operation of a town in which he lived. *Bieluch v. Sullivan*, 999 F.2d 666 (2d Cir. 1993).

9. Officer could be discharged for telling the media and the attorney for the shooting victim's widow that another officer was guilty of second degree murder for failing to provide medical assistance to shooting victim. *Lytle v. City of Haysville*, 138 F.3d 857 (10th Cir. 1998).

10. Employee in sheriff's department who used profane language to chew out a superior in front of other employees could be disciplined. *Morris v. Crow*, 117 F.3d 449 (11th Cir. 1997).

B. Racially Offensive Speech

In *Pruitt v. Howard County Sheriff*, 623 A.2d 696 (Md. Ct. App. 1993), Donald Pruitt was a major in the Howard County Sheriff's Department, and his twin brother Dennis was a sergeant. The twins engaged in "Nazi-like" conduct while on duty, including clicking heels, giving Nazi salutes, and uttering German expressions. Apparently, the Pruitts viewed this conduct as a joke and an imitation of the "Hogan's Heroes" television show. The twins were told to stop this on-duty conduct several times. After repeated orders to stop, they were recommended for demotion and to go to sensitivity training because of unbecoming conduct. They appealed. The new sheriff rejected the recommendation and fired both of the Pruitts.

The Maryland Court of Appeals found that the speech itself was made to other department employees and employees of the Howard County Courthouse. It was intended as a joke rather than a social commentary. Here the speech and conduct remain unprotected because they did not concern a matter of public interest but indicated a personal bias. *Id.* at 702. The court upheld the dismissal. *See also* Edwin J. Delattre & Daniel L. Schofield, *Combating Bigotry in Law Enforcement*, Law Enforcement Bulletin 27 (June 1996).

Other cases where racially offensive speech or expression was the basis of some job action include:

1. A sheriff was authorized to terminate an employee who was an **active** member of the KKK. *McMullen v. Carson*, 754 F.2d 936 (11th Cir. 1985).

2. A sergeant's report of a bottle-throwing incident that included characterizations of residents of a black neighborhood as being of "limited intelligence" and engaging in "animalistic behavior" could be a basis for discipline. *Boone v. Mingus*, 697 F. Supp. 1577 (S.D. Ala. 1988).

3. An off-duty officer attending a Halloween party at a police union lodge dressed in blackface; bib overalls; and a black, curly wig and carrying a watermelon could be disciplined. *Tindle v. Caudell*, 56 F.3d 966 (8th Cir. 1995).

4. The dismissal of a correctional officer for wearing a "White Power" T-shirt to a barbecue on Martin Luther King Day was upheld. *Lawrenz v. James*, 46 F.3d 70 (11th Cir. 1995).

5. County Sheriff's single racist epithet directed at a subordinate employee at police academy firing range may be sufficient to create a hostile work environment under state law and warrants discipline. *Taylor v. Metzger*, 706 A.2d 685 (Sup.Ct. N.J. 1998).

C. Poor Taste Speech

Police officers sometimes say things about others that are in poor taste or could be viewed as offensive. When action is taken, the First Amendment is asserted as a shield. These types of statements are usually found to be matters of personal concern and are not subject to First Amendment protection.

1. An officer's remarks that challenged the authority of the chief and city manager are not protected. *McMurphy v. City of Flushing*, 802 F.2d 191 (6th Cir. 1986).

2. A city officer who called a county officer a "fag," a "piss-assed lieutenant," and a "M--F—"could be disciplined. *Sims v. Baer*, 732 S.W.2d 916 (Mo. Ct. App. 1987).

3. A lieutenant in the fire department who referred to his captain as an "asshole" and to another lieutenant as a "jew cocksucker" could be terminated. *Griggs v. North Maine Fire Dist.*, 576 N.E.2d 1082 (Ill. Ct. App. 1992).

4. Use of the words "bitch" and "whore" cannot be justified as "rough" language of a police officer, but is offensive to women and is not protected under the First Amendment. *Black v. City of Auburn*, 857 F. Supp. 1540 (M.D. Ala. 1994).

5. Suspension of an officer for the use of the word "s---" several times while giving testimony did not violate his First Amendment rights. *Hansen v. Soldenwagner*, 19 F.3d 573 (11th Cir. 1994).

D. False Statements

1. There is no Constitutional right to lie in an internal investigation. *LaChance v. Erickson*, 522 U.S. 262 (1998).

2. Courts are split on whether false statement made recklessly are per se unprotected but at least it is a factor to consider in balancing in favor of the employer. *Johnson v. Multnomah County*, 48 F.3d 420 (9th Cir.) *cert.den.* 515 U.S. 1161 (1995).

E.   Courtroom and Deposition Testimony

1.   An officer who gave voluntary testimony at the bail hearing for the son of a friend who was charged with organized gang activity could be transferred from drug task force. *Green v. City of Philadelphia,* 105 F.3d 882 (3rd Cir.) *cert. den.* 522 U.S. 816 (1997).

2.   Termination of deputy sheriff was unlawful when based upon testimony given at a co-worker's discrimination lawsuit against the sheriff. *Tindal v. Montgomery County,* 32 F.3d 1535 (11th Cir. 1994).

3.   When motive of testimony is for personal benefit, then not protected. *Workman v. Jordan,* 32 F.3d 475 (10th Cir.) *cert.den.* 514 U.S.1015 (1994).

F.   Assignments

The assignments of personnel to certain duties could implicate the First Amendment. Just as speech cannot be prohibited, speech also cannot be **compelled**. A government employer cannot force an employee to agree with a government agency's position. For example, Arlington County, Virginia, sent a contingent of uniformed officers to the Capitol building, along with members of agencies from across the country, to support legislation banning assault weapons. One participant was John Donaggio, who opposed the legislation. He sued for violation of his First Amendment rights. Although Donaggio agreed that the chief had asked for volunteers to actually demonstrate at the Capitol, he contends that his rights were violated because he was in attendance. He relied on the Supreme Court's ruling that an employee need not "stand pat and fight" the forced speech, but merely "object" to it in order to challenge it later. See *Abood v. Detroit Bd. of Education,* 431 U.S. 209 (1977). The court found that because Donaggio was not compelled to demonstrate at the Capitol, there was no compelled speech. *Donaggio v. Arlington County,* 880 F. Supp. 446 (E.D. Va. 1995), *aff'd,* 78 F.3d 578 (4th Cir. 1996) (unpublished).

This theory of compelled speech can be troublesome. If this theory is extended to other assignments, such as protection of demonstrators, or security at political rallies, then the administrator's job will be impossible. Asking for volunteers for every assignment will not work.

POLITICAL ACTIVITY AND AFFILIATION

Political speech is usually analyzed under the *Connick-Pickering* test. However if the position the employee holds requires political or personal loyalty, then the courts are split on whether to use the *Connick-Pickering* test or a different analysis under a line of political patronage cases. This issue usually arises in the area of deputy sheriffs.

In 1976, in *Elrod v. Burns,* 427 U.S. 347 (1976), the Supreme Court declared patronage dismissals unconstitutional, because the practice limited political belief and association, and therefore violated the First Amendments right of freedom of expression and association. However, the Court created a narrow exception to give effect to the political process. The Court allows patronage dismissals of those employees holding policymaking or confidential positions, reasoning that this exception would, in part, advance the important government goal of assuring "the implementation of policies of [a] new administration, policies presumably sanctioned by the electorate." 427 U.S.

at 367. The Supreme Court said that a clerk, a bailiff, and a process server did not meet the criteria for using political affiliation as a basis of employment.

Four years later, in *Branti v. Finkel.*, 445 U.S. 507 (1980) the Supreme Court in deciding if an assistant public defender could be dismissed based upon political affiliation or activity recognized that the labels used in *Elrod* ignored the practical realities of job duties and structure. The Court modified the *Elrod* test: "The ultimate inquiry is not whether the label 'policymaker'or 'confidential' fits a particular position; rather, the question is whether the hiring authority can demonstrate that party affiliation is an appropriate requirement for the effective performance of the public office involved." 445 U.S. at 518. Simply put, *Branti* modified the test in *Elrod* by asking if "there is a rational connection between shared ideology and job performance." *Stott v. Haworth, 916 F.2d 134, 142 (4th Cir. 1990)* (citing *Savage v. Gorski,* 850 F.2d 64, 68 (2nd Cir. 1988)). The Supreme Court found that Assistant Public Defenders could not be fired based upon political affiliation.

Political ideology and personal loyalty cannot be required of most government employees. In the case of *Rutan v. Republican Party of Illinois*, 497 U.S. 62 (1990), the newly elected governor of Illinois imposed a hiring freeze. In order to be hired, transferred, or promoted in any state agency, the Governor's office must approve. The Governor's office required the employee obtain an endorsement of a county Republican Party chairmen. The Supreme Court said this requirement was unconstitutional. Political affiliation cannot be the basis of employment decisions, hiring, promotion, or transfer of lower-level employees. In a later case the United States Supreme Court also ruled that political affiliation is also not appropriate criteria for awarding government contracts. *O'Hare Truck Service, Inc. v. City of Northlake*, 518 U.S. 712 (1996).

The question is whether a deputy sheriff is a position that a sheriff can constitutionally require political support and loyalty. In other words, the wholesale dismissal of deputies who campaigned for the losing candidate establishes that the newly-elected sheriff "elevated political support to a job requirement." *Terry v. Cook*, 866 F.2d 373, 377 (11th Cir. 1989). The federal circuit courts of appeal are split on this issue. For example the Fourth Circuit analyzed the issue of support for a political opponent under the *Connick-Pickering* test. It determined that a captain in the sheriff's office who supported the sheriff's opponent was sufficiently high in he organization that the interests of the department out weighed the First Amendment interests of the captain. His dismissal was constitutional. *Joyner v. Lancaster*, 815 F.2d 20 (4th Cir.1987). The Fourth Circuit subsequently in an *en banc* decision determined that a sheriff has a right to demand political loyalty from all deputies, no matter what their rank or position in the organization. In *Jenkins v. Medford*, 119 F.3d 1156 (4th Cir.). *cert. den.* 522 U.S. 1090 (1998) Bobby Lee Medford was elected sheriff of Buncombe County, North Carolina, in November 1994. The plaintiffs in this action were deputy sheriffs, who were employees under the previous sheriff. Shortly after his election, he dismissed ten deputy sheriffs. These deputies filed suit under *42 U.S.C. §1983,* alleging violations of their rights under the First Amendment to the United States Constitution. They asserted that they were dismissed for failing to support Medford's election bid, for supporting other candidates, and for failing to associate themselves politically with Medford's campaign. Using these criteria as the basis of an employment decision violated their Constitutional rights to freedom of expression and association. The Fourth Circuit Court of Appeals said that in jurisdictions where the sheriff is elected by popular vote, the triumph of one candidate indicates voter approval of the candidate's espoused platform and general agreement with the candidate's expressed political agenda. Some candidates gain office by promising changes in current policy. By choosing a particular candidate to protect the citizens of the county, the electorate vests in the sheriff broad discretion to set and implement the policies necessary to carry out his goals. The sheriff owes a duty to the electorate and the public at large to ensure that his espoused policies are implemented.

The court further said that deputy sheriffs play a special role in implementing the sheriff's policies and goals. The sheriff is likely to include at least some deputies in his core group of advisors. Deputies on patrol work autonomously, exercising significant discretion in performing their jobs. In the course of their duties, deputies will make some decisions that actually create policy. Deputies are often called upon to make on-the-spot, split-second decisions effectuating the objectives and law enforcement policies that a particular sheriff has chosen to pursue.

In addition the court noted that the sheriff relies on his deputies to foster public confidence in law enforcement. Deputies are expected to provide the sheriff with the truthful and accurate information he needs to do his job. In some jurisdictions, the deputy sheriff is the general agent of the sheriff, and the sheriff is civilly liable for the acts of a deputy.

Based upon these findings, the Fourth Circuit Court of Appeals in a 8-5 decision concluded that all deputies, no matter what rank can be terminated by the sheriff merely because the deputy's failed to support the sheriff in the election, supported the sheriff's opponent or failed to participate in the sheriff's campaign. *Jenkins*, 119 F.3d at 1164. There was no violation of the deputies' rights. This opinion has been applied to deputies in Maryland, *Mills v. Meadows*, 1999 U.S. App. Lexis 16895 (4th Cir. 1999)(unpublished) and confidential secretary to a West Virginia sheriff, *Barr v. Barrill*, 199 U.S. App. Lexis 26524 (4th Cir. 1999)(unpublished). The Fourth Circuit has not applied *Jenkins* to an unsworn jailer employed by a North Carolina sheriff. *Knight v. Vernon*, 214 F.3d 544 (4th Cir. 2000).

Jenkins v. Medford overrules the analysis employed in *Joyner v. Lancaster*, 815 F.2d 20 (4th Cir. 1987) and an earlier case in the Fourth Circuit of *Jones v. Dodson*, 727 F.2d 1329 (4th Cir. 1984) which required that the deputy occupy a high ranking position in the agency before political or personal loyalty could be required. The Eleventh Circuit in *Terry v. Cook*, 866 F.2d 373 (11th Cir. 1989) and the Seventh Circuit in *Upton v. Thompson*, 930 F.2d 1209 (7th Cir. 1991), *cert. denied*, 503 U.S. 906 (1992) agree with the Fourth Circuit. On the other hand, the Third Circuit in *Burns v. County of Cambria* 971 F.2d 1015 (3rd Cir. 1992), the Fifth Circuit in *Brady v. Fort Bend County, Texas*, 145 F.3d 691 (5th Cir.), *cert. den.* 525 U.S. 1105 (1999), the Sixth Circuit in *Hall v. Tollett*, 128 F.3d 418 (6th Cir. 1997) and the Ninth Circuit in *DiRuzza v. County of Tehama*, 206 F.3d 1304 (9th Cir.) *cert. den.* 121 S.Ct. 624 (2000) all disagree. The Third, Fifth, Sixth and Ninth Circuits require an analysis of the deputy's position to determine if political or personal loyalty is required.

CONCLUSION

Public employees retain their First Amendment rights. However, the public employer must be able to deliver public services effectively and efficiently. When these two interests collide, there must be a weighing of each and a determination of which should prevail. It is not an easy process or one which can be reduced to a formula. First, an employee's comments on matters of public concern are given the most protection. Second, a law enforcement agency has a heightened interest in discipline and the need for obedience to orders. Speech can be restricted if the employer can show it will adversely affect the employer's interests. Sometimes, the courts will defer to an employer's judgment on the effect, but not always. Finally, speech involving matters of personal concerns or personal bias is protected to a much less extent, and the employee must be prepared to show that such speech will not have an adverse effect upon the agency.

CHAPTER 12

RELIGIOUS FREEDOM
IN THE WORKPLACE

The First Amendment to the United States Constitution prohibits Congress from making any law establishing a religion and prohibiting the free exercise of religion. Both the Free Exercise Clause and the Establishment Clause limit the authority of state and local governments by reason of the Fourteenth Amendment. *Everson v. Board of Education*, 330 U.S. 1 (1947) (Establishment Clause); *Hamilton v. Regents of Univ. of Cal.*, 293 U.S. 245 (1934) (Free Exercise Clause). These clauses involving freedom of religion apply to the workplace, but the right is limited. Managers need to know the general parameters of this Amendment in to avoid legal pitfalls. Policies, rules and decisions may need to be modified in order to accommodate an employee's religious belief. As discussed below, most challenges to rules and policies based upon religion are brought pursuant to Title VII of the Civil Rights Act. In addition, claims may also be brought pursuant to 42 U.S.C. § 1983 that prohibits a person acting under color of law from violating another's Constitutional rights. *See* Chapter 14.

WHAT IS RELIGION?

The first issue is determining what constitutes a religion for purposes of protection by the First Amendment. Clearly an established religion such as Protestant, Catholic, Jewish, or Muslim is protected. But the United States Supreme Court does not limit the coverage to established religions but applies to all "beliefs rooted in religion." *Thomas v. Review Bd. of Indiana Employment Sec. Div.*, 450 U.S. 707, 713 (1981). The Court said "religious beliefs need not be acceptable, logical, consistent, or comprehensible to others in order to merit First Amendment protection." *Id*. at 714. If a belief is "so bizarre, so clearly nonreligious in motivation," it is not entitled to protection. *Id*. at 715. On the other hand, the employee need not show that he or she attends church or that the belief is part of a dogma or tenet of an organized religion, only that it is a "sincerely held religious belief." *Frazee v. Employment Sec. Dep't.*, 489 U.S. 829, 834 (1989). The employee's beliefs must occupy a place in the life of the employee "parallel to that filled by the orthodox belief in God" in religions more widely accepted in the United States. *United States v. Seeger*, 380 U.S. 163, 166 (1964). Unusual rituals can also be part of a religious dogma such as animals sacrifice, *Church of the Lukumi Babalu Aye, Inc. v. City of Hialeah*, 508 U.S. 520 (1993), witchcraft, and casting spells. *Dettmer v. Landon*, 799 F.2d 929 (4th Cir. 1986). The police manager cannot dismiss an employee's assertion of a religious belief merely because it is unusual or not related to an established religion. An employee who has sincerely held religious beliefs qualifies for protection.

FREE EXERCISE CLAUSE

One of the most important rights guaranteed to all of us by the Constitution is the right to freely practice our chosen religion. The fact that a person is employed by government or even incarcerated by government does not make this right any less important. The Free Exercise right is subject to a balancing of interest. Government must be able to effectively and efficiently deliver police services and to insure security within a confinement facility. The manager must balance the interests of the agency with those of the employee. This means accommodating an employee's religious belief and Free Exercise rights whenever possible.

The United States Supreme Court for many years interpreted the Free Exercise Clause of the Constitution as requiring the government to demonstrate that any government action that substantially burdens a person's free exercise of religion was the "least restrictive" means to further a "compelling government interest." In *Sherbert v. Verner*, 374 U.S. 398 (1963), a Seventh-Day Adventist working for a South Carolina company refused to work from sundown on Fridays until sundown on Saturdays, her Sabbath. The employee was fired and applied for unemployment compensation. The South Carolina Employment Security Commission denied her unemployment benefits because of its rule of prohibiting benefits to a person who "without good cause" refused to accept suitable work that had been offered. The Supreme Court of South Carolina affirmed the denial of benefits, and the employee appealed to the United States Supreme Court. The United States Supreme Court reversed and ordered benefits to be paid. The Court said that the rule burdened the free exercise of religion. The employee was forced to choose between following the precepts of her religion and forfeiting benefits or abandoning the precepts of her religion and accepting work. The Court held that the State could not show a compelling state interest in this rule. *See also Hobbie v. Unemployment Appeals Comm'n of Florida*, 480 U.S. 136 (1987) (Cannot deny benefits to an employee who converted to a Seventh-Day Adventist, refused to continue to work on Saturday, and was discharged); *Wisconsin v. Yoder*, 406 U.S. 205 (1972) (Compulsory school attendance law unconstitutional when applied to Amish children).

The Supreme Court has recognized compelling governmental interests in a variety of situations. For instance, the Court found the need for uniformity paramount in a case requiring an Amish employer to pay Social Security taxes for Amish employees, *United States v. Lee*, 455 U.S. 252, 258-59 (1982), and in a case denying Jewish servicemen the right to wear a yarmulke, *Goldman v. Weinberger*, 475 U.S. 503, 508-510 (1986). It found public welfare paramount in a case enforcing the draft against persons who considered a particular war "unjust," *Gillette v. United States*, 401 U.S. 437, 462 (1971), and in a case denying tax exemptions to educational institutions with racially discriminatory policies, *Bob Jones University v. United States*, 461 U.S. 574, 604 (1983). The Court found the public health and safety interest decisive in upholding mandatory vaccination, *Jacobson v. Massachusetts*, 197 U.S. 11 (1905) and in enforcing child labor laws, *Prince v. Massachusetts*, 321 U.S. 158, 168-70 (1944) (Finding that a state's interest in protecting health justified prohibiting a nine-year-old Jehovah's Witness from distributing religious literature). However a compelling state interest is hard to find for many rountine policies which make an agency function efficiently.

In 1990, the United States Supreme Court clarified its view on the Free Exercise Clause and held that laws, policies, or rules that are of general applicability and that "incidentally burden" the free exercise of religion do not need to be justified by showing a compelling state interest. This "compelling interest" requirement is limited to those laws that specifically and intentionally target religious practices. In *Employment Div. v. Smith*, 494 U.S. 872 (1990), a drug rehabilitation organization fired two employees because they ingested peyote for sacramental purposes at a Native American church ceremony. Peyote is a hallucinogenic drug. When the two men applied for unemployment, they were denied benefits. The denial was for work-related misconduct. The United States Supreme Court reversed the Oregon Supreme Court and held that the denial of benefits did not violate the Free Exercise Clause. The Court held that a law of general applicability that was religiously neutral, such as one prohibiting possession of controlled substances (including peyote), did not need to make an exception for religious use. The incidental affect on religion did not require the State to show a compelling need or that this was the least restrictive means of accomplishing this result. The Court said: "We have never held that an individual's religious beliefs excuse him from compliance with an otherwise valid law prohibiting conduct that the State is free to regulate." *Id.* at 878-9.

The *Smith* test for determining violations of the Free Exercise Clause is as follows: (a) does the rule or policy apply generally to employees (does not focus on a particular religion); (b) does it reasonably relate to a matter that the agency can regulate; (c) If yes to both (a) and (b), then the rule or policy is constitutional despite the fact that it burdens or restricts employees free exercise of their religion. The employer or custodian of an inmate is still required to accommodate the religion of the employee or inmate as long as the accommodation does not cause undue hardship or invalidate the effectiveness of the rule or policy.

In response to this perceived change in the standard for Free Exercise Clause, Congress passed the Religious Freedom Restoration Act of 1993 (RFRA). Congress stated that the purpose of the act was "to restore the compelling interest test set forth in *Sherbert v. Verner*, 374 U.S. 398 (1963), and *Wisconsin v. Yoder*, 406 U.S. 205 (1972), and to guarantee its application in all cases where free exercise of religion is substantially burdened." 42 U.S.C. § 2000bb(b)(1). In order to implement this purpose, Congress specifically overruled the distinction between laws that specifically and intentionally target religion and laws of general applicability that have the unintended effect of burdening religion the Supreme Court adopted in *Employment Div. v. Smith*. "Government shall not substantially burden a person's exercise of religion even if the burden results from a rule of general applicability." 42 U.S.C. § 2000bb-1(a).

The term "government" is defined to include federal, state, and local governments; government officials; and agencies. 42 U.S.C. § 2000bb-2(1). The RFRA is applicable only if a law, ordinance, policy, or decision "substantially" affects the free exercise of religion and not simply because it has some impact.

RFRA spawned numerous challenges to many routine government regulations from conduct of confinement facilities, sick leave policies, and zoning and land use policies that applied to churches. The challenge that reached the United States Supreme Court involved applying a city's historic preservation zoning laws to a church that wanted to expand. The church was denied a building permit to expand. The Archbishop sued the city claiming that the zoning laws burdened the church members' Free Exercise rights by prohibiting the expansion of the church. He also claimed that there was no compelling government interest in establishing a historic district or in limiting the expansion of the church. RFRA was declared unconstitutional and unenforceable by the Supreme Court. *City of Boerne v. Flores*, 521 U.S. 507 (1997). The Supreme Court said that Congress overstepped its authority when it enacted RFRA. The Court said that only it has the power to decide what the Amendments to the Constitution mean and not Congress. The Court reasoned that Congress attempted to alter the meaning of the Free Exercise Clause and exceeded its authority. The standard for determining if a policy generally applicable to everyone and which only incidentally burdens religion violates the Free Exercise Clause is whether the policy is rationally related to a government interest. The RFRA can be applied to federal agencies as a policy of the federal government but cannot be applied to other litigants, such as state and local government agencies. The Court reinstated the *Smith* test for state and local government managers.

The *Smith* test, again, is that if an agency has a rule or policy of general applicability and it reasonably regulates an area that the agency can regulate, *e.g.* grooming, sick leave, etc., then an employee must comply with the rule or policy even if it burdens the Free Exercise of religion. The agency must try to accommodate the exercise of the person's religion if it can without undue hardship or nullification of its rule or policy.

ESTABLISHMENT CLAUSE

The Establishment Clause is intended to keep government from choosing a particular religion or granting benefits to people who have certain beliefs. The Supreme Court identified three main evils prohibited by the Establishment Clause, "sponsorship, financial support, and active involvement of the sovereign in religious activity." *Walz v. Tax Commission*, 397 U.S. 664, 668 (1970). There must be a wall of separation between church and state. *The Life and Selected Writings of Thomas Jefferson* (Adrienne Koch and William Peden, eds. 1972). The Supreme Court has developed a series of criteria to determine if a law or policy violates the Establishment Clause. First, the law or policy must have a secular or non-religious purpose. Second, its primary effect must be one that neither advances nor inhibits religion. Finally, the statute or policy must not foster an excessive government entanglement with religion. *Lemon v. Kurtzman*, 403 U.S. 602, 612-3 (1971). The Supreme Court construes the First Amendment to "affirmatively mandate accommodation not merely tolerance, of all religions and forbids hostility toward any." *Lynch v. Donnelly*, 465 U.S. 668, 673 (1984). Religious freedom is the purpose and avoidance of state-sponsored church is the means. The government cannot encourage or promote one religion over others or religion over any non-religion. *See Everson v. Board of Education*, 330 U.S. 1, 15-6 (1947)

Religion and government come into contact. The national motto is "In God We Trust." The question is how must the government manager act when faced with the issue of religion. The manager must accommodate the religion without promoting it. The manager cannot prefer an employee who believes in no religion over those who do believe and vice versa. *Zorach v. Clauson*, 343 U.S. 314 (1952).

The issue of the Establishment Clause arises in the police employment context when an employee or the organization uses government assets to further religious beliefs. An employee who preaches while on duty or the agency allows the use of facilities for one particular religion and not others. Also, selecting employees because of the religious views they hold raises this issue. All of these are examples of potential problem areas. The manager must be religion neutral. Government benefits cannot be given to someone on the basis of religion.

On the other hand, the mere fact that religion is involved or functions are performed by religious people does not necessarily violate the Establishment Clause. Many police agencies have chaplains who help with counseling crime victims and others. The courts have upheld the use of police chaplains if the primary purpose is secular and the department does not favor one religion over another.

Managers must be religion neutral. Encouraging or discouraging religion may lead to legal proceedings.

TITLE VII—RELIGIOUS DISCRIMINATION AND ACCOMMODATION

Title VII of the Civil Rights Act of 1964, 42 U.S.C. § 2000e-1 to -14, prohibits religious discrimination in hiring, promotion, and terms and conditions of employment. 42 U.S.C. § 2000e-2(c)(1). This law also requires an employer, including state and local law enforcement agencies, to make reasonable accommodations to an employee's religious beliefs.

In order to prevail on a claim of religious discrimination, the employee must show that (1) a bona fide religious belief conflicts with an employment requirement; (2) the employer was informed of the belief; and (3) the employee was disciplined, discharged, or otherwise damaged in terms or conditions of employment. The employer must then show that it cannot "accommodate" the employee's religious practice without "undue hardship on the conduct of the employer's business." 42 U.S.C. § 2000e-2(a)(1)(j).

An employer has the legal duty to "accommodate" an employee if it can be done without "undue hardship." These requirements mean that upon request of an employee, the employer must review the policy or decision to determine if the employee's particular request can be accomplished without causing substantial difficulty. As with all such balancing of interests, the courts have an opportunity to strike a different balance. This is especially true when the supervisor cannot point to specific problems or disruption that will occur if the request is granted. The Supreme Court in *Trans World Airlines, Inc v. Hardison*, 432 U.S. 63 (1977), held that it was not reasonable to require the airline to schedule a pilot so that he was not required to work on his Sabbath. The Court said, "To require TWA to bear more than a *de minimis* cost in order to give Hardison Saturdays off is an undue hardship." *Id.* at 84. The Court further opined that to discriminate in favor of Hardison by giving him every weekend off amounts to allocating a benefit according to a person's religious belief and is also illegal discrimination.

A hostile work environment based upon hostility toward the religion or the lack of religion of an employee is also prohibited by Title VII. *See also* Chapter 5, Sexual Harassment. For example, a dispatcher was discharged. She alleged that the chief of police was a born-again Christian and told her that if an employee was unwilling to play by God's rules, he would trade her. He also said that he would not allow the evil spirit that had taken her soul to live in the police department. The Court held that due to the coercive atmosphere a request for reasonable accommodation was not necessary for a claim of a violation of the Establishment Clause and found a violation of the dispatcher's rights. *Venters v. Delphi, Indiana*, 123 F.3d 956 (7th Cir. 1997).

Most claims for violation of religious freedom are brought pursuant to Title VII. EEOC procedures discussed in Chapter 4 apply to such claims.

EXAMPLES

Police Chaplains

The sheriff of Pierce County located in Washington state had a volunteer chaplain program. Preachers from many churches volunteered their time to counsel people who come in contact with the police. The program was challenged. The Washington State Supreme Court upheld the program. *Maylon v. Pierce County, Washington*, 935 P.2d 1272 (WA. 1997). The Washington court applied the *Lemon* test and found the chaplain program was established for a secular purpose. *Lemon v. Kurtzman*, 403 U.S. 602, 612-3 (1971). Even though the chaplains are employed by a church and are religiously trained, the purpose is secular counseling. The court said that the purpose of the program need not be entirely secular but religious concerns cannot be the sole motivation behind the program. The court next determined that the primary effect of the program is not to advance religion. The effect is broad based counseling. The court then noted that an employer could not refuse to hire counselors merely because they are religious. Finally, the court had to determine if there was excessive entanglement. Excessive entanglement occurs when the distinction between the church and the state becomes blurred and it is unclear whether the employee is acting for the church or the state. The court found there is no excessive entanglement between the church and the state. The chaplains worked for the police department when on duty.

On the other side, the court in *Voswinkel v. City of Charlotte*, 495 F.Supp. 588, (W.D. N.C. 1980) held that the chaplain program operated by the Charlotte, North Carolina, police department violated the Constitution. The police department paid Providence Baptist Church half of the chaplain's salary. The chaplain's position was required to be filled by a minister which was an unconstitutional religious test for public employment. The court said that this program led to excessive entanglement. The chaplain was being paid by both the state and the church and it was not clear who the chaplain answered to when working for the police department.

A chaplain program is lawful if the chaplain is selected in a non-discriminatory manner and engages in secular based counseling. The program does not establish a religion at government expense.

Grooming

An agency policy that regulates dress and grooming may be challenged as violating an officer's Free Exercise rights. In *Kelley v. Johnson*, 425 U.S. 238 (1976) the Supreme Court said that a police department regulation prohibiting mustaches or limiting the length of an employee's hair length was unconstitutional. This challenge was based upon the Fourteenth Amendment due process protection of a person's liberty interest in his own appearance. The Supreme Court rejected the challenge and said that a state has a compelling interest in the operation of its police agencies. More recently a similar challenge has been launched against grooming standards, not based upon the Fourteenth Amendment but based upon the First Amendment freedom of religion clause.

The Third Circuit ruled that a policy that prohibited mustaches on officers could not be applied to an officer who had a sincerely held religious belief that his facial hair was a religious symbol. The Newark, New Jersey police department had a no mustache rule with a medical exception primarily for people who have a skin condition called *pseudo folliculitis barbae* which makes it very painful to shave. The Fraternal Order of Police filed a lawsuit on behalf of two officers who are Sunni Muslims. According to the officers the refusal by a Sunni Muslim male who can grow a beard, to wear one is a major sin—as serious a sin as eating pork. The court ruled that since there was a medical exception for facial hair, the agency unconstitutionally discriminated against the officer based upon his religion when an exception was not made for religious reasons. The Court said:

> The Department also suggests that permitting officers to wear beards for religious reasons would undermine the force's morale and esprit de corps. However, the Department has provided no legitimate explanation as to why the presence of officers who wear beards for medical reasons does not have this effect but the presence of officers who wear beards for religious reasons would. And the same is true with respect to the Department's suggestion that the presence of officers who wear beards for religious reasons would undermine public confidence in the force. We are at a loss to understand why religious exemptions threaten important city interests but medical exemptions do not.
>
> *FOP Newark Lodge No. 12 v. City of Newark*, 170 F.3d 359, 366-7 (3rd Cir. 1999)

In *Rourke v. N.Y. Dep't. of Corrections,* 915 F.Supp. 525 (N.D. N.Y. 1994) the court held that a department policy on hair length for correction officers violated the rights of a full-blooded Mohawk Native American who believed his hair symbolized spirituality. RFRA was the basis of this ruling. This case may not accurately reflect the current law.

Drug Use

In *United States v. Bauer*, 84 F.3d 1549 (9th Cir.), *cert. den.* 519 U.S. 1132 (1997) the Ninth Circuit held that under the RFRA the government was required to prove that it had a compelling state interest in enforcing marijuana laws and that universal enforcement was the least restrictive means to accomplish this compelling interest when Rastafarian's are charged with unlawful possession of marijuana. The defendants claimed that as Rastafarians, marijuana use is part of their religious ceremony. This case may not reflect current law.

Assignments

In *Rodriguez v. City of Chicago*, 156 F.3d 771 (7th Cir.) *cert. den.* 525 U.S. 1144 (1998), the Seventh Circuit Court of Appeals was confronted with a lawsuit filed by a Catholic Chicago police officer who was assigned to a special detail to protect employees of abortion clinics. He objected and was originally reassigned. Upon returning from injury leave, he was again assigned to this detail over his objection. He was told that he could transfer to another precinct which did not have an abortion clinic. Otherwise, he had to work the assignment. He appealed, and his appeal was denied. He then filed suit under Title VII for discrimination based upon religion and the RFRA. The court of appeals held that the officer cannot be required to accept an assignment which violates his religious beliefs if the city has the ability to accommodate him. In this case the court said the city did accommodate the officer by giving him the option of transferring to another precinct. They upheld the dismissal of the lawsuit. They did note that the city can refuse to accommodate an officer if it creates an undue hardship on the city and adversely affects its ability to deliver efficient police services. They did not reach this issue because the officer had been adequately accommodated.

Shifts

An officer can be required to work on the officer's Sabbath. *In Beadle v. Hillsborough County Sheriff's Dept*, 29 F.3d 589 (11th Cir. 1994), a deputy was fired for refusing to work on his Sabbath. The department allowed deputies to swap shifts and to take vacation or compensatory time to avoid working on their Sabbaths. The deputy unsuccessfully argued that reasonable accommodation required the department to arrange for a swap of shifts or transfer him to a job as a bailiff or process server, which did not require weekend work. The federal court of appeals defined reasonable accommodation as follows:

> Title VII does not require an employer to give an employee a choice among several accommodations; nor is the employer required to demonstrate that alternative accommodations proposed by the employee constitute undue hardship. Rather the inquiry ends when an employer shows that a reasonable accommodation was afforded, regardless of whether that accommodation is one which the employee suggested.

Id. at 592

Unbecoming Conduct

An employee cannot use religion as a defense to unbecoming conduct. An officer who makes offensive religious remarks cannot complain about discipline. *Hershinow v. Bonamarte*, 735 F.2d 264 (7th Cir. 1984) (Telling a female he had stopped for speeding "All they have in this town are Jewish bitches.").

Leave Policies

A department policy which requires that an employee who is on sick leave must remain at home does not violate the employee's religious freedom by prohibiting the employee from going to church. *Crain v. Board of Police Comm'rs*, 920 F.2d 1402 (8th Cir. 1990).

Witnessing

Employees can be prohibited from attempting to convert other employees or the public while being paid by the government. *Langlotz v. Picciano*, 683 F.Supp. 1041 (E.D.Va.) *aff'd* 905 F.2d 1530(4th Cir. 1999) (Counselor in juvenile court can be dismissed for bring religion into counseling sessions); *Lynch v. Indiana State Univ. Bd. of Trustees*, 177 Ind. App. 172 (1978) (Dismissal of math professor for reading Bible at beginning of class upheld).

CONCLUSION

Freedom of religion is an evolving area of the law. Determining if a belief of an employee is entitled to protection may be difficult. Once the employee is found to have a sincerely held belief, accommodation is required if it can be accomplished without undue hardship. The public manager must give thoughtful consideration to religion in the work place. The manger cannot prohibit an employee from the free exercise of religion, but must not allow one employee to impose religious beliefs on the public or other employees. Being religion-neutral is required.

CHAPTER 13

DRUG TESTING IN THE WORKFORCE: LEGAL RAMIFICATIONS

INTRODUCTION

Drug screening or testing of applicants and employees is an evolving area of law. The law varies from public employees to private employees, state to state, job to job. Prior to implementing any drug-testing program, an attorney should be consulted. There are many potential pitfalls, plus many benefits.

CONSTITUTIONAL PROTECTION—PUBLIC EMPLOYEES

Generally, the United States Constitution protects persons from action by the federal, state, or local government. Such action can be in the form of government agencies or employees, or of laws, ordinances, or rules enacted by a government or agency. The United States Constitution does **not** normally restrict actions between a private employer and a private individual.

The Fourth Amendment to the United States Constitution protects federal, state, and local employees or applicants for employment from unreasonable searches. A drug test is a search. The question is whether it is reasonable.

The United States Supreme Court, in *Skinner v. Railway Labor Executives Ass'n*, 489 U.S. 602 (1989), held that a regulation for testing of breath, blood, or urine for any employee involved in train accidents is constitutional. The Court found that the government's compelling interest in public safety outweighed any privacy interest. The Court said that "particularized suspicion" of drug use was not required when there had been an accident.

The United States Supreme Court also upheld a regulation of the United States Department of Treasury that required mandatory drug testing for Customs Service employees who are directly involved in drug interdiction or enforcement or who carry firearms. The Court did not uphold the requirement for employees who "handle classified material." The Court was unclear which jobs the last category covered and sent it back for further review. The Court used a balancing test between the interest of the government and the privacy of the employee. The Court found that the government's interest in law enforcement outweighed the employee's right to privacy. *See Treasury Employees v. Van Roab*, 489 U.S. 656 (1989). Subsequently, the Supreme Court upheld random urinalysis testing of public school students participating in interscholastic athletics. *Vernonia Sch. Dist. 473 v. Acton*, 115 S. Ct. 2386 (1995).

The trend is for courts to uphold drug testing without reason for employees in law enforcement, public safety, and sensitive positions. Applicants for employment have less of a privacy interest than incumbent employees. Mandatory drug testing for applicants for a wider range of public employment positions is allowed. *Willner v. Thornburg*, 928 F.2d 1185 (D.C. Cir.) (Drug testing of attorney applying with United States Department of Justice Antitrust Division), *cert.*

denied, 502 U.S. 1020 (1991); *National Federation of Federal Employees v. Cheney*, 884 F.2d 603 (D.C. Cir. 1989) (Random drug testing of civilian police officers who work for the Army); *Thomson v. Marsh*, 884 F.2d 113 (4th Cir. 1989) (per curiam) (Army drug testing of civilian employees at chemical weapons plant); *AFGE Council 33 v. Barr*, 794 F. Supp. 1466 (N.D. Cal. 1992) (Random drug testing of Bureau of Prison employees who have access to firearms).

DRUG TESTING IN PRIVATE SECTOR

Federal Contractors

Under the Drug-Free Workplace Act of 1988, 41 U.S.C. §§ 701-707, all employers with federal procurement contracts of $25,000 or more must certify to the contracting agency that they will provide a drug-free workplace. The employer must publish a statement notifying employees that the manufacture, distribution, possession, or use of a controlled substance is prohibited in the workplace and specifying the consequences for violating the policy.

In addition, employers must establish a drug-free awareness program to inform employees about the dangers of drug abuse, the employer's policy concerning drug use, any available counseling and rehabilitation programs, and the penalties that may be imposed upon employees for drug-abuse violations. The employer's statement must require employees engaged in contract-related work to notify the employer of any criminal conviction for a drug violation occurring in the workplace within five days of the conviction. Contractors receiving such notices must, within thirty days, either take appropriate action against the employee, up to and including discharge, or require the employee to satisfactorily complete an approved rehabilitation program. Employers must also notify the contracting agency within ten days after receiving notice of an employee's conviction.

Failure to comply with these requirements can lead to proceedings to suspend payments, terminate the contract, or suspend or debar the contractor. A debarred contractor is ineligible for any federal contract for a period not to exceed five years.

On January 31, 1989, the Office of Management and Budget issued a government-wide rule for the purpose of implementing the statutory requirements of the Drug-Free Workplace Act. The rule, which amends the Federal Acquisition Regulations, *48 C.F.R.* subparts *9.4, 23.5,* and *52.2,* is the sole authority for implementing the Act—there are no separate agency guidelines. Although the government-wide implementing regulations do not require contractors to conduct drug testing of employees, Department of Defense rules *48 C.F.R. 223* and *252* (interim regulation) remain operative. The Defense Department rule **requires** drug testing of selected contractor employees in sensitive positions.

Commercial Motor Vehicles—Interstate Commerce

Regulations issued by the United States Department of Transportation (DOT) impose on private employers a duty to test any person who operates a commercial motor vehicle in interstate commerce. *See 49 C.F.R. parts 40, 391, 394.* The regulations apply to "motor carriers" and persons who operate a "commercial motor vehicle." A motor carrier is defined as a for-hire or a private motor carrier of property. *49 C.F.R. § 390.5.* A "commercial motor vehicle" includes a vehicle designed to transport more than fifteen passengers. *49 C.F.R. § 391.85.* Under the regulations, testing for illicit drug use is required in the following situations: First, employees must be tested upon reasonable cause for the use of controlled substances. *49 C.F.R. § 391.102.* The employer must also test each driver during the first medical examination after implementation of the program and implement a random drug-testing program in which the total number of tests conducted in a twelve-month period must be equal to at least fifty percent of the drivers subject to testing. *49 C.F.R. §§ 391.105, 391.109.* Finally, a driver who is involved in a reportable accident must be tested no more than thirty-two hours after the accident. *49 C.F.R. § 391.113.* DOT further requires covered employers to establish an Employee Assistance Program that includes education and training components addressing the effects and consequences of substance abuse. *49 C.F.R. §§ 391.119, 391.121.* The Ninth Circuit upheld these regulations in their entirety in *International Brotherhood of Teamsters v. Department of Transp.*, 932 F.2d 1292 (9th Cir. 1991).

Union Employees

Drug testing has been ruled to be a mandatory subject of collective bargaining. *See Brotherhood of Teamsters Engineers v. Burlington N. R.R. Co.*, 838 F.2d 1087 (9th Cir. 1988). Preemployment drug testing may not be. *Star Tribune v. Div. of Cowles Media Co.*, 295 N.L.R.B. No. 63 (1989).

Recovering Alcoholics and Drug Abusers

The Americans with Disabilities Act (ADA) and the Federal Rehabilitation Act, 29 U.S.C. §§ 701-796i state that a disabled individual does not include an alcoholic or drug abuser whose current use prevents him or her from performing the duties of the job in question or whose employment, by reason of current alcohol or drug abuse, would constitute a direct threat to property or to the safety of others. In such cases, neither of these laws apply. 42 U.S.C. § 12211; 56 C.F.R. § 1630.16(d)(e).

Note, however, that **reformed** alcoholics and drug abusers who have successfully completed supervised drug rehabilitation programs and are no longer using drugs **are** protected by the Rehabilitation Act, as are persons who are erroneously regarded as current alcoholics and drug abusers. Under the ADA, however, employers who hire former drug users may institute reasonable procedures, including drug testing, to ensure that the worker remains drug-free. *56 C.F.R. § 1630.3(a), (b).*

Some state and federal agencies and courts have leaned toward protecting drug addicts under the Rehabilitation Act. *See, e.g., Johnson v. Smith*, 39 E.P.D. § 36,020 (D.C. Minn. 1985). However, the federal government's new drug-free workplace statute and regulations suggest a trend in the opposite direction. In *Travnor v. Turnage*, 485 U.S. 535 (1988), four justices opined that the Rehabilitation Act did not conflict with a Veteran's Administration regulation defining alcoholism as "willful misconduct" while three dissenting justices felt that the regulation did conflict with the act. (Justices Scalia and Kennedy did not participate in the decision.)

Discrimination

Title VII of the Civil Rights Act of 1964, 42 U.S.C. § 2000e, prohibits discrimination on the basis of race, color, creed, national origin, or sex. This law apples to employers who have fifteen or more employees. Any condition of employment or preemployment requirement that impacts on members of one of the protected groups at a substantially higher rate than nonprotected groups (females vs. males) is said to have "adverse" or "disparate" impact. When such drug testing eliminates a substantially higher percentage of one group over another, an employer must demonstrate that the drug-testing rule is necessary to assure future job performance or workplace safety. *New York City Transit Auth. v. Beazer*, 440 U.S. 568 (1979) (Excluding from employment all methadone users serves a legitimate goal of safety and efficiency, even though some were prescribed the drug as part of a drug-rehabilitation program).

State Constitution and Statutory Protection

State legislatures or agencies may have established restrictions on drug testing. Also, state courts may have interpreted state constitutional provisions to provide more protection for employees. State law must be consulted before implementing any drug testing.

For example, the North Carolina Constitution and General Statutes have not been interpreted to authorize or limit who is subject to drug testing in the workplace. North Carolina does have a Handicap Protection Act, N.C. Gen. Stat. §§ 168A-1-12, and antidiscrimination statutes, N.C. Gen. Stat. §§ 143-422.1-422.3. There are limitations on labs for analyzing for drugs and mandatory procedures to follow, N.C. Gen. Stat. §§ 95-230-235, but the law does not control when testing is authorized.

The North Carolina Court of Appeals said that a policy requiring all airport employees who drive motor vehicles to be tested for drug use was not unconstitutional and upheld the dismissal of an employee who refused to submit to the test. The court held that an employee who was authorized to drive was in a position where the safety of others was an overriding concern, and there was a legitimate reason to implement a drug-testing program. *Boesche v. Raleigh-Durham Airport Auth.*, 111 N.C. App. 149, *disc. rev. improvidently allowed and appeal dismissed*, 336 N.C. 304 (1994) (*per curiam*).

Drug Testing of Applicants

The Americans with Disabilities Act (ADA) takes a neutral stand on whether employers should test employees or applicants for the illegal use of drugs. Drug tests are not encouraged, authorized, or prohibited. Should a drug test be administered, the results may be used as a basis for disciplinary action, including termination. 42 U.S.C. § 12114(d).

Tests for the illegal use of drugs are not considered medical examinations, so they can be given as part of the application process. Employers are not required to wait until after they have made a conditional offer of employment before testing for **illegal** drugs.

If the results reveal information about a person's medical condition beyond whether the person is currently engaging in the illegal use of drugs, this additional information is to be treated as a confidential medical record. An applicant cannot be required to reveal information about a medical condition prior to a conditional offer of employment. (Current employees cannot be forced to undergo tests for medical conditions unless such tests are job related.)

Consequently, there are two approaches an employer can follow that can reconcile the ADA's provisions with regard to applicants:

1. The employer could give drug tests after a conditional offer of employment has been made. Any job offer would be strictly contingent on the person's not testing positive on the drug test for the illegal use of drugs.
2. Alternatively, the employer could ensure that the drug tests given prior to a conditional offer of employment are solely for the illegal use of drugs and do not identify drugs taken pursuant to medical supervision.

There are limitations on employers' use of drug testing that are not mentioned in the ADA or the Rehabilitation Act. The ability to conduct tests is limited by and must be in conformance with applicable federal, state, or local laws or regulations regarding permitted testing, quality control, confidentiality, and rehabilitation. Furthermore, a person may challenge a positive drug-test result by invoking the protection of the ADA, that is, by claiming that he or she is erroneously regarded as an illegal user of drugs as a result of a false-positive drug test. People who take medication under medical supervision and those who are erroneously regarded as illegal drug users are protected against discrimination.

REQUIREMENTS FOR PERFORMING TESTS

Drug-screening tests are inexpensive but have an unacceptably high number of false positives. Drug screenings are not sufficiently reliable to justify taking job action. A confirmatory drug test using a gas chromatography with mass spectrometry or similar type test should be used.

When the drug test shows positive, then the applicant or employee can only prevent the employer from taking action by showing that the test procedures were unreliable or that the results were a false positive. The employer will usually have the burden of showing that the results of the test were reliable. The employer must first show that the sample analyzed was from the person challenging the results. Just as in a criminal case, a chain of custody must be shown. The chain of custody was adequate in one case where the employer showed that the unnamed courier was given an intact sample with bar-coded seals on the container, and the container was placed in a sealed, tamper-proof bag, which was placed in a protective box and was received by the lab in the same box without any signs of tampering. *Logan v. Personnel Bd. of Jefferson County*, 657 So. 2d 1125 (Ala. Civ. Ct. App. 1995).

North Carolina law regulates controlled substance examinations. N.C. Gen. Stat. §§ 95-230-235. Controlled substances include all narcotic drugs, prescription drugs, and illegal drugs. It does **not** include alcohol. The requirements are:

1.   Samples for examination must be collected under "reasonable and sanitary" conditions with individual dignity preserved. Collection must be calculated to prevent substitution of sample. N.C. Gen. Stat. § 95-232(b).

2.   Only laboratories approved by the United States Department of Health and Human Services or the College of America Pathologists may be used. N.C. Gen. Stat. §§ 95-231(1), 95-232(c).

3.   An approved laboratory must confirm any sample that proves a positive result by a second examination of the sample utilizing gas chromatography with mass spectrometry or an equivalent scientifically accepted method. N.C. Gen. Stat. § 95-232(c1).

4.   Every sample producing a confirmed positive result must be preserved at least ninety days after the confirmation. N.C. Gen. Stat. § 95-232(d).

5.   Chain of custody must be maintained. N.C. Gen. Stat. § 95-232(e).

6.   An employee or applicant, at such person's expense, has a right to retest a confirmed positive sample at the same or another approved laboratory. N.C. Gen. Stat. § 95-232(f).

For any violation of this act, the North Carolina Commissioner of Labor may assess a civil penalty of up to $250.00 per affected examiner, with a maximum of $1,000 per investigation. N.C. Gen. Stat. § 95-234.

LEGAL PITFALLS

The legal pitfalls for an employer on the issue of drug testing are numerous. An employer who adopts a drug-testing program may face litigation from applicants or current employees claiming either no justification for a random testing program or no reason for a particular test. This potential for litigation also applies to an employer who adopts a drug-testing program and does not follow the applicable state law and regulations. Incorrectly reporting a person to have used drugs may allow a claim for negligent infliction of emotional distress or defamation. An illegally requested drug test may result in a claim for invasion of privacy.

On the other hand, an employer who does not implement drug testing or some other method to identify users of illegal drugs may be sued by innocent third persons injured by the employee. Such a claim will be limited to those jobs that pose a significant risk to the safety of others. *See Welsh Mfg. Div. of Textron v. Pinkerton's Inc.*, 474 A.2d 436 (R.I. 1984) (Security firm negligently hired security guard with criminal background).

CONCLUSION

The area of drug testing is unsettled. There is no person who can, with assurance, answer all the questions. Strict adherence to current laws and regulations as interpreted by the courts is essential. Drug-testing requirements must be job specific. Only those where public health or safety are at risk should be included.

CHAPTER 14

LITIGATION UNDER 42 U.S.C. § 1983

INTRODUCTION

The term "1983" should be known to every law enforcement supervisor and public manager. This term refers to federal statute Section 1983 of Title 42 of the United States Code. Section 1983 is the basis for most litigation filed against government agencies and employees. It is the statute that is used to apply the rights guaranteed by the United States Constitution to the everyday decisions and policies of state and local government agencies. The public manager must be familiar with the law and the policies under which the agency operates in order to avoid liability for violation of constitutional rights.

Section 1983 is a portion of the Civil Rights Act of 1871 known as the "Ku Klux Klan Act." It was designed to provide a redress for violations of federally protected rights committed by persons acting under color of state law. *Adicikes v. S.H. Kress & Co.*, 398 U.S. 144 (1970). It creates no substantive rights, but merely provides a remedy for deprivations of rights established elsewhere by the Constitution or federal law. *City of Oklahoma City v. Tuttle*, 471 U.S. 808 (1985). Violations of federal statutory rights as well as federal constitutional law **may** be enforced under § 1983. Not all constitutional provisions have been found to provide a proper basis of liability under Section 1983. *Chapman v. Houston Welfare Rights Org.*, 441 U.S. 600 (1979) (Supremacy Clause is not grounds for Section 1983 liability). Rights under the First Amendment, *Pickering v. Board of Education*, 391 U.S. 563 (1968), and the Fourth, Eighth, and Fourteenth Amendments, *Graham v. Connor*, 490 U.S. 386 (1989), may, however, be enforced pursuant to § 1983.

NATURE OF REMEDY

42 U.S.C. § 1983 provides in part:

> Every person who, under color of any statute, ordinance, regulation, custom or usage . . . subjects or causes to be subjected any citizen of the United States or other person within the jurisdiction thereof to the deprivation of any rights, privileges or immunities secured by the constitution and laws shall be liable to the party injured.

The elements of a claim for money damages under § 1983 which the party bringing the lawsuit must prove are:

1. that the defendant is a "person" within the meaning of the statute;
2. that the defendant was acting under color of statute, ordinance, regulation, custom, or usage; and

3.   that the actions of the defendant deprived the party bringing the lawsuit of a right secured by the federal Constitution or laws.

The Supreme Court has held that § 1983 actions may be brought in state as well as federal courts. *Maine v. Thiboutot*, 448 U.S. 1 (1980). There is no requirement that a person bringing the lawsuit exhaust or use state-provided remedies prior to filing a § 1983 lawsuit. *Patsy v. Florida Bd. of Regions*, 457 U.S. 496 (1982). Furthermore, a state cannot require that a litigant filing a § 1983 action follow a state notice of claim procedure prior to filing the action. *Felder v. Casey*, 487 U.S. 131 (1988). On the other hand, a § 1983 action cannot be used to challenge the fact or duration of confinement in a penal institution. *Preiser v. Rodriquez*, 411 U.S. 475 (1974).

WHO IS A "PERSON"?

A state government employee may be sued for money damages in his or her **individual or personal** capacity for acts performed while discharging duties as a state government employee. *Hafer v. Melo*, U.S. 2d (1991). But a suit against a state employee in his or her "official" capacity imposes liability against the entity that he or she represents and cannot be brought because the Eleventh Amendment prohibits lawsuits against states. *Brandon v. Holt*, 469 U.S. 464 (1985).

No state or any of its departments or agencies may be sued for money under Section 1983. Since such a case is in reality a suit against the state and is prohibited by the Eleventh Amendment, Congress did not intend to include states or state agencies within the meaning of "persons" for purposes of money damages. *Will v. Michigan Dep't of State Police*, 491 U.S. 58 (1989). A state and its agencies may be sued for prospective injunctive relief to prevent continuous or future constitutional violations, however. *Kentucky v. Graham*, 473 U.S. 159 (1985). When a person suing prevails for injunctive relief, the state may be required to pay attorneys' fees under 42 U.S.C. § 1988. *Hutto v. Finney*, 437 U.S. 678 (1978).

Local governments and their employees are treated differently. A city, county, or non-state entity is not a "state" within the meaning of the Eleventh Amendment, even though it is created by the state. *Monnell v. Department of Social Serv.*, 436 U.S. 658 (1978). A local government employee may be sued in his or her personal or individual capacity, the same as a state employee, for an act committed under the authority of state law and local ordinance. A local government employee can be sued in his or her "official" capacity, but this is in essence a suit against the local government employer; to recover, the party suing must show that the local government employer had a policy that was followed by the employee and that, as a result, a constitutional right of the party suing was violated. A policy may enforce a local ordinance that prohibits parades that violate the First Amendment, or it could be a policy of allowing police to arrest homeless people for no reason. But absent such a policy, neither the local government employer nor the local government employee in his or her official capacity can be held liable.

The use of the terms "individual capacity" or "personal capacity" does not mean that an officer must defend himself or herself or that any judgment rendered must be paid by the officer. This legal concept of individual versus official capacity is unrelated to the issue of representation or payment of judgment, which will be discussed later.

COLOR OF LAW OR STATE ACTION

For a person to be liable under § 1983, he or she must be acting under color of state law at the time of the act in question. *Polk County v. Dodson*, 454 U.S. 312 (1981). "Color of law" or "state action" under § 1983 is when there is a misuse of power possessed by virtue of state law or local ordinance and made possible only because the wrongdoer is clothed with the authority of the government. *West v. Adkins*, 487 U.S. 42 (1988). The question is whether the conduct causing the deprivation of federally protected rights can be fairly attributed to the state. *NCAA v. Tarcanian*, 488 U.S. 179 (1988). Off-duty action by a police officer cannot be the basis of a lawsuit under § 1983 unless the officer uses police equipment or uses his or her authority as a government employee.

CONSTITUTIONAL RIGHTS

The party suing must show that the conduct of the public employee or the policy of the local government resulted in a violation of a right protected by the Constitution or a federal law that can be enforced through § 1983. The first step in any § 1983 lawsuit is to identify the exact contours of the underlying Constitutional right or federal law claimed to have been violated. *Graham v. Connor*, 490 U.S. 386, 394 (1989). The kinds of conduct that may be included are denial of a parade permit because of the nature of the group requesting the permit, e.g., Nazis wanting to march in a predominantly Jewish neighborhood; denial of due process by taking of a drivers license without a hearing either before or after the taking; towing of vehicles; use of force; etc. Any government action may result in a claim of a violation of constitutional rights. The party suing must be able to point to a specific constitutional provision that was violated by the conduct of the officer.

STATE LAW VIOLATIONS AND TORTS

Violations of state laws may **not** be the basis of liability under § 1983, only federal constitutional and statutory violations may be. *Gryger v. Burke*, 334 U.S. 728 (1948). The negligent act of an official causing unintended loss of or injury to life, liberty, or property cannot be brought under § 1983 but must be brought in state court under normal tort law. *Daniels v. Williams*, 474 U.S. 327 (1986). A 'tort' is a civil wrong which entitles the person wronged to compensation for any injuries caused. The tort may also amount to a violation of the criminal, but not always. A slip and fall in a store may be a tort, but not violate the criminal law. On the other hand, hitting someone with a fist for no reason is an assault or battery under both criminal law and amounts to a tort. Unless the action results in a violation of a Constitutional right, § 1983 does not apply.

The most common tort is negligence. Negligence occurs when a person owes a legal duty to be careful to another person and breaches that legal duty causing injury to another. For example, a driver runs a stop sign and causes a vehicle crash. The law imposes a duty on the driver to stop at the stop sign and he breached this duty. He is, therefore, responsible for the injury caused under state tort law. He did not violate a Constitutional right of the other person, so § 1983 does not apply. *Daniels v. Williams*, 474 U.S. 327 (1986).

Some state law torts mirror Constitutional rights. For example, the state tort of false arrest can also amount to a violation of the Fourth Amendment when the false arrest is based upon a lack of probable cause to make the arrest. However, if the false arrest tort is based upon a violation of state law, e.g. arresting a person outside the officer's territorial jurisdiction, then there is no constitutional violation as long as there is probable cause.

Most lawsuits against law enforcement officers for violating a person's Constitutional right will also include state torts. State tort law is varies from state to state and is beyond the scope of this chapter.

FOURTH AMENDMENT SEARCH AND SEIZURE

The Fourth Amendment prohibits "unreasonable" searches and seizures and the issuance of warrants on less than probable cause. The term "unreasonable" refers not only to the fact that a search or seizure occurred but also the manner in which law enforcement officers conducted the search or seizure.

The first issue to determine is whether a search or seizure occurred. Next, was there justification for the search or seizure under the rules that are usually applied in the criminal law context? Even if there was justification for the search or seizure, a search or seizure undertaken in an unreasonable manner violates the Constitution. The manner of the search or seizure will be the final issue.

A seizure occurs when an individual is stopped by the very instrumentality set in motion or put in place in order to achieve that result. A seizure occurs when there is a termination of freedom of movement through means intentionally applied by the government. *Brower v. Inyo County*, 489 U.S. 593 (1989) (Establishing a roadblock that is designed to and does result in the offender crashing into it amounts to a seizure for purposes of the Fourth Amendment). Attempting to stop or seize someone does not amount to seizure. *California v. Hodari D.*, 499 U.S. 621, 626 (1991). A search occurs when a person's reasonable expectation of privacy is invaded. *Treasury Employees v. Von Rabb*, 489 U.S. 686 (1989) (Drug test).

The rules to justify a seizure are the same as applied in the criminal law context. A stop must be based upon reasonable suspicion unless there is an exception such as a roadblock. An arrest must be based upon probable cause. An arrest warrant is not required if the arrest is in a public place. Absent consent an arrest warrant is required to enter the defendant's home and a search warrant and arrest warrant are needed to enter a third person's home. A frisk requires reasonable suspicion to believe the person is armed. A search in the workplace for a non-criminal investigation requires reasonable suspicion. Criminal investigations require probable cause to search and may require a search warrant. The failure to follow the rules for a search or seizure establishes liability under § 1983, the only question is what is the amount of damages or injury caused to the person.

Finally, even when justification for the search or seizure is shown, a search or seizure performed in an unreasonable manner is unlawful and allows for damages. The rules governing the manner in which a search or seizure is conducted are based upon balance the interests of the government against the interests of the individual. The court will consider what a hypothetical "reasonably well-trained officer" facing the same situation would do.

FOURTH AMENDMENT—STOPS

A stop of either a pedestrian or a vehicle is a seizure within the meaning of the Fourth Amendment and must be based upon reasonable suspicion. *Delaware v. Prouse*, 440 U.S. 648 (1979). The test for reasonable suspicion is an objective one based solely upon the facts know to the officer. The intent of the officer is irrelevant in determining whether reasonable suspicion exists. *Whren v. United States*, 517 U.S. 806 (1996). Reasonable suspicion exists when the facts show "a particularized and objective basis for suspecting the particular person stopped of criminal activity." *United States v. Cortez*, 449 U.S. 411, 417 (1981). If an officer lacks the requisite reasonable suspicion when a stop is made, then a violation of the Fourth Amendment has occurred and a lawsuit pursuant to § 1983 can be brought. *Whren v. United States*, 517 U.S. at 809-10. On the other hand, if the requisite reasonable suspicion is present, then a Fourth Amendment violation cannot be brought for a stop of a pedestrian or vehicle.

Of course, a stop which is legal at its inception can become illegal if the detention is longer than is necessary to carry out the purpose of the stop or the investigative techniques are too intrusive for the reason for the stop. *Martinez v. Nygaard*, 831 F.2d 822, 827 (9th Cir. 1987). A frisk for weapons must be based upon reasonable suspicion that the person stopped is armed. *Terry v. Ohio*, 392 U.S. 1 (1968). If the frisk for weapons is not based upon suspicion or exceeds the scope of a search for weapons, even if contraband is found, is unconstitutional. *Minnesota v. Dickerson*, 444 U.S. 85, 93-4 (1993).

FOURTEENTH AMENDMENT—STOPS

A claim for an unconstitutional stop can also be brought under the Fourteenth Amendment Equal Protection Clause when improper motives are the basis of the stop, such as race. The United States Supreme Court said "the Constitution prohibits selective enforcement of the law based upon considerations such as race. But the constitutional basis for objecting to intentional discriminatory application of laws is the Equal Protection Clause, not the Fourth Amendment. Subjective intentions play no role in ordinary, probable-cause Fourth Amendment analysis." *Whren v. United States*, 517 U.S. at 813. A claim of "racial profiling" can be brought against an officer, supervisors or the agency alleging a policy of targeting persons based upon their race. A claim of race based stopping in violation of the Fourteenth Amendment must be supported by proof of intentional discrimination based upon race. Such evidence will include racial statistics of stops, charges, and searches. Discrimination in employment claims and any other evidence of racial problems within the agency will be used to show that racial discrimination is the policy of the agency not only in stops but in other aspects of management. A lawsuit claiming racial profiling will be expensive to defend and can be very divisive. The suing party will seek money damages and an injunction to prevent such policy in the future. To assure compliance with an injunction, record keep for the court will be required. *Price v. Kramer*, 200 F.3d 1237 (9th Cir 2000) (City of Torrance, California); *Rodriguez v. California Highway Patrol*, 89 F. .Supp. 2d 1131 (N.D. CA); *Maryland State Conference of NAACP*

Branches v Maryland Department of State Police, 72 F. Supp. 2d 560 (D. Md 1999); *United States v. State of New Jersey*, http://www.usdoj.gov/crt/split/documents/jerseysa.htm.

The claim of a constitutiornl violation for racial profiling is usually accompaniedby a claim for violation of Title VI of the Civil Rights Act of 1964. *See* 42 U.S.C. § 2000d. Title VI says that "No person in the United States shall, on the ground of race, color, or national origin, be excluded from participation in, be denied the benefits of , or be subjected to discrimination under any program or activity receiving Federal financial assistance." Since most police agencies receive some federal money, some courts have allowed this claim to be pursued. *Rodriguez v. California Highway Patrol*, 89 F. Supp. 2d 1131 (N.D. CA); *Maryland State Conference of NAACP Branches v Maryland Department of State Police*, 72 F. Supp. 2d 560 (D. Md 1999).

FOURTH AMENDMENT—ARRESTS AND SEARCHES

An arrest to be a reasonable seizure under the Fourth Amendment must be based upon probable cause. *Whren v. United States*, 517 U.S. 806 (1996). A search must be based upon probable cause and in some cases be accompanied by a search warrant. The rules that apply in criminal court are applied in a civil proceeding. The failure to follow the established rules may result in liability after the criminal court surpresses the evidence.

FOURTH AMENDMENT—USE OF FORCE

Although § 1983 protects numerous federal constitutional rights, the use of force is unique to law enforcement officials. Law enforcement officials are entitled to use force to perform their duties. Only when that use of force is "excessive" does the Constitution prohibit it.

A § 1983 claim of excessive force during arrest by a law enforcement officer is analyzed under the Fourth Amendment standard of whether the "seizure" was reasonable under the totality of the circumstances. *Graham v. Connor*, 490 U.S. 386 (1989). The reasonableness of an officer's actions is based on actions of the suspect at the time of the incident and what can be inferred from his or her actions. *Sherrod v. Berry*, 856 F.2d 802 (7th Cir. 1988). Some of the considerations include (1) the crime for which the suspect was being seized, (2) whether he or she posed an immediate threat to the safety of the officer or others, (3) whether the suspect was actively resisting arrest, and (4) whether the suspect was attempting to evade arrest by flight. *Graham v. Connor*, 490 U.S. at 396.

The reasonableness of a particular use of force must be judged from the prospective of a reasonable officer on the scene, rather than with the 20/20 vision of hindsight. The calculus of reasonableness must embody an allowance for the fact that police officers are forced to make split-second judgments in circumstances that are tense, uncertain, and rapidly evolving. *Id*. The extent of the physical injuries may be evidence of the amount of force used. *Dean v. City of Worcester*, 924 F.2d 364 (1st Cir. 1991).

Deadly force may be used to seize a suspect where the officer has probable cause to believe the suspect (1) poses a threat of serious physical harm either to the officer or to others, (2) threatened the officer with a weapon, or (3) has committed a crime involving infliction or threatened infliction of serious physical harm. Some warning should be given, if feasible. *Tennessee v. Garner*, 471 U.S. 1 (1985).

FOURTH AMENDMENT—MALICIOUS PROSECUTION

Malicious prosecution is a state tort which involves the filing criminal charges without probable cause or continuing prosecution when probable cause no longer exists. The person suing must show that the charges were terminated in his favor and not the result of a plea bargain. A criminal conviction or sentence cannot be attacked or challenged by suing under §1983, but a federal habeas corpus action must be filed. *Heck v. Humphrey*, 512 U.S. 477, 487 (1994). A criminal prosecution without probable cause in which the defendant is found not guilty may allow a §1983 lawsuit for violation of the Fourth Amendment. *Albright v. Oliver*, 510 U.S. 266 (1994).

EMERGENCY VEHICLE OPERATION

Emergency vehicle operation does not implicate the Constitutional rights of another absent using the vehicle intentionally to stop another vehicle or otherwise as a weapon. The United States Supreme Court was faced with the case of a deputy sheriff who responded to a disturbance. He saw a motorcycle approaching at high speed. It was operated by a young male with a young male, Lewis, riding as a passenger. The deputy turned on his blue light and called for the driver to stop and tried to block the motorcycle. The driver maneuvered through the police cars and drove off. The deputy activated his emergency lights and siren and began a pursuit. The chase lasted about 75 seconds over a course of 1.3 miles in a residential neighborhood. The motorcycle wove in and out of traffic forcing vehicles off the road. The patrol car followed the motorcycle at speeds of up to 100 m.p.h. at a distance as short as 100 feet when the stopping distance was 650 feet. The chase ended when the motorcycle tipped over while trying to make a sharp left turn. The deputy slammed on brakes but could not avoid hitting the passenger at approximately 40 m.p.h. The patrol car knocked the passenger 70 feet from point of impact, killing him.

The family of the 16 year-old victim sued the County alleging a violation of the substantive due process clause of the Fourteenth Amendment to Constitution. The substantive due process clause is violated by action is characterized as arbitrary or shocks the conscience of the court. In a police pursuit the Supreme Court said that even if the deputy's conduct violated "the reasonableness held up by tort law or the balance struck in law enforcement's own codes of sound practice, it does not shock the conscience." *County of Sacramento v. Lewis*, 523 U.S. 833 (1998).

QUALIFIED IMMUNITY

Even if a person can show a violation of a constitutional right by an officer, the person may not be entitled to money. An officer is entitled to qualified or "good-faith" immunity unless clearly established federal rights, of which a reasonable person would have known, are shown to have been violated. *Mitchell v. Forsyth*, 472 U.S. 511 (1985). This immunity defense provides ample protection to all but the plainly incompetent or those who knowingly violate the law. *Malley v. Briggs*, 475 U.S. 335 (1986). Even though an officer is mistaken about what is reasonable, his or her perception may nevertheless have been "objectively reasonable" under the circumstances. *Collinson v. Gott*, 895 F.2d 994 (4th Cir. 1989). The question is whether the officer's actions could reasonably have been thought to be constitutional. *Anderson v. Creighton*, 483 U.S. 635 (1987). If the conduct has not previously been declared unlawful, then the unlawness must be apparent. *Id.* Courts must consider cases of controlling legal precedent. *Wilson v. Layne*, 526 U.S. 603 (1999) (Media ride-along was unconstitutional but law was not clearly established). The controlling legal precedent is limited to the U.S. Supreme Court, the Federal Circuit Court of Appeals for the officer's state and the highest court from the officer's state, e.g., N.C. Supreme Court, but not N.C. Court of Appeals. *Wilson v. Layne*, 141 F.3d 111 (4th Cir. 1998), *affirmed on other grounds* 526 U.S. 603 (1999)

Qualified immunity is intended to protect public employees in those decisions where it is not clear what the parameters of a person's constitutional rights are. This gray area occurs on occasions when: (1) at the time the decision is made, it is not clearly established that a constitutional right exists; or (2) the right was clearly established, but the public employee could not reasonably know that this decision or conduct was unlawful and would violate a constitutional right. An example of (1) is *Tennessee v. Garner*, 471 U.S. 1 (1985). The State of Tennessee had a law that authorized a law enforcement officer to use deadly force to arrest a fleeing felon, no matter what the felony. Nondangerous and dangerous felonies were treated the same. A Memphis police officer was dispatched to a breaking and entering. A fifteen-year-old youth had broken into and entered a house and had stolen a purse. The officer saw the youth fleeing and attempting to climb a fence. Since the officer knew he could not catch the fleeing felon, and relying on the Tennessee statute, he shot and killed the fifteen-year-old. The family sued. The United States Supreme Court, in a landmark decision, held that a person's Fourth Amendment rights to be free from unreasonable seizures is violated by using deadly force to seize a fleeing felon who poses no immediate danger to the officer or another person. Of course, at the time the decision was made by the officer, it was not clearly established that the fleeing felon had such a constitutional right. The United States Supreme Court did not address the issue of qualified immunity. On remand to the lower court, the lower court held that the officer in his individual capacity was entitled to qualified immunity, since he made the decision to shoot based upon the fact that this constitutional right was not clearly established. The lower court also ruled that a city is not entitled to qualified immunity. Therefore, the family could sue the city, but not the officer. Of course, had the officer been a state officer and not a city officer, the family would have recovered nothing, since the state cannot be sued at all.

The second occasion occurs when the law is clearly established, but a reasonable person in the employee's position would believe that his or her conduct is constitutional. The employee need only have a "reasonable perception" that the conduct is constitutional, even if the perception is incorrect. In *Tarantino v. Baker*, 825 F.2d 772 (4th Cir. 1987), B.R. Baker was a detective with the Avery County Sheriff's Department in the western part of North Carolina. He received an anonymous phone call saying that Tarantino was growing marijuana in an old general store. Baker went to the store at 10:00 p.m. and found the front door padlocked and the windows covered. He walked around to the back porch, knocked on the door, and received no response. He then noticed, as the caller had reported, that a crack ran along the back wall roughly three feet above the level of the porch floor. Believing that looking through the crack would amount to a constitutional "plain view" search, Baker shined his flashlight through the crack and saw marijuana plants. Tarantino was arrested and at trial moved to suppress the evidence. The evidence was suppressed by the court, which held that Baker's conduct exceeded the scope of a "plain view" search and violated Tarantino's Fourth Amendment rights. The charges were dismissed, and Tarantino sued in federal court for money for a violation of his Fourth Amendment rights. The Fourth Circuit Court of Appeals dismissed his lawsuit, finding that although the "plain view" doctrine was clearly established, a reasonable officer in Baker's position would not know that his conduct was a violation of the plain view doctrine.

This case shows that if the conduct is close to the constitutional line, the courts do not want a public employee to hesitate because some court later may determine the employee made a wrong decision. The courts will not hold the employee responsible for what the law is in the future, only for what is clearly established now.

STATUTE OF LIMITATIONS

A statute of limitations sets the time in which a lawsuit may be brought. If the lawsuit is not brought within the time specified, the lawsuit is barred and cannot be brought, no matter how meritorious it is. There is no federal statute of limitations for Section 1983 claims. For lawsuits brought pursuant to Section 1983, the courts will use the state statute of limitations for personal injury lawsuits. *Owens v. Okure*, 488 U.S. 235 (1989). The statutes of limitations for Section 1983 are as follows: (1) North Carolina, three years, *National Advertising Co. v. City of Raleigh*, 947 F.2d 1158 (4th Cir. 1993); (2) Maryland, three years, *Gratton v. Burnett*, 710 F.2d 160 (4th Cir. 1988); (3) South Carolina, three years, *Simmons v. S.C. State Ports Auth.*, 694 F.2d 63 (4th Cir. 1982); (4) Virginia, two years, Va. Code Ann. Э 8.01-243(A). The statute of limitations must be considered when establishing retention schedules for records. Records of critical incidents should be saved until the statute of limitations expires.

DAMAGES

A person suing under 42 U.S.C. Э 1983 may be entitled to nominal, compensatory, and punitive damages, *Carey v. Phiphus*, 435 U.S. 247 (1978), and to attorneys' fees, 42 U.S.C. Э 1988. Nominal damages are minimal amounts, such as one dollar. These damages are awarded when a defendant violated a person's rights, but the person suing was not hurt. Compensatory damages are to pay a person for what he or she lost, such as property damage, medical bills, pain and suffering, or permanent disfigurement. Punitive damages are awarded to punish a defendant so that the defendant will not do the same thing again and to make him or her an example so that others will not do it either.

Nominal damages are presumed from any violation of rights, but compensatory damages must be proved. *Carey v. Phiphus*, 435 U.S. 247. The abstract value or importance of constitutional rights is not a permissible element of compensatory damages. *Memphis Community Sch. Dist. v. Stachura*, 477 U.S. 299 (1986). Punitive damages may be awarded only upon a showing of either a malicious intent or a reckless disregard. *Smith v. Wade*, 461 U.S. 30 (1983).

SUPERVISORY LIABILITY

Under Section 1983, a supervisor can be held responsible for the acts of people supervised. The supervisor is not liable just because an employee violates another's constitutional right. The supervisor is responsible for failing to do the job of supervising when the failure results in a violation of constitutional rights.

The doctrine of *respondeat superior* means that the employer is responsible for the acts of its employees. This doctrine cannot be the basis of liability for a state employee under 42 U.S.C. § 1983, *Polk County v. Dodson*, 454 U.S. 312 (1981), or otherwise. Generally, to be liable under § 1983 or otherwise, a state official must have personally participated in the deprivation of a person's constitutional rights, or there must be some direct, causal link between the acts of the individual officers and those of the supervisory defendants. *Rizzo v. Goode*, 423 U.S. 362 (1976).

However, supervisors can be liable under § 1983 if they establish or enforce a policy or custom that causes a constitutional deprivation. *City of Oklahoma City v. Tuttle*, 471 U.S. 808 (1985). Liability usually cannot be based solely on a single incident of misconduct. *Id.* The official policy must be the moving force of the constitutional violation. *Polk County v. Dodson*, 454 U.S. 312. A policy exists only when a course of action is established by the official responsible for the final policy with respect to the subject matter involved. *Pembaur v. City of Cincinnati*, 475 U.S. 469 (1986). If the employee acted constitutionally, then the supervisor cannot be held liable. *City of Los Angeles v. Heller*, 475 U.S. 796 (1986).

The failure to train and/or supervise a trooper may also be the basis of liability if such failure amounts to "deliberate indifference." *Shaw v. Stroud*, 13 F.3d 791 (4th Cir.), *cert. denied*, 513 U.S. 813 (1994). In order to impose liability, a plaintiff must prove three elements. First, the plaintiff must show that the supervisor had actual or constructive knowledge that his or her employee engaged in conduct that posed "a pervasive and unreasonable risk of constitutional injury to citizens like the plaintiff." *Id.* at 799. The courts have relied upon the following to establish such knowledge that an officer posed an unreasonable threat:

1. official verbal and written complaints about the officer to the local office and to headquarters;
2. complaints by citizens to the local office even when the citizens state they do not want to make a complaint;
3. counseling cards for rudeness;
4. complaints that were investigated, either by the local office or by headquarters, for which the officer was exonerated;
5. a high percentage of charges of assault on a law enforcement officer when compared to other officers;
6. a high percentage of charges of resisting arrest when compared to other officers.

The person suing must next prove that the supervisor's response to that knowledge was so inadequate as to show "deliberate indifference to or tacit authorization of the alleged offensive practices." *Id.*

Deliberate indifference means that the action was so grossly incompetent, inadequate, or excessive as to shock the conscience or to be intolerable to fundamental fairness. Deliberate indifference may be demonstrated by either actual intent or reckless disregard. A supervisor acts recklessly by "disregarding"a substantial risk of danger that is either known to the supervisor or that would be apparent to a reasonable person in the supervisor's position. Mere negligence is insufficient. *See Miltier v. Beorn*, 896 F.2d 848 (4th Cir. 1990). The only basis for such liability is if the supervisor remains "indifferent" to the allegation or conduct of an employee. *See Wellington v. Daniels*, 717 F.2d 932 (4th Cir. 1983). Mere negligent training is insufficient to establish deliberate indifference. *Mateyko v. Felix*, 924 F.2d 824 (9th Cir. 1991) (three to four hours of training by Los Angeles Police Department in use of Tazer stun gun may have been inadequate but insufficient to establish deliberate indifference).

Finally, the plaintiff must show an "affirmative causal link" between the supervisor's inaction and the particular constitutional injury suffered by the plaintiff. *Shaw*, 13 F.3d at 799. Causal connection is not difficult to show if there are previous use of force complaints and if the person suing is injured by the officer.

In *Shaw v. Stroud*, a North Carolina trooper attempted to arrest a driver for driving while impaired and resisting arrest. An altercation broke out. The driver took the trooper's metal flashlight and struck him in the head. He pursued the trooper and hit him again and was attempting to strike the trooper again when the trooper shot several times, killing the driver.

The family sued the trooper and two of his supervisors. One sergeant had supervised the trooper for five years but had transferred eighteen months before this shooting. The second sergeant had taken over and was the supervisor at the time of the shooting. Because of the high-profile nature of the shooting, many people complained of past abuse by the trooper, and some claimed that they had complained to one or the other sergeant. The court held that the first sergeant, who had transferred, could be sued even though the shooting occurred eighteen months after he left. The court said that the evidence that the sergeant had received complaints and done nothing was sufficient to allow this lawsuit for failure to supervise. The court, however, dismissed the lawsuit against the second supervisor because that supervisor had reacted to complaints by sending other supervisors to monitor court cases and by riding with the trooper, personally observing his conduct. Ultimately, a civil jury found that the trooper had acted properly. Therefore, since the trooper acted properly, no supervisor can be held liable.

LOCAL GOVERNMENT LIABILITY

Local governments and their officers are treated differently from states and state employees. A city, county, or non-state entity is not a "state" within the meaning of the Eleventh Amendment, even though it is created by the state and are persons for purposes of § 1983. *Monnell v. Department of Social Serv.*, 436 U.S. 658 (1978). A local government cannot be sued under § 1983 absent a showing by the plaintiff that the government had a custom or policy which resulted in a violation of the constitutional right of the plaintiff. Absent such a policy or custom, the local government employer cannot be held liable. The official policy must be the moving force behind the violation. *Polk v. Dodson*, 454 U.S. 312 (1981). *Monnell*, 436 U.S. at 691. A single incident of misconduct by a police officer is generally insufficient to establish a policy or custom. *Oklahoma City v. Tuttle*, 471

U.S. 808 (1985). A single action or decision which is unconstitutional can impose liability if made by the official with the final authority to establish municipal policy. *Pembaur v. Cincinnati,* 475 U.S. 469 (1986). Who is the final decision-maker is a question of state law. *City of St. Louis v. Praprotnik,* 485 U.S. 112 (1988). To prove a custom, a widespread, pervasive practice must be shown. *Adickes v. S.H. Kress Co.,* 398 U.S. 144 (1970). The doctrine of *respondeat superior* does not apply so that the local government is not liable merely for employing an officer who violates the plaintiff's rights. A police department or sheriff's department cannot be sued--only the city or the county. See *Coleman v. Cooper,* 89 N.C. App. 188, 366 S.E.2d 2, *disc. rev. den.* 322 N.C. 834, 371 S.E.2d 275 (1988)(Raleigh Police Department is not an entity capable of being sued); *McMillian v. Moore County, Alabama,* 520 U.S. 781 (1997)(Under Alabama state law, the sheriff represents the State of Alabama and not Moore County. The sheriff in his official capacity is entitled to Eleventh Amendment immunity.); *But see Harter v. Vernon,* 101 F.3d 334 (4th Cir. 1996) (A North Carolina sheriff can be sued in his or her official capacity and is not entitled to Eleventh Amendment immunity).

The Supreme Court has held that a city may be liable for damages for failure to train its policy officers. In *City of Canton v. Harris,* 489 U.S. 378 (1989), a citizen who was arrested and denied treatment for an emotional problems she was suffering at the time of the arrest sued the city of Canton, Ohio for failure to train its police officers to recognize a person in need of medical attention. The Supreme Court said that such a lawsuit can be brought, but only if the person suing can show that the "failure to train amounts to deliberate indifference to the rights of persons with whom the police com into contact." *Id.* at 388. The court also required that the deficiency in the training program must be closely related to the ultimate injury.

The Supreme Court recently addressed the liability of a local government for improperly screening and hiring a deputy sheriff. In *Board of Cty. Comm'rs of Bryan County v. Brown,* 520 U.S. 397 (1997), Brown was injured during an arrest by a reserve deputy Burns. Brown alleged that the background of the Deputy Burns included an assault conviction and traffic violations. Brown asserted that the only reason that the deputy was hired as a reserve is that he is the son of the Sheriff Moore's nephew. The Supreme Court held that the county could not be sued for the Sheriff's improper screening of this applicant. The Court said that the local government cannot be sued unless it can be shown that "...in hiring Burns, Sheriff Moore disregarded a known risk or obvious risk of injury." *Id.* at 412. The Court concluded that "Bryan County is not liable for Sheriff Moore's isolated decision to hire Burns without adequate screening, because respondent [Brown] has not demonstrated that his decision reflected a conscious disregard for a high risk that Burns would use excessive force...." *Id.* at 415. The Court requires that the hiring decision is highly likely to result in a constitutional violation before the local government will be liable.

AVOIDING LIABILITY

A supervisor can never avoid being named as a defendant in a civil action. A supervisor can, however, reduce the likelihood of being named a defendant and, consequently, being found liable for damages by exercising supervisory responsibility. A supervisor must not be "just one of the boys." A supervisor is responsible for the actions of the employees under his or her supervision and must actually manage and supervise them. A supervisor must not be so busy doing paperwork that he or she is unaware of what the employees are doing. A supervisor should take affirmative steps to learn how employees perform their jobs and take action when an employee does not meet the high standards of conduct expected. Some ways to avoid liability include:

1.   observe the employee on the job;
2.   investigate all complaints (formal or otherwise);
3.   observe the employee in court;
4.   routinely discuss the employee's job performance with the employee and your supervisor;
5.   review with the employee each critical incident (significant use of force, shootings, pursuits, etc.) to assure compliance with policy;
6.   note number and frequency of charges of resisting arrest and assault on law enforcement, especially those cases where the only charge filed is resisting arrest or assault;
7.   be aware of each officer's reputation within the criminal justice system.

DEFENSE OF EMPLOYEES

The defense of officers and other employees is provided by statute, association or union contract, or insurance policy. As a general rule, the employer will provide for defense of employees who were acting within the course and scope of their employment at the time the events giving rise to the lawsuit occurred. The determination of acting in the course and scope of employment is made by the chief administrator of the agency. If an insurance policy is involved, the policy usually requires defense of the employee unless a court declares that the policy does not cover the employee. An employee who is denied defense can usually file a grievance to contest the denial. For example, North Carolina state employees are defended by the North Carolina Attorney General's office if the employee requests representation. The Attorney General can decline to defend if an employee acted with malice, if the employee acted outside the course and scope of employment, if there is a conflict, or if it is not in the best interest of the state to represent the employee. N.C. Gen. Stat. § 143-300.4. Under certain circumstances, the Attorney General may request that the Governor appoint an attorney at state expense to represent an employee. N.C. Gen. Stat. § 147-17. This usually occurs when there are two state employees sued, and there is a conflict between the employees. The Attorney General will represent one employee, and a private attorney paid for by the state will represent the other. Also, if an employee is charged with a criminal offense and the head of the agency determines that there is no basis for the charge, the Attorney General will petition the Governor to have an attorney hired at state expense, since the Attorney General's office handles all criminal appeals. In such cases, the employee usually selects the attorney, and the agency pays. The decision whether to represent or to appoint private counsel rests with the Attorney General and not the employee. Finally, the State of North Carolina has an automobile insurance policy. Traveler's Insurance Company will provide the attorney under the provisions of that insurance policy.

Certain associations provide for an attorney for a law enforcement officer sued as a result of law enforcement duties. The Police Benevolent Association (PBA) dues pay for an attorney to represent the officer. Usually, a PBA attorney will work with attorneys provided by the employer or the insurance company. The employer or insurance company will want its attorney in control since it will be required to pay any judgment rendered against the employee. The PBA does not pay the judgment; it only provides an attorney.

A judgment is a court order entered at the conclusion of a lawsuit. It will either dismiss the lawsuit or order one of the parties to pay the other money. Whether the employer or the employee pays the judgment will depend upon the circumstances and the statutes involved. Generally, if the employer provides an attorney, either by hiring one or through an insurance policy, the employer will pay up to the limits of the insurance policy or a figure set by statute or local ordinance. For example, in North Carolina judgments rendered against state officers will be paid by the agency up to the limits of the Tort Claims Act, which is currently $500,000. *See* N.C. Gen. Stat. §§ 20-194, 143-291, 143-300.6. In cases involving actions other than the operation of a motor vehicle, boats or aircraft, an additional $11,000,000 coverage is provided by an excess insurance policy.

CONCLUSION

Litigation under 42 U.S.C. § 1983 is a fact of life within the law enforcement community. There is no way to prevent lawsuits from being filed. A supervisor who is familiar with agency policy and who stays aware of the conduct of the employees under his or her supervision will reduce the likelihood of such a lawsuit being filed. If filed, the likelihood of a judgment being entered should also be reduced. Supervisors should not make decisions based upon the threat of a lawsuit, but should be aware that in our litigious society, one may well be filed.

CHAPTER 15

FAILURE TO PROTECT

The job of law enforcement officer is summarized in many agencies as "to serve and to protect." The question then arises, can an officer or agency be held responsible to pay money to someone who is neither protected nor served? The answer is usually no. Because neither the police nor another government agency can ensure that a person will not become a crime victim or be hurt in an accident and because the taxpayers cannot afford to pay for all such injuries, the law recognizes only limited circumstances when government will be responsible for injuries of crime and accident victims. Generally, a law enforcement officer or agency will be liable if the officer uses the authority of the position of law enforcement officer: (1) to place a person in a position where injury occurs, e.g., place a person in custody or leave a person stranded in a dangerous area; or (2) to prevent a person from avoiding injury by assuring the person of the assistance or to prevent a rescue by another. In other words, if the officer acts affirmatively to expose a person to danger, then the courts will, in limited circumstances, hold the officer responsible. Even if the officer is not legally responsible, the public may blame the officer, and this reaction may negatively affect the agency. This chapter will discuss the legal responsibility of the officer to protect a citizen.

CONSTITUTIONAL RIGHT TO PROTECTION

There is no constitutional right to protection. The Due Process Clause of the Fourteenth Amendment does not protect citizens from the actions of other private individuals. It does protect citizens from the government abusing its power or using the power as an instrument of oppression. Consequently, only an injury that is the result of affirmative actions of a government official gives rise to a claim under the Constitution.

The United States Supreme Court discussed the constitutional obligation of the government to protect its citizens. In *DeShaney v. Winnebago County*, 489 U.S. 189 (1989), Joshua DeShaney lived in Winnebago County, Wisconsin. He was born in 1979. In 1980, his parents were divorced, and his father was awarded custody. During the father's second divorce in January 1982, the father's second wife complained to the police that the father hit Joshua, causing marks, and was a prime case for child abuse. The father was interviewed and denied the allegations. Nothing was done. In January 1983, Joshua was admitted to the local hospital with multiple bruises and abrasions, consistent with child abuse. A "Child Protection Team" consisting of a physician, social worker, police, and others reviewed the case and determined there was insufficient evidence of abuse and returned Joshua to his father, with a recommendation of counseling. A month later Joshua, was treated again. Social services made home visits, but nothing was done. In March 1984, Joshua's father beat him so severely that Joshua suffered permanent brain damage and must be confined for the rest of his life to an institution for the profoundly retarded. The father was convicted of child abuse. The natural mother reappeared and, along with Joshua, sued the county department of social services for depriving Joshua of his liberty without due process of law in violation of the Fourteenth Amendment.

The Supreme Court first stated that this case involves a claim that invokes the substantive, rather than procedural, component of the Due Process Clause. There was no allegation of a lack of adequate procedures, only that the county had an obligation to protect Joshua and failed to do so. The Court then noted one of the basic tenets of constitutional law:

> But nothing in the Due Process Clause itself requires the State to protect the life, liberty, and property of its citizens against an invasion by private actors. The Clause is phrased as a limitation on the State's power to act, not as a guarantee of certain minimal levels of safety and security.

Id. at 195

The Court finally stated:

> As a general matter, . . . we conclude that a State's failure to protect an individual against private violence simply does not constitute a violation of the Due Process Clause.

Id. at 197

The Court then discussed when a claim under the Due Process Clause may arise. The Court held that the Due Process Clause protection attaches when a "special relationship" is established between the government and a citizen, but this situation is limited to when the citizen is placed in custody by acts of a government official. The Court limited failure to protect to custodial situations and held that the county was not constitutionally responsible for the injuries to Joshua. *See Buffington v. Baltimore County*, 913 F.2d 113 (4th Cir. 1990) (Due Process Clause imposes an affirmative obligation on the county to prevent a detainee in the county jail from committing suicide).

The Court in a later case reiterated this rule when it held that the failure to train a municipal employee about workplace hazards that resulted in his death did not violate the Fourteenth Amendment Due Process Clause. *Collins v. Harker Heights*, 503 U.S. 115 (1992). The Court said that the acceptance of employment and being bound by the rules of the workplace are not comparable to custody for purposes of a claim of failure to protect.

ADDITIONAL THEORIES OF LIABILITY

While the United States Supreme Court has limited constitutional liability to custodial settings, the lower courts still struggle with imposing liability on a government agency when a citizen is injured. Many of the previous cases could not be brought under the Constitution but may still be brought under a tort theory based upon state law. Negligence under state tort law involves the person suing showing: (1) a legal duty of care by the defendant to the person suing, (2) a breach of that duty of care by failing to act as a reasonable person would under those circumstance, and (3) injuries that were caused by the breach of the duty. Under tort law, law enforcement officers do not owe a duty to each citizen, but only to all citizens in general. A law enforcement officer can establish a duty of care to a specific individual by interacting with the person and exercising authority in relation to a person, thereby creating a "special relationship" with the person. Once the "special relationship" is established, then the officer has a legal duty to act as a reasonable officer would under those circumstances. If the officer does not and the person is injured, then the court may find the officer negligent and impose liability for the failure to protect the person.

This area of the law is still evolving, which is a lawyer's way of saying that the rules are constantly changing. The law enforcement manager must learn of these new theories and adjust training and policy to avoid this liability.

LEAVING STRANDED MOTORIST

Numerous lawsuits have arisen out of the arrest of a driver of a motor vehicle and the subsequent injury to the passengers. Although the courts do not usually hold an officer responsible for an adult male passenger, leaving children or women stranded is more likely to impose legal responsibility. Besides the moral obligation, the adverse publicity and cost of litigation can have a substantial adverse impact on the agency. This litigation can usually be avoided by policies that require the arresting officer to protect the passengers before leaving the scene.

In *Walton v. City of Springfield*, 995 F.2d 1331 (6th Cir. 1993), a police officer arrested the driver of a vehicle for driving while license suspended. He allegedly left the driver's fifteen-year-old daughter and two-year-old granddaughter in the parked car, despite the pleas of the driver to take the children into protective custody. The driver and the children sued, claiming the children remained in the car for six hours with only twenty cents and no way to contact anyone. The trial court originally said that their allegations were sufficient to allow a suit. The court of appeals reversed and dismissed the constitutional rights claim based upon qualified immunity. This decision means that there was no clearly established constitutional right that the officer violated by leaving the children in the car and no clearly established constitutional requirement to take the children into protective custody. This ruling involved only the constitutional right and did not involve the question of liability under state tort law. This decision is, however, the rule in the majority of states and is consistent with the *DeShaney* decision. *Moore v. Marketplace Restaurant, Inc.*, 754 F.2d 1336 (7th Cir. 1985) (Officers not liable when they arrested minor's parents and gave the child the option of staying in the patrol car or sleeping in the family camper alone overnight, and the minor selected the camper). Note that in both the *Walton* and *Moore* cases, the minors were not injured, only left alone. Even when the stranded passenger is severely injured, the majority of jurisdictions do not impose liability. *Gregory v. City of Rogers*, 974 F.2d 1006 (8th Cir. 1992) (Officers are not liable when sober driver arrested; keys left in car; and one drunken passenger drove and wrecked, injuring others); *Courson v. McMillian*, 939 F.2d 1479 (11th Cir. 1991) (Officers not liable when a passenger was left on the side of the road at night after the companion was arrested and vehicle was towed); *Hillard v. City & County of Denver*, 930 F.2d 1516 (10th Cir.), *cert. denied*, 502 U.S. 1013 (1991) (No clearly established right to personal security where there is no element of state-imposed custody; officers could not be held liable for rape and beating of a passenger by a third party when passenger was left in the vehicle after the intoxicated driver of the vehicle was arrested).

On the other hand, some courts have said that a jury must decide. In *Wood v. Ostrander*, 879 F.2d 583 (9th Cir.), *cert. denied*, 498 U.S. 938 (1990), the Ninth Circuit Court of Appeals, before *DeShaney* was decided, held that the officers were not entitled to qualified immunity and that they could be sued for arresting a drunk driver and leaving a female passenger stranded in the car. She was subsequently attacked and raped by a third party. The court held that the officers exposed her to danger and could be held responsible for her injuries.

The stranded passenger who is injured will probably not be entitled to recover for a violation of constitutional rights because the *Deshaney* decision limited such claims to custodial situations. The potential for liability still remains under state tort law for failure to protect or negligence or a state constitutional claim. This litigation can be avoided by proper policy and training, even if liability is usually not imposed.

FAILURE TO ARREST

The question invariably arises, if the officer does not arrest a person who the officer has probable cause to arrest and there is a subsequent injury to another, is the officer liable? The answer is generally no, provided the officer can show that the decision not to arrest was a good-faith exercise of discretion and not made for some arbitrary reason. The arbitrary reasons listed include failing to arrest based upon the race, sex, color, national origin, or personal relationship with either the offender or the victim.

In *Estate of Simthasomphone v. City of Milwaukee*, 785 F. Supp. 1343 (E.D. Wis. 1992), the City of Milwaukee and several officers were sued by the parents of one of Jeffery Dahmer's victims. The facts of this case showed that citizens called the police saying that a fourteen-year-old boy was naked in the street, drugged and bleeding. The police arrived and questioned the boy and Dahmer. Dahmer claimed that he and the boy were adult homosexual partners. The police, over the protestation of citizens, returned the boy to Dahmer. It was later discovered that Dahmer mutilated and killed this boy as his thirteenth victim.

The court originally refused to dismiss the case against the officers but subsequently granted summary judgment on the basis of qualified immunity. 838 F. Supp. 1320 (E.D. Wis. 1993). The court, however, refused to dismiss the claim against the city. The court said that if the estate could show that the police department had a policy of not taking action because of intentional discrimination based upon race, color, national origin, or sexual orientation, the estate would have a claim for the jury to pass upon. 878 F. Supp. 147 (E.D. Wis. 1995). The estate supported its claim of alleged discrimination by showing a finding by the court of racial discrimination in hiring and promotion of police officers, use of excessive force against minorities, and even statements that the department discriminated against minorities by former chiefs of the department. Before the case was brought for trial, the city settled for $850,000.

In another failure to **promptly** arrest case, the North Carolina courts did not find a constitutional violation or a "special relationship" between the state and the local officers sued in *Lynch v. N.C. Dep't of Justice*, 93 N.C. App. 57 (1989). In this case, the State Bureau of Investigation, Forsyth County Sheriff's Department, and Greensboro Police Department and officers were sued for failing to arrest Frederick R. Klenner, Jr. This case was the basis of the book *Bitter Blood* and arose when Klenner began living with his cousin Susie Lynch. Susie was the mother of two children and was involved in a bitter custody battle with their father. Klenner, who at one time or another passed himself off as a doctor or a Vietnam war veteran, which he was neither, murdered five people, including Susie's mother, father, grandmother, mother-in-law, and sister-in-law. They were all slated to testify against Susie in the custody hearing. Some of the killings occurred in Forsyth County, and some in another state. The police finally put the case together and were preparing to arrest Klenner at the couple's apartment in Greensboro, North Carolina. The officers saw Klenner and Susie load the two children into a Chevrolet Blazer, along with weapons. They attempted to block the Blazer and arrest Klenner, but he drove around them. A pursuit started, with Klenner shooting at the police with a machine gun as they chased him. The chase covered several miles. The Blazer suddenly stopped in the roadway and was immediately blown apart by a bomb detonated by Klenner. An autopsy of the children revealed that they had been given a lethal dose of cyanide and had been shot in the head by either Klenner or Susie. The father of the children sued. The Court of Appeals dismissed the case, finding no constitutional violation and no "special relationship" between the police and the children. The court quoted the long-recognized legal axiom that no one has a "constitutional right to be protected by the state against being murdered by criminals or madmen." Bowers v. DeVito, 686 F.2d 616, 618 (7th Cir. 1982).

Another twist of this question is whether the police have a duty to arrest a lawbreaker to protect the law breaker from his own acts. The answer is usually no, but once the court finds the police interacted with a citizen, the court could also find a special relationship. In *Sellers v. Baer*, 28 F.3d 895 (8th Cir. 1994), *cert. denied*, 513 U.S. 1084 (1995), officers removed a man from the fairgrounds after observing this obviously drunk individual urinating in public and randomly grabbing women by the buttocks. There were more than 600,000 people attending the fair, so the officers decided not to charge him but took him to the nearest police station, which was ten blocks away, and released him in the parking lot. The drunk was later struck and killed after he wandered onto an interstate highway a mile and one-half from the police station. The court found no constitutional violation, but did discuss whether the police could be liable if they placed the man in a more dangerous position by leaving him in the parking lot.

FAILURE TO RESCUE

When a police officer does not increase the danger to a citizen, it is unlikely that the officer will be responsible for injuries suffered by the citizen. On the other hand, what if an officer prevents private citizens from helping or fails to assist a person in danger? Is it a defense that the officer interfered with a rescue or failed to assist because of danger to the rescuer? This situation has produced conflicting results, and a general rule of conduct is not entirely clear. If the police officer chooses not to attempt a rescue because of danger or because of any nondiscriminatory reason, the courts will not impose liability. On the other hand, if the police actively interfere with a rescue attempt by another, liability may be imposed. If the attempted rescuer creates an additional danger to the rescuer or others, the police can exercise authority and prevent the attempt.

In *Ross v. United States*, 910 F.2d 1422 (7th Cir. 1990), a twelve-year-old boy disappeared into Lake Michigan. Citizens were attempting to locate him, and the sheriff's office was called. The county had an agreement with the city that the city fire department would perform all rescue services at the lake. The sheriff adopted a policy that required his deputies to stop all citizen rescue efforts so that the city fire department could perform its job. The deputies stopped all rescue efforts. The city fire department arrived twenty minutes later and eventually pulled the child's lifeless body from the lake. The mother sued, and the court held that arbitrarily cutting off present rescue efforts without having an alternative available violated the child's Fourteenth Amendment rights. *Id.* at 1431. This case may not have survived the Supreme Court's ruling in *DeShaney*, but the defendants were not willing to gamble and settled the case for $1.29 million. *See Chicago Daily Law Bulletin*, p. 3 (Jan. 31, 1995).

It is possible for police officers to be held liable for failure to attempt a rescue if the reasons given seem inappropriate. In *Doe v. Calumet City*, 641 N.E.2d 498 (Ill. 1994), police were called to a possible burglary and found an adult woman who said a man had entered her apartment and climbed onto her. He began grabbing her clothing and touching her breasts and genital area. He said he was going to rape and kill her. She broke away as he threatened to kill her two children; she ran out of her apartment clothed only in undergarments and slammed the door, which locked. She did not have her keys and could not let officers into the apartment. The officer in charge declined to break the door down and rescue the children because he did not want to be responsible for paying for the property damage. The woman also claimed the officer rudely questioned her about why she would leave her kids alone with a potential killer and indicated he thought it was merely a domestic dispute. An investigator finally entered the back door and arrested the intruder, who was in the act of raping the woman's daughter. The daughter said that the intruder had repeatedly raped her and forced her to perform deviate sexual acts and had threatened and choked the male child. The court said that there was no special relationship established here, but said liability may be shown under a theory of negligent infliction of emotional distress. Declining to break down the door for fear of liability for property damage could be found to be utter indifference or conscious disregard for the safety of the children and, under Illinois law, a basis for liability. In support of this conclusion, the court noted that other officers on the scene were not allowed to do anything to help because of the actions of the officer in charge.

INJURIES TO INNOCENT THIRD PARTIES

Injuries to innocent third parties, who are not involved with the police or the offender but who are merely in the wrong place at the wrong time, always raise difficult legal and moral issues. The police are to serve and protect. When an innocent person is injured or killed while the police are attempting to enforce the very rules designed to protect the individual, the public cries for compensation may be very loud. The public may also demand changes in policy or tactics to prevent similar situations in the future. The general rule is that the police are not responsible for injuries to innocent third parties caused by an offender, absent outrageous conduct. If the police officers cause the injuries to innocent third parties, then the rules of liability discussed in other chapters apply, and the issue is not failure to protect.

The cases where this issue arises most often are police pursuits where an officer is attempting to stop a violator, and the violator flees. If the violator injures an innocent third party, the violator is clearly liable. The question of whether the police are liable under the Constitution was conclusively decided in *Sacramento County v. Lewis*, 523 U.S. 833 (1998). The United States Supreme Court held that pursuing by police did not violate the Fourteenth Amendment standard of "shock the conscious of the court." If the officer uses the car to stop the pursuit by ramming and such conduct amounts to a seizure, the Fourth Amendment will apply. The prevailing rule is that state tort law applies, and officers can be held liable only if there is a duty of care and a breach of such duty. The North Carolina courts, for example, do not impose liability on an officer when the offender causes the injury, absent gross negligence of the officer, S*ee Bullins v. Schmidt*, 322 N.C. 580 (1988), and recently applied the same standard to a situation where a police vehicle struck and injured an innocent motorist. Gross negligence is the same standard as used to impose criminal liability under manslaughter statutes and involves a violation of obvious standards of care to the point of reckless disregard for the rights and safety of others. Much more than mere negligence must be proved. *See Young v. Woodall*, 343 N.C. 459 (1996). Rules in other states may differ, however.

Other innocent third-party cases include allowing a drunk to drive a vehicle. In *Reed v. Gardner*, 986 F.2d 1122 (7th Cir. 1993), an Illinois state trooper arrested a driver and left an obviously drunk passenger in the car with the keys. The drunk passenger drove off. Two hours later, a deputy sheriff tried to stop the vehicle. The drunk driver, while attempting to flee, crossed the centerline and struck a Chevrolet Suburban, killing a pregnant woman and her fetus, causing permanent brain damage to another child, and severely injuring four other people. The court refused to dismiss the case at the early stages, saying that if the injured person could show that a sober driver was arrested and that a drunk passenger was left in the car with the keys, then the police may have created a dangerous situation where the police could be held liable. The court held that the affirmative act of the state trooper in arresting the driver and leaving an obviously drunk passenger access to the car distinguished this case from *DeShaney*. Here, the allegations are that the police created the danger, not that they merely failed to protect a person, as was the case in *DeShaney*. The court expressed doubt that the injured persons can establish that a sober driver was replaced with a drunk and said:

> While we do not seek to expand any existing duties for police officers, we do suggest that officers may be subject to suit under section 1983 if they knowingly and affirmatively create a dangerous situation for the public and fail to take reasonable prevention steps to diffuse that danger. Thus, removing one drunk driver and failing to prevent replacement by another drunk will not subject the officers to section 1983 liability, any more than an initial failure to remove the first drunk would.

Id. at 1127

The courts still struggle with the issue of injury to an innocent third party, and attorneys attempt new theories to get cases to a jury. The sympathy for the innocent victim can result in huge problems for an administrator.

PROMISES OF ASSISTANCE

Many citizens first contact with law enforcement officials is through the dispatcher by calling "911." Even this contact can lead to a special relationship and liability if the dispatcher or officers fail to exercise good judgment. The general rule is that no "special relationship" exists by simply calling the police. It is only when assurances of help or when instructions are given that this relationship is established. For example, in *DeLong v. County of Erie*, 469 N.Y.S. 611 (1983), New York's highest court held the city and county liable for injuries suffered by a citizen who called 911 for help. In this case, a female victim called 911 and told the dispatcher that a burglar had broken into her house. The dispatcher told her to remain in the house, that help was on the way. The dispatcher did not repeat the address to the victim or ask her name but dispatched a car to the wrong address. The victim stayed in the house as the dispatcher suggested rather than running to the local police station 1,300 feet away. The burglar subsequently stabbed and killed the victim. The jury awarded $800,000 against the county. In another case involving ambulance service, a jury in Chicago awarded $2.5 million to a boy and his family. The boy was injured playing at school. The school officials called 911 and were assured an ambulance was being dispatched. The school was located near a hospital, but the school officials decided to wait on the ambulance. The ambulance did not arrive until after three phone calls over a one-hour period. The doctor testified that the boy's injuries were made worse by this delay. *Barth v. Board of Education*, No. 85-538, *Chicago Daily Law Bulletin* (February 21, 1986), *aff'd*, 490 N.E.2d 77 (Ill. App. Ct. 1986). The usual rule is that mere assurance that help is on the way does not create this special relationship. There must be specific assurance or instructions given for this relationship to arise. *See Galuszynski v. City of Chicago*, 475 N.E.2d 960 (Ill. 1985) (Dispatcher's telling 911 caller that police were on their way and to watch for the police did not create a special relationship).

There must be contact between government officials and the victim for this special relationship to arise. In a case out of Georgia, a man went to his sister-in-law's house and demanded to speak to his estranged wife. The sister-in-law spoke to the wife by phone, telling her that her husband was present. The wife told the sister-in-law to let her husband in and that she would call the police. The wife called the police and was told the police would be sent. The wife called the sister-in-law back and was told the police had not arrived. The wife called the police several times before a car was finally dispatched. During that time, the sister-in-law was sexually assaulted several times by the husband. The sister-in-law sued, but the court said that there could be no special relationship between the sister-in-law and the police because the sister-in-law did not talk with the police, only the wife. *City of Rome v. Jordan*, 426 S.E.2d 861 (Ga. 1993).

FAILURE TO INTERVENE

There is one area where the courts have consistently allowed a lawsuit against an officer, and it falls in line with the motto of "to serve and to protect." That is, the failure to intervene to prevent another officer from violating a citizen's constitutionally protected rights. "A police officer may not stand by idly while a citizen's constitutional rights are violated by another officer; he has an affirmative duty to intercede on the citizen's behalf" *Browning v. Snead*, 886 F. Supp. 547, 551 (S.D. W. Va. 1995).

The courts reasoning is that since the officer violating the citizen's rights is exercising the authority of the state, other state officers are involved by their mere presence and must intervene to prevent a constitutional violation. This failure to respond is referred to as an act of omission and is subject to a lawsuit the same as an act of commission. This duty to intervene applies not only to supervisors, but also to co-workers, either from the same or different agencies, *Byrd v. Clark*, 783 F.2d 1002 (11th Cir. 1986), and even if the excessive force is by a higher ranking officer, *Webb v. Hiykel*, 713 F.2d 405 (8th Cir. 1983). It is usually applied in a use-of-force situation, but could be applied to any other constitutional violation, such as an unconstitutional arrest.

Of course, the mere fact that another officer uses excessive force in the presence of other officers does not make them all liable. The violation of a citizen's constitutional rights must be of sufficient duration to provide an opportunity for other officers to intervene. *Mathis v. Parks*, 741 F. Supp. 567 (E.D. N.C. 1990). In *Browning*, 886 F. Supp. 547, Officers Snead and Adkins stopped Dennis Browning for driving his father's unregistered pickup truck. Snead approached the driver's side. Browning did not have a license and was intoxicated. Browning's evidence was that he was handcuffed while in the truck and was then jerked out of the truck and slammed to the ground by Snead. He says that Snead kicked him several times, jerked him up, threw him into the passenger side of the patrol car, and shoved him into the back seat of the patrol car. Browning claims he hit his head on the top of the patrol car. All of this abuse occurred while he did not resist. His evidence also was that while this abuse was occurring, Adkins stood and watched and did not try to stop it. The court said that this evidence is sufficient to create a jury question and that the lawsuit against Adkins must go to trial with the one against Snead.

Officers must not stand back while another uses force in an arrest. The other officers must intervene. Standing back and saying that it is the other officer's arrest will not provide protection from a civil suit. An officer on the scene may as well intervene and help; the courts will hold the officer responsible, even the officer does nothing.

CONCLUSION

The general rules relating to liability for failure to protect are:

1. Government officials are **not** civilly liable for failing to prevent crime or injury, and no one has a constitutional right to protection from the actions of criminals and madmen.
2. In a custodial or other setting where the freedom of an individual is taken away by the government, and the government has limited the individual's ability to protect himself, the government must take reasonable steps to prevent injury.
3. When a government official affirmatively places a particular individual in a position of danger or creates a more dangerous situation, then the official must protect the individual who is endangered.
4. When a government official gives assurances of help or protection and the individual relies upon such assurance, the government official must protect the individual.

5.   When a government official violates the clearly established law, then the official will be responsible for the injuries caused.
6.   An officer who observes unconstitutional conduct by another officer and who has the opportunity to intervene but fails to do so will be held responsible for the violation of the citizen's rights.

The fact that bad things happen and that people are injured does not make law enforcement officials legally responsible. In many failure-to-protect cases, however, good training, policy, or the exercise of good judgment could avoid injury. Law enforcement agencies may not be legally responsible for certain injuries, but the public may hold them morally responsible.

CHAPTER 16

FEDERAL CRIMINAL VIOLATIONS

INTRODUCTION

Although the likelihood of a law enforcement officer being charged with a federal crime is remote, it is more likely that a member of a law enforcement agency will be the target of an investigation by federal law enforcement agents. The supervisor needs to be aware of federal law enforcement procedures and the federal criminal statutes that are generally used as a basis of an investigation of state and local law enforcement officials.

Law enforcement officers are familiar with the concept that evidence seized pursuant to an unconstitutional search or seizure may be excluded at the criminal trial of a defendant. Law enforcement officers are also aware of civil liability associated with even unintentional violations of constitutional rights by law enforcement officers. Officers who violate a person's constitutional rights expose themselves, their supervisors, and their employing municipalities and counties to the potential for a large money judgment based upon 42 U.S.C. § 1983. In addition, there is a potential for criminal liability for **intentionally** violating a person's constitutional rights while acting under color of law. *See* 18 U.S.C. § 242. Also, an officer who uses the position of police officer to obtain something of value can be charged pursuant to the Hobbs Act. *See* 18 U.S.C. § 1951.

It is incumbent upon public managers to ensure that each officer supervised is aware of the ever-present potential for federal criminal sanctions. There are steps that a manager can take to reduce the risk that such officers will be unjustly indicted as a consequence of exaggerated or false allegations of wrongdoing. Additionally, officers must be aware of their rights should they become the focus of a federal criminal investigation. There are certain legal requirements for a manager which must be followed during a criminal investigation.

FEDERAL CRIMINAL CIVIL RIGHTS LIABILITY

A civil lawsuit brought pursuant to 42 U.S.C. § 1983 is intended to compensate a person suing for injuries caused by an officer's unconstitutional conduct. The federal government may, either in conjunction with or without the civil suit, seek criminal charges against an officer to vindicate the U.S. government's interest in assuring that a public official adheres to the Constitution and the laws of the United States.

Background

Historically, grand jury indictments and federal prosecutions of law enforcement officers for criminal civil-rights violations have been rare. The federal government has, for more than one hundred years, relied primarily on state and county prosecutors in cases where state and local officers have been accused of wrongdoing, even where such wrongdoing involved allegations of civil-rights violations. In the wake of the Rodney King case, however, it may reasonably be anticipated that federal criminal civil-rights investigations will increase and that, consequently, there will be more federal prosecutions and, presumably, more convictions of law enforcement officers for federal civil-rights violations.

According to the statistics maintained by the United States Department of Justice (DOJ), Civil Rights Division, that agency received 9,620 complaints alleging violations of civil rights during fiscal year 1993. Of these complaints, 3,026 were turned over to the Federal Bureau of Investigation for investigation. Of the total number of complaints received, approximately only one percent actually resulted in prosecution and subsequent conviction. Unfortunately, the statistics maintained by the DOJ do not specify how many of the total complaints received involved law enforcement officers. They do maintain statistics, however, with respect to the number of law enforcement officers whose cases went to the grand jury or were tried pursuant to a criminal information filed by DOJ prosecutors. Those statistics reveal that approximately fifty percent of the cases that went to trial involved law enforcement officers. A total of fifty law enforcement officers were tried during fiscal year 1993, and thirty-seven percent of those cases resulted in conviction. Based upon the above-given statistics, the likelihood that an officer will be tried and/or convicted for federal civil rights violations is remote. On the other hand, the possibility that allegations will be made against an officer is far from remote.

Jurisdictional Basis

Federal criminal civil-rights actions are prosecuted jurisdictionally by the DOJ pursuant to 18 U.S.C. §§ 241 and 242. These statutes, which have existed since 1870, provide for independent federal criminal jurisdiction for conduct in which an individual either acting alone or conspiring with others willfully deprives another person of any right, privilege, or immunity secured or protected by the Constitution of the United States or by federal law. These statutes make it a federal crime to conspire to violate an inhabitant's constitutionally protected rights or to act under color of law to deprive an inhabitant of a guaranteed right, privilege, or immunity secured by the Constitution.

Federal prosecution is possible under these statutes even if the defendant was previously prosecuted in state court, and it makes no difference whether he or she was convicted or acquitted in state court. The prior state court prosecution does not serve as a bar to federal prosecution under the principle of double jeopardy. The Double Jeopardy Clause prohibits a second prosecution by the same government, not by a different one. In addition, the elements of the charges may also differ.

The federal criminal civil-rights statute, 18 U.S.C. § 242, reads as follows:

> Whoever, under color of any law, statute, ordinance, regulation, or custom, willfully subjects any inhabitant of any state, territory, or district to the deprivation of any rights, privileges, or immunities secured or protected by the Constitution or laws of the United States, or to different punishments, pains, or penalties, on account of such inhabitant being an alien, or by reason of his color, or race, than are prescribed for the punishment of citizens, shall be fined not more than $1,000 or imprisoned for not more than one year, or both; and if death results, shall be subject to imprisonment for any terms of years or for life.

The elements of the offense are:

1. defendant's act deprived someone of a right secured or protected by federal law or the Constitution;
2. defendant's act was committed under color of law;
3. the person deprived of the constitutional right(s) is an inhabitant of a state, territory, or district; and
7. defendant acted willfully.

The elements are similar to those required to prove civil liability under 42 U.S.C. § 1983. The additional element of willfulness has been added to ensure the necessary *mens rea*, or guilty mind, traditionally required in serious criminal offenses.

First, the rights protected by 18 U.S.C. § 242 include any right or privilege secured to persons by the United States Constitution or by any law of the United States. Included within the "rights and privileges" phrase are those rights of persons to be free from excessive force as provided in the Fourth Amendment for arrestees and Fifth Amendment for pretrial detainees; due process of law violations (substantive and procedural) as provided in the Fourteenth Amendment; unlawful arrest, search, seizure, false arrest, or imprisonment as provided in the Fourth Amendment; and cruel and unusual punishment for persons convicted of crimes as provided in the Eighth Amendment.

The element of acting under color of law occurs when an officer acts under the pretense of law. This includes but is not necessarily limited to "under authority of law," whether real or apparent. In other words, the unlawful use of an officer's authority to stop, arrest, search, or seize is "under color of law." An officer who uses an unreasonable amount of force during the apprehension of a suspect normally does so without the authority invested in him by virtue of his status as an officer of the law. Nonetheless, his conduct may be deemed to be "under color of law."

18 U.S.C. § 242 applies to a deprivation of rights of any "inhabitant" of a state territory or district. The victim need not be a citizen. An illegal alien may qualify as an "inhabitant" under this statute.

In order to be convicted under 18 U.S.C. § 242, the government must show that the defendant law enforcement officer acted "willfully." In a **civil** excessive force case, however, the willfulness requirement may be met merely by proving an intentional application of unreasonable force. In a **criminal** excessive force case, the United States Supreme Court in *Screws v. United States*, 325 U.S. 91, 105 (1945), explained that to "act willfully in the sense in which we use the word [is to] act in open defiance or reckless disregard of a constitutional requirement that has been made specific and definite."

Consistent with the above-stated definition, an officer who conducts a warrantless search of a residence, absent the existence of exigent circumstances to justify the search, may be deemed to be in violation of this statute. The warrant requirement for the search of a residence is so clearly established in law that the jury may infer that the officer willfully violated the victim's constitutional rights if it concludes that no reasonable law enforcement officer could believe that, under the circumstances, a warrantless search of a residence could be constitutionally permissible.

There is no requirement in 18 U.S.C. § 242 that the defendant's alleged wrongful conduct results by reason of (the victim's) color or race. This requirement applies only to specific situations where a "different punishment, pain, or penalty" is imposed on account of or by virtue of the status of the victim. Racial discrimination is not a requirement for a violation of 18 U.S.C. § 242 in any other context. Therefore, a white law enforcement officer who allegedly uses excessive force while arresting a white subject may be prosecuted under this statute.

If no bodily injury results, the permissible punishment is a $1,000 fine and/or one year imprisonment. If bodily injury results, then an unspecified fine or imprisonment for not more than ten years or both may be imposed. If death results, then imprisonment for any term of years or for life is authorized.

In addition to violating a person's rights, 18 U.S.C. § 2 allows a charge of aiding and abetting. This statute makes it a federal crime for an individual to assist, aid, or abet another in the commission of a civil rights violation. This statute is oftentimes used in conjunction with 18 U.S.C. § 242. 18 U.S.C. § 2 provides in pertinent part: Whoever commits an offense against the United States or aids, abets, counsels, commands, induces or procures its commission is punishable as a principal. The elements of aiding and abetting are:

1.   specific intent to facilitate crime by another,
2.   guilty knowledge on the part of the accused,
3.   offense committed by someone else, and
4.   accused assisted or participated in commission of the offense.

18 U.S.C. § 2 does not create a discrete criminal offense. It merely allows an officer to be found guilty of the underlying substantive offense even though the officer did not personally commit all of the acts constituting the offense. The aider and abettor is punished the same as the principal.

Of course, under federal law, if the government cannot prove that the officer did anything, the government need prove only that the officer "agreed" to violate another's rights. 18 U.S.C. § 241, Conspiracy Against Rights, provides as follows:

> If two or more persons conspire to injure, oppress, threaten, or intimidate any inhabitant in the free exercise or enjoyment of any right or privilege secured to him by the Constitution or laws of the United States or because of his having so exercised the same; or if two or more persons go in disguise on the highway, or on the premises of another, with intent to prevent or hinder his free exercise or enjoyment of any right or privilege so secured—they shall be fined not more than $10,000 or imprisoned not more than ten years, or both; and if death results, they shall be subject to imprisonment for any terms of years or for life.

A conspiracy is defined, as it is under most state criminal statutes, as an agreement by two or more persons to commit an unlawful act. No overt act toward committing the offense is required for conspiracy. (This is the same as under North Carolina some others state's criminal conspiracy law.) Unlike with 18 U.S.C. § 242, there is no requirement that the defendant act under color of law. A person may be prosecuted under this statute even if the person was acting as a private individual as long as someone within the conspiracy is acting under color of law. The rights and privileges protected are the same as with 18 U.S.C. § 242.

The federal statute does have a statute of limitations for bringing federal criminal prosecutions. After the expiration of this time, no prosecution can be brought. The statute of limitations is four years from the date of the incident to the date of the charge. Reports and physical evidence need to be preserved for this period of time. If federal authorities express interest in the conduct of an officer involved in a particular incident, the agency should conduct its own investigation and preserve the report and evidence until the statute of limitations expires.

Rodney King

One of the most notorious federal criminal civil-rights trials involved the prosecution of Los Angeles police officers for the beating of Rodney King. On March 3, 1991, Rodney King, who has a prior criminal record, led the Los Angeles police and others on a high-speed chase. At the conclusion of the chase, King's passengers surrendered, but King ran and resisted. The Los Angeles police officers used a Tazer and repeatedly struck King with PR-24 batons. All of this was captured on videotape by a citizen watching from his balcony. The videotape was broadcast worldwide. The public was incensed by what they viewed as unnecessary force. There were also radio transmissions made with racially derogatory statements.

On March 15, the four officers involved—Lawrence Powell, Timothy Wind, Theodore Briseno, and Sergeant Stacey Koon—were charged with the state offenses of assault with a deadly weapon and use of excessive force. The mayor called for Los Angeles Police Department (LAPD) Chief Daryl Gates' resignation, which Gates rejected. May 7, Gates fired one officer and suspended the three others. King was arrested again on suspicion of assault on a vice officer, but no charges were brought. On July 9, the independent Christopher Commission released a report of widespread abuses within the LAPD and called for Gates to resign. On March 5, 1992, the state trial of the four officers began. While the trial was progressing on April 16, Willie Williams was named to replace Gates, who had yet to resign. On April 29, the jury acquitted each officer of all but one minor charge. South Central Los Angeles erupted into three days of riots. On May 2, the Justice Department announced the convening of a grand jury to investigate the officers. On June 26, King was arrested when his wife accused him of hurting her in a domestic dispute and again on July 16, on suspicion of drunk driving. In each case, no charges were filed. Williams was sworn in as the new chief of LAPD on June 30.

The federal grand jury indicted the four officers on August 4. The indictment read as follows:

COUNT ONE

On or about March 3, 1991, in Los Angeles, California, within the Central District of California, defendants LAWRENCE M. POWELL, TIMOTHY E. WIND and THEODORE J. BRISENO, then police officers with the Los Angeles Police Department, while acting under color of the laws of the state of California, aiding and abetting each other, did willfully strike with baton, kick, and stomp Rodney Glen King, an inhabitant of the state of California, resulting in bodily injury to Rodney Glen King, and thereby did willfully deprive Rodney Glen King of the right preserved and protected by the Constitution of the United States not to be deprived of liberty without due process of law, including the right to be secure in his person and free from the intentional use of unreasonable force by one making an arrest under color of law, all in violation of Title 18, United States Code, Sections 2 and 242.

COUNT TWO

On or about March 3, 1991, in Los Angeles, California, within the Central District of California, defendant STACEY C. KOON, then a sergeant with the Los Angeles Police Department, while acting under color of the laws of the state of California, did willfully permit other Los Angeles Police Officers in his presence and under his supervision, namely Lawrence M. Powell, Timothy E. Wind, and

Theodore J. Briseno, unlawfully to strike with batons, kick, and stomp Rodney Glen King, an inhabitant of the State of California, while Rodney Glen King was in the custody of those officers, and did willfully fail to prevent this unlawful assault; resulting in bodily injury to Rodney Glen King, and thereby did willfully deprive Rodney Glen King of the right preserved and protected by the Constitution of the United States not to be deprived of liberty without due process of law, including the right to be kept free from harm while in official custody, in violation of Title 18, United States Code, Section 242.

On February 3, 1993, the federal criminal trial began. On April 17, Officers Wind and Briseno were acquitted, and Officer Powell and Sergeant Koon convicted. Powell and Koon were sentenced to two and one-half years in prison. Subsequently, King won a multimillion dollar damage award against the city.

The effect on the agency, the city, and the other officers within the LAPD will never be completely known. It is clear that the entire country was affected by the arrest of Rodney King and the subsequent events that took place.

FBI POLICY REGARDING CRIMINAL CIVIL RIGHTS INVESTIGATIONS

According to officials of the Federal Bureau of Investigation (FBI), the specifics related to the policy and procedures followed by them regarding the initiation and conduct of investigations are classified material, which they refuse to divulge. Despite this shroud of secrecy, however, the policy and procedures were generally described in an article in *FBI Law Enforcement Bulletin*, distributed nationwide to most law enforcement agencies. It is evident from that article that the Department of

Justice (DOJ) has established a more aggressive stance with respect to the investigation/prosecution of alleged civil rights violations.

Federal criminal civil-rights investigations are conducted by special agents assigned to the local office of the FBI. These investigations can be initiated in one of several ways. First, whenever local FBI agents discover independently that an incident such as a riot, shooting, or other critical incident has occurred that they feel may merit some federal monitoring, the local office can "self-initiate" an investigation and can monitor what occurs in a state criminal prosecution that may have civil-rights overtones. At the present time, DOJ policy provides that the FBI **must** initiate an investigation if an allegation of excessive force appears in the local press (newspapers/TV/radio). Second, a citizen's complainant may cause an investigation. An investigation will be initiated whenever a citizen files a complaint with either the DOJ, the United States Attorney's office, or the local FBI office. Finally, an anonymous complaint is sufficient to initiate investigation.

The investigation is, in no uncertain terms, a criminal investigation. Normally, the investigation is conducted by a local FBI agent unless that agent has a routine working relationship with the officer's department. In such cases, the investigation may be assigned to a federal agent outside the immediate area in order to avoid future conflict and tension between the individual officer and the agent and their respective agencies.

It is the responsibility of the investigating special agent to gather information and to file a report with the Civil Rights Division of DOJ in Washington, DC. The agent may, in that report, express an opinion that the initial complaint is unfounded, or in the alternative, he may recommend that there is a need for further investigation or that a federal grand jury is necessary for the commencement of a criminal prosecution.

The Civil Rights Division of DOJ is the federal agency that will review the facts documented by the investigating agent and that will make the ultimate decision on further action or federal prosecution. This decision is usually made within sixty to ninety days of the initial interview with the involved officer. If the Civil Rights Division determines that federal prosecution is appropriate, the matter will be turned over to the United States Attorney for presentation to a grand jury and possible prosecution. In some cases, the prosecutor from the Criminal Section of the Civil Rights Division will be assigned to prosecute the case rather than the local United States Attorney.

HOBBS ACT

The Hobbs Act, 18 U.S.C. § 1951, is used by federal authorities to prosecute state and local officials for corruption in office. Generally, the Hobbs Act prohibits demanding or accepting money to perform or not perform official acts. It is referred to as extortion under color of law. The punishment for violating the Hobbs Act is up to twenty years in federal prison and a fine.

A charge under the Hobbs Act requires the federal government to provide that the defendant:

1.   was a public official;
2.   obstructed, delayed, or affected commerce; and
3.   either:
     a.   knew the demand for money was made in return for an official act, or
     b.   knew the payment was in return for an explicit promise or undertaking by the official to perform or not perform an official act.

A "public official" includes any public employee, elected or appointed, who exercises an official's powers or creates a reasonable impression that he or she possesses such power. *United States v. Freeman*, 6 F.3d 586 (9th Cir. 1993).

The element of obstructing, delaying, or affecting commerce merely requires a showing of some direct or indirect effect on interstate commerce. Actions of a police officer will usually affect interstate travel or commerce, but not always. In one case, a defendant attempted to extort money from a wealthy businessman when he tried to sell him an audiotape of the businessman's sexual encounter with a female defendant in a state criminal case. The court said that the government failed to prove an effect on interstate commerce because the businessman was rich enough to pay the extortion without selling stock in his business. The federal charges were dismissed. *United States v. Buffey*, 899 F.2d 1402 (4th Cir.1990).

Accepting a payment or thing of value can be direct or indirect. In one case, a sheriff was convicted because he issued honorary deputy sheriff's commissions that contained a badge identical to those carried by sworn deputies, in exchange for a $500.00 campaign contribution. *United States v. Farley*, 2 F.3d 645 (6th Cir.), *cert. denied*, 510 U.S. 1030 (1993).

The payment can be either for an explicit promise to perform or not perform an act or for acceptance of a payment for which the official is not entitled, knowing the payment was in return for official acts. In South Carolina, the FBI set up a sting operation that focused on a bill in the South Carolina House of Representatives intended to legalize parimutuel betting. An undercover FBI agent recorded (on audio- and videotape) payment to several legislators in exchange for an implicit or explicit agreement for an affirmative vote. Several legislators were indicted and some convicted. *See United States v. Taylor*, 993 F.2d 382 (4th Cir.1993).

Such payments are not limited to elected officials. In *United States v. Crowley*, 504 F.2d 992 (7th Cir.1974), a police officer was convicted of violating the Hobbs Act for accepting payments from an owner of a bowling alley and promising to improve delivery of police services to the business. On the other hand, a deputy sheriff could not be charged with a Hobbs Act violation for accepting money from litigants in order to "influence" or "fix" cases, since the deputy had no authority or ability to "fix" the cases. *United States v. Kaye*, 593 F. Supp. 193 (N.D. Ill. 1984).

FEDERAL CRIMINAL PROCEDURE

Federal government investigatory procedures differ from many state criminal procedures by the length of time the investigation will take and the use of the grand jury in order to learn the testimony of witnesses and to view evidence prior to trial. First, the FBI is very thorough in its investigations; consequently, the investigation may take months or years to complete. Hobbs Act investigations may take years to complete and require the agency to produce numerous records and explain procedures to the investigators.

The use of an investigatory grand jury also makes such an investigation difficult for the public manager. The United States Attorney may subpoena records or individuals to appear before the grand jury. Unlike most state grand juries, under the federal system, a witness is sworn and questioned by the United States Attorney, without the benefit of the presence of an attorney or a judge. The testimony is transcribed and will be used in any subsequent criminal proceeding or by FBI agents in the investigation.

This procedure requires decisions by public employees prior to any formal charges. The issue is, to what extent does an employee cooperate in the investigation? First, no one should obstruct an investigation. On the other hand, the mere fact that the person being investigated is a law enforcement officer does not change the Constitution. The officer has the right to remain silent, and the agency cannot require the officer to cooperate. *Garrity v. New Jersey*, 385 U.S. 493 (1967). The officer under investigation needs to consult an attorney outside the agency to advise the officer at this critical juncture. The consequences of testifying before the grand jury are significant. Any material discrepancies in the testimony before the grand jury and the statement given to the FBI may be the basis of either an obstruction-of-justice charge or a perjury charge. On the other hand, the United States Attorney may only desire information on the conduct of others, and the employee may want to cooperate. It is the officer's choice, and the agency should only allow the testimony, not compel it.

Although not required by law or policy, oftentimes a federal investigator will call the agency and request to set up an interview with the involved officer(s) to try to prevent damage to future relationships. The manager should promptly and courteously respond to the investigator but should require a written request, addressed to the agency head. The written request should, at a minimum, set out the nature and extent of the investigation and the purpose of the meeting. This will alert the officer to the nature of the allegation and assist him or her in determining whether to meet with the investigating officer as requested and, if the officer chooses to do so, to be better prepared for that meeting. Upon receipt of the written request, the agency should acknowledge receipt and the fact that it has been delivered to the officer.

Internal Affairs File

On occasion, federal investigators will ask to see a copy of any statement previously provided by the suspected officer(s) during the internal investigation. Information contained in an officer's internal affairs file is generally protected by state law. Compliance with state law is necessary; but, generally, a federal subpoena or court order will be sufficient to authorize release. The release of this report, if it contains the suspected officer's statement, will cause the investigator *Garrity* problems because the officer gave the internal statement under threat of discipline. The investigator may choose to exclude this statement or obtain a *Garrity* waiver from the officer. It is the investigator's job—not the manager's—to make this decision.

Once the written request is given to the involved officer(s), there is no need for further communication between the agency and the federal investigator. If the officer chooses to seek legal counsel, the federal investigator should communicate directly with counsel. If the officer, for whatever reason, chooses not to seek legal counsel, the federal investigator should be instructed to communicate directly with the officer, thereby avoiding any appearance that the agency is either: (1) interfering with the investigation, or (2) applying undue pressure to cooperate on the officer being investigated.

Dealing With the Involved Officer(s)

The involved officer(s) should be given a copy of the written request for interview and a copy of the department's policy. Once informed of the impending investigation, the officer should be afforded the right to consult with legal counsel. Under no circumstances, even where the allegations appear facially frivolous, should the officer be discouraged from consulting with counsel prior to making a decision whether or not to meet with the investigator. The officer's right to consult with counsel should not be overshadowed by the agency's desire to cooperate with the investigator, by a perception (or representation) that the investigation is "purely routine," or by a concern that a refusal to meet with the federal investigator may give the appearance that the officer has something to hide. No pressure whatsoever should be exerted on the officer by the officer's agency to meet with federal agents or not to consult with legal counsel.

The investigator will need to make a determination of whether the allegations against the officer(s) are true. If an officer refuses to talk, the only information the investigator may have is that of the complaining party. An alternative procedure is to prepare a third-party, hearsay statement for the investigator. By requiring the officer to give a statement to internal affairs and having a second statement prepared in the third person and signed by the head of internal affairs, the investigator will learn the position of the officer but cannot use it against the officer.

A tactic sometimes used by federal investigators to circumvent this limitation is to attempt to meet with the officer and then ask him to "affirm" the accuracy of information contained in the third-party statement, including his previously compelled statement. Most prudent attorneys would advise the officer that there is no need to do so, however, and, accordingly, would likely advise the officer not to make any statement whatsoever. It has been this writer's practice to provide the third-party statement **in lieu of**, not in addition to, an interview or statement from the involved officer(s). This alternative procedure is not always agreeable to the officer or the federal investigator, but it should be considered.

Providing Counsel for Involved Officer(s)

Advising an affected officer(s) of the opportunity to consult with legal counsel prior to determining whether to meet with federal investigators may be less than meaningful unless the agency agrees to provide such counsel at no expense to the involved officer(s). Most agencies have a method of providing attorneys either by appointment by the agency or through a union or association. For example, a state law enforcement officer in North Carolina who requires legal advice can request it. The head of the department will request the Attorney General to provide an attorney. Since the Attorney General may have a conflict with representing an employee in a criminal proceeding, the Attorney General will usually petition the Governor to appoint an attorney at state expense to advise the officer involved. *See* N.C. Gen. Stat. §§ 143-300.4, 147-17. Local officers can obtain counsel under a local procedure. N.C. Gen. Stat. § 160A-167. The manager needs to be familiar with the requirements within the agency.

In deciding to cooperate, the officer may be confronted with the terminology used by the federal officials. There are three categories of persons in a criminal investigation. They are (1) a target, (2) a subject, or (3) a witness. A person who is a "target" is a person who is the focus of the investigation or one the federal government expects to charge with a crime. A "subject" is a person who is not a target, but whom the government believes may become a target of the investigation. A "witness" is a person who the government believes has relevant evidence, but whom the government does not believe is otherwise involved. Absent a grant of immunity by the United States Attorney, a witness can become a target and ultimately a defendant. The fact that the officer was told that he or she was a witness is not a defense to the use of grand jury testimony to indict the officer.

CONCLUSION

Criminal procedures in federal court are complex and difficult for persons who have not worked within the system. The agency must be prepared to react to such an investigation to reduce disruption on the agency without obstructing the federal government's investigation.

CHAPTER 17

WHAT HAS O.J. DONE FOR US?

(USE OF INTERNAL AFFAIRS FILES IN CRIMINAL PROCEEDINGS)

INTRODUCTION

Whether the verdict in the O.J. Simpson trial spoke the truth or not, the "trial of the century" showed the criminal justice system at its worst. From the allegations of planting evidence to racial discrimination in the prosecution, the effects of this trial have been felt throughout the country. The conduct of one officer, Mark Fuhrman, has been and will be used to drag down all law enforcement officers. This trial, coupled with court decisions, requires the Internal Affairs investigator to take great care not only to investigate complaints thoroughly, but to assure that the agency identifies those officers who have lost credibility and will adversely affect the overall mission of the agency-- the delivery of efficient law enforcement services. The attitude that Internal Affairs' files are "ours" and will not be disclosed outside the agency is no longer workable.

USE OF INTERNAL AFFAIRS FILES IN CRIMINAL PROCEEDINGS

Traditionally, Internal Affairs files have not been used in criminal proceedings. These files were not deemed relevant to any criminal trial. The adage that "the defendant is on trial, not the officer" has been substantially eroded. In certain circumstances, the officer's prior conduct is relevant.

Constitutional Standard

The United States Supreme Court has addressed the issue of the evidence which must be released. The Court held that there is no constitutional right to pretrial discovery or for the defendant to know everything the prosecutor knows. *United States v. Agurs*, 427 U.S. 97, 106 (1976). However, the prosecutor may not unfairly convict the defendant by hiding favorable evidence. The Court imposed an affirmative duty to disclose "exculpatory" evidence on the prosecutor. The Supreme Court said failure to produce evidence showing trial testimony of a prosecution witness to be perjured, or other favorable evidence which is material on the issue of guilt or punishment, requires a reversal of the conviction. *Brady v. Maryland*, 373 U.S. 83 (1963). The next logical question: Must evidence which does **not** show the defendant to be innocent but merely casts doubt on the testimony of the prosecuting witness be released?

The Supreme Court answered in the affirmative. In *United States v. Bagley*, 473 U.S. 667 (1985), the Court concluded that there is no distinction between "exculpatory" evidence and "impeachment" evidence. If it is favorable to the defendant by reason that it can make the prosecution's witness less believable, it must be disclosed by the prosecutor.

"I see Nothing, Nothing," Sergeant Schultz

The evidence in the prosecutor's file is the first place the prosecutor must look. Are there inconsistent statements from the same witness? However, the prosecutor cannot stop here. There is a "DUTY TO LEARN." The Supreme Court in *Kyles v. Whitley*, 514 U.S. 419 (1995), discussed in detail the obligation of the prosecutor. The Court was faced with a 1984 robbery/murder case in which the defendant received the death penalty in a second trial after the jury could not reach a verdict in the first trial. There were six witnesses to the accosting of 60-year-old Dolores Dye in the parking lot of a grocery store. The gunman struggled with her as she was putting groceries in the trunk of her car. He shot her in the left temple and stole her car. The witnesses gave varying descriptions of the perpetrator. Three days later, a person with several aliases, being called "Beanie," came forward and claimed to have purchased the dead woman's car from defendant Kyles. Physical evidence was found in Kyles' residence. Beanie gave several conflicting statements. Kyles' defense was that Beanie had planted the evidence. In fact, some of the witnesses' descriptions could have been of Beanie. The prosecutor did not turn over any of the inconsistent information to the defendant or report the fact that Beanie received $1,600 in reward money. The Court, in a 5-4 decision, reversed the conviction and sent the case back for a new trial.

The Court first said that there is no constitutional requirement that the prosecutor have an open file policy and allow the defendant to search the files. 514 U.S. at 437. On the other hand, the Court said a prosecutor cannot limit the search for exculpatory evidence to the prosecutor's file or those items submitted by the law enforcement agency.

> [T]he individual prosecutor has a duty to learn of any favorable evidence
> known to the others acting on the government's behalf in the case,
> **including the police.**

> *Id.*, 514 U.S. at 437 (Emphasis added)

The Court said that the responsibility for revealing *Brady* evidence is that of the "government." The fact that the lawyer for the government does not know about the evidence does not excuse the "government" from complying with Brady.

"No #%&@ DA is Going to Look at My Files!"

The Supreme Court has placed the responsibility on the prosecutor to first decide if the information is favorable or material to the defense. *Kyles,* 514 U.S. at 437-439. The unanswered question is whether the prosecutor is required to review all files or can the prosecutor rely upon an evaluation by the police.

This issue has not been decided in this jurisdiction. In other jurisdictions, the courts have held that the prosecutor can rely upon the police agency to review the files and make an initial determination if there is potential *Brady* information in the files. The prosecutor must then decide if the information is to be released. This is the policy adopted by the United States Department of Justice. *See United States v. Herring*, 83 F.3d 1120 (9th Cir. 1996).

What Is "Potential Brady" Material?

The information to be disclosed to the prosecutor is much broader than the information that will be disclosed to the court or that the court will allow to be used against the officer. The court will require disclosure of material which affects the officer's credibility. The categories of conduct are:

> ➢   untruthful
> ➢   biases
> ➢   crimes

Untruthful

The term "untruthful" means false statements, false reports, or incomplete reports. The false statements involve all aspects of the job, not just in criminal investigations. *See Dreary v. Gloucester*, 9 F.3d 191 (1st Cir. 1993) (Ten-year-old disciplinary finding that officer falsified overtime records). *United States v. Williams*, 1997 WL 335794 (D.D.C. 1997) (New trial ordered because FBI failed to disclose that an agent who was a witness fifteen years earlier received a letter of reprimand for forging an informant's signature on a receipt and lying about the forgery under oath).

Bias

"Bias" is the Mark Fuhrman case. Prior records show his bias against an identifiable group, e.g. African-Americans, women, etc. Bias could also be shown toward a particular person or family, such as prior conduct with this defendant.

Crimes

"Crimes" include any crimes other than motor vehicle misdemeanors or infractions. Even motor vehicle offenses must be disclosed to the prosecutor when the criminal case involves similar conduct.

The information is not limited to Internal Affairs files. It could include background investigations, applications for disability, and training files. The Court will look at the category, not the location.

Do We Disclose Complaints for Which the Officer Was Exonerated?

The best policy is to disclose to the prosecutor and let the prosecutor decide. If the evidence of commission of the conduct is strong, a judge may order it disclosed. The fact that the agency chooses to believe the officer does not relieve the agency of the responsibility to disclose the information--at least to the prosecutor. *See United States v. Booker*, 1997 WL 214850 (E.D. Pa. 1997) (Nine IAD complaints of verbal and physical abuse for which the officer was exonerated were not admissible. There was no prejudice for failing to disclose this information).

Are Pending Investigations Subject to Disclosure?

Again, disclosure will protect the integrity of a criminal conviction. The general rule is that unverified or speculative information is not subject to disclosure. However, the decision to disclose such information is best left to the prosecutor. *See United States v. Agurs*, 427 U.S. 97 (1976); *United States v. Diaz*, 922 F.2d 998 (2nd Cir. 1990), *cert. den.* 500 U.S. 925 (1991).

STATE LAW REQUIREMENTS

Discovery in Criminal Trials

The State courts usually do not allow a defendant to request an officer's personnel file for a fishing expedition to determine if there is relevant information. *See, State v. Cunningham*, 344 N.C. 341, 474 S.E. 2d 772 (1996). However, a request for *Brady* material will require the prosecutor to reveal information listed above.

Confidentiality of Records

Personnel records may are confidential under State law. For example, under North Carolina law personnel records of state and local government employees are confidential. N.C.G.S. §§ 126-24 (State Officers); 153A-98 (County Officers); 160A-168 (City Officers). These records can be released to another State agency, e.g. the District Attorney, when necessary to the proper functioning of the requesting agency. N.C.G.S. §§ 126-24(5); 153A-98(c)(5); 160A-168(c)(5). On the other hand, personnel records in Florida are public records under most circumstances.

USE OF INFORMATION

Information must be disclosed to the prosecutor and from the prosecutor to the defense attorney, but it is possible that information may not be used in court. Only evidence which the court finds to be relevant for impeachment purposes can be used. This requires a balancing of the probative value against its prejudicial effect. *See* Rules 403, 608, 609, North Carolina & Federal Rules of Evidence; *United States v. Ortiz*, 5 F.3d 288 (7th Cir. 1993) (Within court's discretion to exclude a letter from officer's personnel file that he falsified the number of hours spent in court); *Dreary v. Gloucester*, 9 F.3d 191 (1st Cir. 1993) (Court can allow in a ten-year-old disciplinary action for falsification of overtime records).

CONCLUSION

Each agency must be prepared to provide a prosecutor with information showing that an officer is untruthful, biased, or that he or she committed crimes of the type that could be used to impeach the officer. The requirement to disclose information to a criminal defendant is a Constitutional one. The prosecutor must disclose the information, even without a request, and has a duty to learn if there is such information held by the police agency that investigated the crime. The police agency cannot hide behind personnel privacy laws and local precincts or district offices cannot hide behind the fact that the records are not available to them, but held by internal affairs or the personnel office.

Managers need to consider these disclosure requirements in determining the type of discipline that is appropriate for particular policy violations. For example, an officer is accused of lying to his supervisor. If the lying is substantiated by the agency, then disclosure will be required. If disclosure is required, then how effective is this officer going to be? Can the agency assign this officer to general investigative work and hope that he or she is not the first officer at the scene of the crime of the century? Can this officer be assigned to investigations where it will be the officer's word against the defendant's? The question then arises, should officers who lie be dismissed? A manager needs to determine the effect that this policy violation will have not only on the internal workings of the agency, but its interaction with the prosecution and court system. Once the information is disclosed in open court, how will the public view the other officers in the agency?

The same is true of policy violations that demonstrate bias toward a particular group or involve criminal law violations that are not prosecuted. Must this information be disclosed? If so, how effective will this officer be?

The impact of some personnel investigations will not be limited to the internal workings of the agency. They will impact the criminal justice system and the way the public views its police. A police manager must consider this issue in determining the level of discipline imposed for a certain policy violations. This is part of what O.J.'s trial did for all of us.